Havana Hardball

UNIVERSITY PRESS OF FLORIDA

Florida A&M University, Tallahassee
Florida Atlantic University, Boca Raton
Florida Gulf Coast University, Ft. Myers
Florida International University, Miami
Florida State University, Tallahassee
New College of Florida, Sarasota
University of Central Florida, Orlando
University of Florida, Gainesville
University of North Florida, Jacksonville
University of South Florida, Tampa
University of West Florida, Pensacola

Jackie Robinson sliding into the base during a spring training game against the Havana Cubans at El Gran Stadium in March 1947. By permission of the National Baseball Hall of Fame Library, Cooperstown, N.Y.

Havana Hardball

Spring Training, Jackie Robinson, and the Cuban League

César Brioso

University Press of Florida
Gainesville Tallahassee Tampa Boca Raton
Pensacola Orlando Miami Jacksonville Ft. Myers Sarasota

20 19 18 17 16 15   6 5 4 3 2 1

Library of Congress Control Number: 2015938073
ISBN 978-0-8130-6116-0

The University Press of Florida is the scholarly publishing agency for the State University
System of Florida, comprising Florida A&M University, Florida Atlantic University, Florida
Gulf Coast University, Florida International University, Florida State University, New College
of Florida, University of Central Florida, University of Florida, University of North Florida,
University of South Florida, and University of West Florida.

University Press of Florida
15 Northwest 15th Street
Gainesville, FL 32611-2079
http://www.upf.com

For my dad, César, who started me on this journey
with his stories about baseball in Cuba

Contents

Preface

Many years ago, I came across some old family photographs in my parents' South Florida home. Among the dozens of sepia-tinted images stuffed into a large manila envelope, the one that stood out was a black-and-white photo of my father from the late 1940s. He could not have been much more than ten years old. I could have been looking at a picture of myself at that age. In the photo, a baseball cap sat tilted at a slight angle on my father's head. A sharp crease split the middle of the bill, and a stylized *A* adorned the low crown. The cap symbolized Almendares, the winter-league baseball team my father rooted for as a child in pre-Castro Cuba.

As a youngster, my father attended Cuban League games at El Gran Stadium in Havana, brought to the ballpark by his uncle Raúl. One of the photos I found that night illustrated the effort it must have taken him to introduce my father to the game. Having lost both legs below the knee—a train had severed them when he passed out on the tracks after a night of drinking—Raúl often used an elaborate wheelchair with handles above the armrests connected to the wheels with what looked like bicycle chains. Later he "walked" on his knees using foam pads that allowed for easier movement through the stadium with my father.

The images that poured out of that envelope brought back the many stories I had heard growing up. Over the years, my father told me about players—from Cuba, the major leagues, and the Negro leagues—who had played in Havana, players such as Monte Irvin, Ray Dandridge, Tommy Lasorda, Roberto Ortiz, Agapito Mayor, and Max Lanier. Discovering those photos reignited my interest in baseball on the island of my birth. It drove me to learn more about the players from my father's stories about Cuban baseball in the 1940s and 1950s.

Pre-Castro Cuba was home to Nobel Prize–winning author Ernest Hemingway, island refuge to gangsters Meyer Lansky and Lucky Luciano, and tropical playground for Americans, both famous and not. Passion for baseball defined the island nation's culture as much as its language, music, and history. Like New York of the 1950s—where the labels Yankees fan, Dodgers fan, and Giants fan carried as much weight as Irish, Italian, or Jewish—Cuba had its own ingrained system of identification, based on the team you supported. You were *almendarista* or *habanista*; you rooted for Cienfuegos or Marianao. To fully appreciate Cuban baseball prior to Castro's revolution, imagine the New York of the 1950s, which writer Roger Kahn described as an era when "the Yankees, Giants, and Dodgers ruled the world." Now throw in the New York Mets. Have those four teams play games only against one another. And have them play all their games in a newly built Yankee Stadium.

My research led me to focus on the 1946–47 Cuban League season. The most dramatic finish in league history unfolded in the closing days of February 1947. It ignited a wild celebration that spread through the streets of Havana and across Cuba. Amid the excitement of the final week of the season, Pan American Clippers carrying members of the Brooklyn Dodgers and minor-league Montreal Royals landed in Havana. Among those arriving: Jackie Robinson. As Brooklyn Dodgers president Branch Rickey embarked upon breaking baseball's color barrier, he relocated the team's spring training base from Jim Crow–era Florida to Cuba, where interracial baseball had flourished since 1900.

With a narrative that alternates between the 1946–47 Cuban League season and Robinson's spring training in Havana, this book explores a pivotal winter-league season in Cuba that dovetailed with the tenuous start to Robinson's historic 1947 campaign. Against the backdrop of Major League Baseball's strong-arm efforts to bring all Latin leagues under the control of "organized baseball," Havana in the spring of 1947 became the nexus of divergent baseball worlds: Major League Baseball under threat by raiders from the Mexican League, the Cuban League under threat of being blackballed by organized baseball, and the Dodgers about to change the face of the game by elevating Robinson to the majors and sounding the death knell for the Negro leagues.

Acknowledgments

Outside of the Cuban restaurants, bakeries, and coffee shops that dot West Tampa, the obituary in the local newspaper likely went unnoticed across the Tampa Bay area. "Agapito Mayor, 89 . . . passed away April 18, 2005," read the item on page 8 in the metro section of the *Tampa Tribune*. The notice included references to Mayor's forty-year baseball career as a player, coach, and manager in leagues from Cuba throughout the Caribbean, from South and Central America to the United States. But even the mention of his induction into the Cuban Baseball Hall of Fame barely begins to explain the left-handed pitcher's place in Cuban baseball history. Mayor carved his name alongside those of his Almendares teammates Max Lanier and Andrés Fleitas in the pantheon of Cuba's winter league. For their exploits on the field at El Gran Stadium, in what is still celebrated as the greatest pennant race in the history of that league, their names will be forever linked.

Six years before his death, Mayor stood in his modest one-story West Tampa home showing off his prize possession and declared, "When I die, I want to be buried in my Almendares jersey." His wife, Gloria, honored his request. "He was given that uniform one night at a gathering at the [Tampa landmark] Columbia Restaurant," she said. "The uniform had number eighteen, which was always his number with Almendares. It was exactly like the one he wore with Almendares, identical, with its cap, the socks, everything. . . . I had a suit for him, thinking to put it on him [for the funeral], but my daughter and a longtime family friend said, 'Remember what he always said.' I said, 'How can I dress him like a baseball player?' They said, 'Well, that's what he always wanted.' . . . So I found the suitcase where he kept the uniform and I took it to the funeral home. And with his uniform he left. A little boy who he would help practice baseball when he was little put a baseball in his hand. The boy asked me for permission, and he put the ball in his hand, so he left with the baseball as well."

Lanier, who had lived in the town of Dunnellon, less than a ninety-mile drive along Florida's Gulf Coast from Mayor, died on January 30, 2007, at age ninety-one. He always spoke fondly of Mayor and fellow Almendares teammate and catcher Andrés Fleitas. Lanier once sent me a note to pass on to Fleitas, who was living in Miami at the time. Dated June 17, 1999, the note, written on St. Louis Cardinals stationery, read: "Dear Andres. How are you doing? Sure would like to see you. You were a great person as well as a great catcher. I couldn't have won those two games without you behind home plate. My health is not too good as I have had two heart attacks and a stroke. Take care and hope you are in good health. Your friend. Max Lanier." Fleitas, who would die on December 18, 2011, at age ninety-five, was grateful to receive the note.

And I remain forever grateful to Mayor, Lanier, Fleitas, and all the others who consented to interviews over the years, such as *Baltimore Afro-American* sportswriter Sam Lacy, Cuban broadcaster Felo Ramírez, former Negro leagues star Buck O'Neil, Hall of Famer Monte Irvin, and former Dodgers Don Newcombe, Bobby Bragan, Buzzie Bavasi, and Mike Sandlock. Their recollections brought a bygone era of Cuban baseball back to life in vivid detail. This book would not have been possible without their willingness to share their experiences.

I am also grateful for the help of former *USA Today* colleague Bob Kimball, who offered his services in back-reading my chapters. Bob is extremely knowledgeable and well-read about baseball history. I knew I had to be doing some things right with this project when I kept hearing "I didn't know that . . ." as he read over the various chapters.

Research for this book was greatly facilitated by online access to the archives of the *Sporting News* and the *New York Times*. The *Sporting*

News covered the Cuban League of the 1940s in remarkable detail and chronicled nearly every development in the battle between organized baseball and the Mexican League. The *New York Times* followed the Brooklyn Dodgers, Montreal Royals, and Jackie Robinson on a daily basis as the spring training schedule of 1947 took them through Cuba, Venezuela, and Panama. I also was able to access crucial articles from two Cuban daily newspapers, *Diario de la Marina* and the *Havana Post*, thanks to the Library of Congress, which graciously shared its microfilm reels through its interlibrary loan service. Equally invaluable were the writings of the *Pittsburgh Courier*'s Wendell Smith and the *Baltimore Afro-American*'s Sam Lacy. These two members of the black press were embedded with Robinson throughout spring training in 1947, and their weekly dispatches provided great insight into Robinson's efforts to earn a roster spot on the Dodgers and break baseball's color barrier that season.

Havana Hardball

The Year of Dick Sisler

El Grito de Yara rang out from Carlos Manuel de Céspedes's plantation La Demajagua on October 10, 1868. With this "Cry of Yara," he freed his slaves and launched Cuba's Ten Years' War against Spain.[1] The island's first major conflict in pursuit of independence from the Spanish crown also set in motion the eventual abolition of slavery in Cuba. From the start, Cuba's fight for independence and its interest in baseball were inextricably linked. "Baseball," according to historian Louis A. Pérez Jr., "became a means by which Cubans disaffected from Spain could give one more expression to their discontent."[2] Introduced to Cuba in 1864 by Nemesio Guilló, the son of a wealthy Cuban family who brought baseball home with him after studying in the United States, the game became an integral element of the war effort against Spain. Despite periodic bans by Spanish authorities, baseball games often were organized—in Havana, and in Florida cities such as Key West and Tampa—as a means of raising funds for the cause of independence. Perhaps the leading figure among "patriot players" was Emilio Sabourín.[3]

One of the founders of Cuba's first professional baseball league in 1878, Sabourín was born on September 5, 1853, in Havana. In his youth, he and his friends prepared a field for games in the Havana neighborhood of Vedado, future site of the first league game, and bought arms and munitions to bring to Cuban rebels. Sabourín's baseball and rebel activities continued until December 15, 1895, when he was arrested for conspiring against Spain and imprisoned at La Cabaña fortress. After a year, Sabourín was deported to a presidio in Ceuta in the then-colony of Spanish Morocco, where he died on July 5, 1897, never having seen the goal for which he fought become reality.[4] Independence from Spain came in 1898. A royal decree had already ended slavery in Cuba on October 7, 1886—more than twenty-one years after the Thirteenth Amendment to the U.S. Constitution outlawed the practice in America.

But on one level Cuba was far ahead of the United States. Cuba's professional baseball fields integrated in 1900, more than four decades before Major League Baseball accomplished the same feat. Not that Cuba was an island free of prejudice and racial strife. Social status, in which skin color was often a factor, sharply divided the population. The sugar mills that powered much of Cuba's economy in the early twentieth century were largely the property of white landowners of European descent, while blacks labored in the fields for *la zafra*, the harvest. This was the world into which Saturnino Orestes Arrieta Armas was born on November 24, 1925. "Discrimination and segregation were very much alive and flourishing in the Cuba of my birth,"[5] the man who became better known as "Minnie" Miñoso wrote years later in his autobiography.

Orestes, as he was then called, was born in El Perico in Matanzas Province to Carlos Arrieta and Cecilia Armas. Cecilia was the mother of four children from a previous marriage, and Carlos Arrieta was one of fifteen black men who cut sugarcane on white landowner Carlos Lopez's ranch La Lonja. Arrieta's duties also included loading the cane onto donkey- or bull-drawn carts and driving the carts to a nearby factory, where the sugar was processed. The family didn't have much: no radio, no electricity; they "used gas light and would make our own lamps." By the time Orestes was eight, his parents divorced, his father moving to Camagüey, while he and his mother moved to Havana to live with his half sister Juanita. Cecilia's death two years later led to an itinerant existence for the boy, who shuttled between Havana, Perico, and Camagüey for the next several years.[6]

In Perico, Orestes often shadowed his much older, baseball-playing half brothers, Cirilo and Francisco Miñoso, which explains how the boy became known by their last name instead of his own. Their father, Cecilia's first husband, was Julián Miñoso. Local fans referred to the trio as the Miñoso brothers and to young Orestes as Little Miñoso, and the name stuck. (The "Minnie" nickname came years later in the majors, often with a tilde-less Minoso.) Cirilo and Francisco were good players with the local factory team. Before long, Little Miñoso started organizing a team on the sugar plantation to play against teams from other plantations and the sugar factory. "I was the big boss of the ranch," he wrote, "and believe me, I was tough. I'd fine the other kids fifty cents for each missed sign."[7]

As good as he was at running a sugar mill team, Orestes Miñoso aspired to more. But amateur baseball wasn't an option. Cuba's amateur-league teams were tied to private social clubs, and "club simply meant whites only," Miñoso wrote.[8] Later in life he acknowledged he preferred the codified discrimination he experienced in the United States to Cuba's more subtle racism. "Where there are laws that say this is as far as you go, to me is more correct," Miñoso said. "Where they don't but when you arrive, they ask, 'Are you a member?' and if you weren't a member you couldn't enter, that to me is more discrimination, more under the table than to just say blacks are not allowed."[9] Unlike Cuba's amateur leagues, the Liga de Base-Ball Profesional Cubana, the Cuban Professional Baseball League, had been open to players regardless of skin color since the turn of the twentieth century. Reaching that level, to be sure, was a long shot for a kid from the Cuban countryside in the 1930s. But plenty of opportunities existed in Cuba's semipro ranks. For Miñoso, seeking those opportunities meant a return to Havana. "I wanted to play baseball, the best caliber of baseball," Miñoso wrote, "and there was lots of baseball in Havana."[10]

One of the first professional baseball scouts to evaluate future New York Giants pitcher Sal Maglie needed to see just three pitches before reaching his conclusion. "Next," he yelled, having decided the semipro hurler didn't have what it took to pitch for the then Class-AA International League's Rochester Red Wings. Another scout, after watching one of Maglie's semipro games, asked if he was going to school. When Maglie said he was, the scout quipped, "Keep going."[11]

Despite these first impressions, Maglie managed to escape the semipro ranks of his hometown Niagara Falls in 1938, signing with the Buffalo Bisons of the International League for $275 a month. He spent three shaky seasons in Buffalo, marked by nerves, ineffectiveness, and shattered confidence. When his record dropped to 0–7 and his earned run average ballooned to 7.17 in 1940, Buffalo sent him down to the Class-D Jamestown (New York) Falcons of the Pennsylvania–Ontario–New York League. It was organized baseball's lowest outpost. Failure there likely would have ended his baseball career. But a partial season in Jamestown led to a season at Elmira (New York) in the Class-A Eastern League, which led to the New York Giants assigning the right-hander to Jersey City of the Class-AA International League in 1942. Maglie got his first taste of baseball in Cuba that spring when he and his Jersey City teammates joined the Giants in Havana for a pair of spring training games. Maglie's duties were limited to throwing batting practice and watching the Giants lose twice to the Brooklyn Dodgers.[12]

Once the regular season got under way in Jersey City, Maglie's baseball career finally seemed to get on track. Yet as he compiled a 9–6 record and 2.78 ERA, the specter of being drafted into World War II loomed. So a career of fits and starts came to a sudden halt after his 1942 preinduction physical. He was spared from military service, given a deferment because of a chronic sinus condition. But with so many other men from Niagara Falls serving in the war, the draft board gave Maglie a choice: lose his deferment or give up baseball and go into defense work. Thus began Maglie's brief career as a pipefitter for the International Paper Company. Worse than that, it was back to semipro ball, this time with the Welland Atlas Steels, a Canadian team in Welland, Ontario, across from Niagara Falls.[13]

Three years away from the minors did not dull Maglie's desire for a career in professional baseball once the war ended. After Nazi Germany surrendered on May 8, 1945, he returned to the Jersey City Giants. By July the New York Giants called up Maglie, along with Cuban left-hander Adrián Zabala. With so many players still not back from the war, a paltry 3–7 record and 4.09 ERA were sufficient to warrant Maglie's first promotion to the big leagues. Following the bombings of Hiroshima and Nagasaki, Japan surrendered on August 14. Maglie made his first major-league start that day. In front of 3,038 fans at the Polo Grounds in New York, he beat the Cincinnati Reds 5–2. Amid the war headlines, sports accounts chronicled his outing, employing the stereotypes common to the sportswriting of that era. The *New York Daily News*'s Dick Young referred to Maglie as "the Giants' new spaghetti and curve ball bender," while the *New York Herald Tribune*'s Jesse Abramson dubbed Maglie "swarthy Sal."[14]

For a guy who didn't reach the majors until age twenty-eight, Maglie's rookie season had to be considered a success. He went 5–4 with a 2.35 earned run average. But most important, the Giants' cantankerous pitching coach, Adolfo Luque, had taken Maglie under his wing. Luque had been the first truly successful Cuban-born pitcher in the majors, compiling a 194–179 record with a solid 3.24 ERA in twenty seasons with the Boston Braves, Cincinnati Reds, Brooklyn Dodgers, and the Giants. As a pitcher, Luque earned a reputation for pitching high and inside. During the 1945 season he began imparting that aggressive brushback style to Maglie. At season's end, Luque asked Maglie to join him in Cuba, where Luque would manage the Cienfuegos Base Ball Club of the Cuban League. Luque's sales pitch was enticing: winter ball would keep Maglie sharp for the challenge of fending off veteran players returning from the war the following season, and a $400-per-month salary was good money for the time.[15]

George Sisler might be one of the least heralded great hitters in baseball history. This despite a .340 career batting average, which is tied for 16th in major-league history with fellow Hall of Famer and New York Yankees legend Lou Gehrig. Twice Sisler batted over .400 to lead the American League for the St. Louis Browns—.407 in 1920 and .420 in 1922. His 2,812 career hits in a fifteen-year career rank 48th all time.

Six times he collected at least 200 hits in a season. Given that pedigree, the St. Louis Cardinals had high hopes for Sisler's son Dick.

At six foot two and 205 pounds, the younger Sisler was bigger and stronger than his speedy father, who had compiled 327 career stolen bases. Dick Sisler's first two seasons in the minors hinted at his power potential. In 1939 he hit 16 home runs in 373 at-bats with the Washington Red Birds of the Class-D Pennsylvania State Association. Sisler followed that up by driving in 83 runs in 105 games with the Class-C Lansing Lancers of the Michigan State League the next season. But Sisler bounced around the Cardinals' lower minor-league affiliates between 1940 and 1942. Then the U.S. Navy came calling prior to the 1943 season.

Stationed at Bainbridge, Maryland, Sisler played against major leaguers who had joined the war effort such as Bob Feller and future Philadelphia Phillies teammate Jim Konstanty during his three-year absence from professional ball. But such matchups were no substitute for real games. When the navy discharged Sisler in 1945, Cardinals owner Sam Breadon wanted his minor-league prodigy to "re-acclimate to professional baseball and learn to play first base."[16] So he sent Sisler to Cuba to play for Cardinals third-base coach Miguel Ángel González's Habana Base Ball Club in the winter of 1945–46. Sisler would amass a total of 55 major-league home runs in his career, never managing more than 13 in any of his eight big-league seasons. But in his lone season in Cuba, Sisler would leave an indelible mark on the Cuban League.

Sisler, Maglie, and Miñoso all embarked upon their first seasons in the Cuban League in the fall of 1945. They arrived in Havana from divergent backgrounds: Sisler the son of a great major-league player, hoping to carve out his own legend in the game; Maglie a journeyman minor leaguer who had arrived in the majors late in life, using a winter in Cuba to reinvent himself into an intimidating pitcher; Miñoso the native-born semipro player, aspiring to succeed at the highest level of baseball in his homeland. Each arrived for the 1945–46 season as the Cuban League was about to enter its most turbulent period—one that would be marked by change, conflict, and a schism among the country's best ballplayers.

Gran Stadium Cerveza Tropical, popularly known as La Tropical, didn't look much like a baseball park. Its dimensions were cavernous: 498 feet to left field, 447 feet to the scoreboard in left-center, 505 feet to center, 426 feet to the clock in right-center, and 398 to right.[17] The infield diamond sat at one end of a soccer field. The encircling running track cut a swath through the left- and center-field grass. The grandstands, mostly built onto a hill along the left-field and third-base line, did not stretch from foul pole to foul pole. Its pastoral surroundings included beer gardens, a dance hall, a brewery, and an ice factory, La Compañia Nueva Fábrica de Hielo, which owned the Tropical brewery. Owner Julio Blanco Herrera had built the stadium on the west bank of the Almendares River and "donated" it to host the second Central American Games in 1930.[18]

The concrete-and-steel structure at number 4409, Avenue 41 in Marianao, a suburban municipality just west of Havana, officially opened for baseball on October 10, 1930. On the sixty-second anniversary of El Grito de Yara, La Tropical played host to the first game of a seven-game exhibition series between two traveling major-league all-star teams: Las Estrellas de Jewel Ens, or the Jewel Ens Stars, and Las Estrellas de Dave Bancroft, or the Dave Bancroft Stars.

Ens had managed the Pittsburgh Pirates to a fifth-place finish in the National League in 1930. Bancroft, a future Hall of Fame shortstop, had completed his final season with the New York Giants. The team's manager, John McGraw, well known to Cuban baseball fans since an 1891 visit during his playing days, served as home-plate umpire. Despite its 9:30 a.m. start, some 20,000 fans attended the opening game, in which Larry French outdueled Carl Hubbell for a 2–0 victory by the Ens Stars.[19] The series, won five-games-to-two by the Ens Stars, featured nine future Hall of Famers: Bancroft, Hubbell, Heinie Manush, Rabbit Maranville, Paul Waner, Al Lopez, Pie Traynor, Chuck Klein, and Bill Terry. French went on to win three games and be named the series's "most outstanding figure."[20] The schedule also featured two exhibition games against local teams, including one in which the Bancroft Stars' Hubbell beat Habana's Ramón Bragaña 2–1.

The 1930–31 Cuban League season began far less auspiciously at La Tropical on October 25, lasting only six days. A contract dispute between teams and the stadium brought the season to an abrupt end with Almendares leading the standings at three wins and one loss. Within two weeks the league hastily organized another season, Campeonato Único, which was played at Almendares Park, the home field of the Almendares Base Ball Club since 1918. A Marianao entry replaced the Santa Clara team. And Almendares, under the name Almendarista, claimed the pennant with a 9–4 record on the strength of pitchers Martín Dihigo, Isidro Fabré, and Basilo "Brujo" Rosell.[21]

Dihigo, his life in danger over his public opposition to General Gerardo Machado's government, was forced to leave Cuba following the 1931–32 season,[22] missing the next three winter seasons in his homeland. The 1932–33 season concluded in a tie between Almendares and Habana, the league's Eternal Rivals since professional play began in Cuba in 1878. A planned playoff series never materialized after a revolution toppled the Machado regime. The ongoing political turmoil also forced cancellation of the following season.[23] The Cuban League resumed play in 1934–35, and Dihigo finally returned for the 1935–36 season, leading the Santa Clara team to the league championship.

The remainder of the Cuban League's tenure at La Tropical was not without hiccups. Over the next fifteen years, teams continued to fluctuate slightly from season to season, but overall the league thrived at La Tropical. During World War II attendance soared, making La Tropical more and more obsolete.

In his seminal work *The Pride of Havana: A History of Cuban Baseball*, Roberto González Echevarría explained: "The bucolic setting and enormous expanses needed to accommodate track and field and other sports made La Tropical a beautiful sports arena. But it was not suited for expansion without changing its character completely." Yet change was needed. Owners of the Cuban League teams supposedly threatened to build a new stadium if La Tropical owner Julio Blanco Herrera failed to upgrade the facility. Herrera refused, reportedly saying "nobody 'built a stadium on him.'"[24]

That was the opening Roberto "Bobby" Maduro needed. He and colleague Miguel "Miguelito" Suárez, whom González Echevarría described as "scions of new Cuban millionaire families,"[25] formed the Compañia Operadora de Stadiums. Its purpose: building a more modern baseball stadium in Havana's working-class neighborhood of El Cerro. The stadium would be built on a patch of land about two miles east of the city's famous Cristóbal Colón Cemetery, named for Christopher Columbus, who landed on Cuba in 1492. Havana residents could easily reach La Tropical by trolley or bus, but the new stadium would be in the heart of the city and would easily surpass the 20,000 fans the rural park was designed to hold. So as the Cuban League's final season at La Tropical unfolded, construction crews broke ground, poured concrete, and erected steel girders for the league's future home.

Once Sal Maglie arrived in Cuba in October 1945, Cienfuegos manager Adolfo Luque began molding the twenty-eight-year-old right-hander in his own image. During his playing career, Luque was known in the United States as Havana Perfecto, the Pride of Havana, after the cigar. (In Cuba, he was known as Papá Montero, after a legendary Afro-Cuban rumba dancer and pimp.)[26] As the first Latin American star in the majors, Luque had no compunction about shaving hitters with inside fastballs. And he was not above resorting to fisticuffs to defend his honor as ferociously as he defended the inside half of the plate—something future Hall of Fame manager Casey Stengel discovered as a young player during Luque's remarkable 1923 major-league season, in which he won 27 games with just 8 losses and a 1.93 earned run average for the Cincinnati Reds.

Despite being white, Luque often was the target of racially tinged bench jockeying from opposing teams. During a midsummer game against the New York Giants at Cincinnati's Redland Field, utility outfield Bill Cunningham led taunts that included slurs such as "Cuban nigger." When Luque finally reached his breaking point, he dropped his glove, came off the mound, and stormed the Giants dugout. Luque took a swing, decking Stengel, who had been sitting next to Cunningham. Despite four Cincinnati police officers dragging Luque back to the Reds dugout, the Cuban pitcher broke free and returned to the Giants bench for more—this time with a bat. Police finally escorted Luque to the Reds clubhouse.[27]

In almost every imaginable way, Maglie was the polar opposite of

Luque. Maglie biographer Judith Testa described him as "a big, good-natured bundle of pitching potential . . . a quiet, gentle, self-effacing man who . . . after more than a decade of effort, had just begun learning how to pitch." And out of that clay, Luque envisioned creating a kindred spirit. He saw Maglie as a potential "mound menace . . . who, with little effort, could look thoroughly threatening."[28] But whatever facial contortions Luque could teach Maglie, they were no substitute for the intimidation of a head-high, inside fastball. So he drilled into Maglie the importance of owning the plate, the entire plate. And Luque, who had learned his own devastating curve ball from Christy Mathewson, worked with Maglie to hone his already good curve ball by using different arm angles to deliver the pitch.[29] The results were instantly noticeable from the outset of the 1945–46 Cuban League season. In his first start for Cienfuegos on October 31, Maglie tossed a complete game, scattering eight hits, although he lost 2–0 to Habana. From November 1945 through January 15, 1946, he lost only once in fourteen appearances. And even though that loss also came against the Leones (Lions) of Habana, Maglie became a thorn in their side throughout the first half of the season.

After bouncing from city to city for several years, Orestes Miñoso returned to Havana in 1941, staying in a $7-per-month one-bedroom apartment with his half sisters, Juanita and Flora. To pay his share, Miñoso earned $6 a month delivering food to the upper-class Vedado neighborhood. He also continued playing baseball, first for the Partagás Cigarette Factory's semipro team, then for the Ambrosía Candy Factory. His big break in semipro ball came when he once again left Havana to play for the Cuban Mining team in Oriente, Cuba's easternmost province.[30]

He made the most of it. In his debut with the Miners, one of Cuba's best semipro teams, Miñoso went 3-for-3 with three runs batted in against future Pittsburgh Pirates pitcher Lino Donoso. Miñoso's performance in his first season with the Miners prompted the team to pay him $100 per month plus expenses to return for another. He never made it to the end of that season. While he was celebrating his birthday with his girlfriend at the Plaza de Marte in Santiago de Cuba, manager Juan Solís brought Miñoso a telegram. "They want you in Havana," Solís said. "Marianao wants you to play professional baseball."[31] Taken aback, Miñoso reported for the next stage of his baseball career with the Marianao Base Ball Club of the Cuban League. Growing up, Miñoso had idolized Cuban League legend and future Hall of Famer Martín Dihigo.[32] Now Miñoso would don the uniform of one of the teams Dihigo had played with during his illustrious career.

Miñoso made his Cuban League debut on December 6, 1945, against Almendares, entering the game in the seventh inning for Marianao third baseman Tony Castaño, who hurt his knee chasing after a foul ball. "I didn't have a number on my [uniform] back," Miñoso recounted. "I was in the dugout. It had been two days since I arrived from Oriente. [Manager Armando] Marsans called my name. 'Hey, kid. Miñoso, go to third.'" With the score tied at 1–1, the ninth inning belonged to Miñoso. In the top of the inning, he lined a single between first and second base off Almendares pitcher Ramón Bragaña. Miñoso's first hit in his first professional at-bat gave the Monjes Grises, the Gray Monks, a 2–1 lead. "That was my debut," Miñoso said. "The first hit of my professional life, and it was against 'El Profesor' Bragaña, who was one of the best pitchers in Cuba."[33] In the bottom of the inning, he saved the game with his glove. With an Almendares runner on second, Miñoso fielded a bunt attempt and threw to first base to record the first out. On the next batter, he speared a ball hit between third and short and threw out the runner at first. A fly ball to right field ended the game, giving Marianao the victory. Later when Miñoso stepped off the streetcar back in El Vedado, friends and neighbors who had heard the game on the radio rushed to congratulate him.[34]

In a game later that month, Miñoso displayed the speed that would earn him the nickname "the Cuban Comet." Again it was a tie game against Almendares. Miñoso came to the plate against Negro leagues star Raymond Brown. There were two outs in the bottom of the ninth inning, and the bases were loaded. With a full count, Brown threw a knuckleball that Miñoso chopped to second baseman Beto Ávila. Unaware of Miñoso's speed, Ávila fielded it like a routine grounder, and Miñoso beat Ávila's throw at first base, allowing the runner to score from third and give Marianao an 8–7 victory.[35] In the stands, Jorge Pasquel was taking notice of the impressive twenty-year-old rookie.

⚑

Described as "charismatic, dapper, dynamic, eccentric, and wealthy," Jorge Pasquel was one of the most powerful men in Mexico in the 1940s. Born in Veracruz on April 23, 1907, Pasquel was the fourth of five brothers whose diverse import-export business included cigars, liquor, banking, real estate, ranches, oil drilling, and steamship lines. He and his brothers also served as agents for General Motors in Mexico, and Jorge Pasquel even exerted influence as a customs official.[36] Despite all that power, Jorge Pasquel's passion was baseball. In that sphere, Pasquel achieved infamy while trying to raise the Mexican League to its aspirational pinnacle.

In 1940 Jorge Pasquel became owner of the Veracruz Blues of the Mexican League. He and his brothers also owned the Mexico City Reds, and reportedly those teams were backed by upwards of 40 million dollars. They also had some controlling interests in the league's other six teams.[37] Using his deep pockets, Pasquel recruited Negro league star players such as "Cool Papa" Bell, Leon Day, Ray Dandridge, Josh Gibson, and Willie Wells to his Veracruz team. Not satisfied with this, he set his sights on enticing major-league players to break their contracts and jump to the Mexican League with the lure of more lucrative deals south of the border.

It began with lower-level players such as New York Giants outfielder Dan Gardella, who jumped in February of 1946 for $8,000 (almost twice what the Giants had paid him in 1945) plus a $5,000 bonus, and Cuban major leaguers such as Napoleón Reyes, Adrián Zabala, and Roberto Estalella.[38] But as time went on, reports began to surface about Pasquel targeting top-level players such as Bob Feller, Hank Greenberg, Stan Musial, Phil Rizzuto, and Ted Williams. Pasquel was engaging in a baseball-style Mexican-American War, and Major League Baseball commissioner Happy Chandler would take notice and act forcefully.

⚑

Cienfuegos showed early during the 1945–46 Cuban League season that it would be a team to reckon with. The Elefantes, or Elephants, ran their record to 8–3 on November 10 to tie Habana for the lead in the standings. By the end of the month, Cienfuegos's record stood at 16–5 for a .761 winning percentage. Sal Maglie won five of those games, Adrián Zabala won four, and Martín Dihigo, Luis Tiant Sr., and Jean Roy each won two. Luis Tiant Jr., who went on to win 229 games in the major leagues, remembers watching his father pitch at La Tropical stadium, brought to games by an uncle when he was a young boy. "Adrián Zabala, who was a good friend of my father's," the younger Tiant said, "he would see me with my uncle and he would call me over and sit me down in the dugout to watch the game."[39] The elder Tiant, who had been a star in the Negro leagues since 1930 with the Cuban Stars (West), Cuban House of David, and New York Cubans,[40] was winding down his Cuban League career but was still an effective left-handed starter and reliever for Cienfuegos.

No Cienfuegos starter, however, was more effective early on than Maglie. His run during the first two and a half months of the season was nothing short of phenomenal, better than any stretch he had ever experienced in semipro ball, the minors, or his short stint in the majors. After losing a well-pitched game to Habana's Cecil Kaiser in his first start, Maglie rattled off six consecutive victories. He eventually won nine games against just two losses during that run. Maglie pitched complete games in all but two of the nine wins, and seven victories came against Habana. He also pitched all twelve innings of a game that ended in a 2–2 tie against Almendares. The impressive run began on November 4 with Maglie pitching eight innings in a 13–3 win against Habana. He followed that up with a complete-game 10–2 victory against Habana that allowed Cienfuegos to tie Habana for first place in the standings. Maglie then beat Habana 2–1 on November 20, 4–1 on November 25 (while allowing just three hits), and 3–1 on December 10, missing Dick Sisler's impressive Cuban League debut by one day.

On December 16 Maglie again beat Habana, this time tossing 6⅓ innings for a 6–1 victory that ran his record to 6–1. The Lions roughed up Maglie for five runs in 1⅔ innings for a 6–2 loss in his next start on December 22. But he bounced back to beat Habana 1–0 on December 30. In his next three starts, Maglie took to stymieing Almendares, tossing a two-hit 1–0 victory on January 4 and a complete-game 4–3 victory on January 15. Sandwiched between those two starts was a twelve-inning no-decision on January 10. On January 19 Habana earned just its third victory in twelve games against Maglie as the Lions tagged him for five runs in four innings of a 5–3 victory. Maglie did not win again during the 1945–46 season. But no loss compared to what Habana—and specifically Dick Sisler—did to him in his next start.

After serving thirty-seven months in the U.S. Navy, Sisler reported for baseball duty in Havana in early December of 1945. The St. Louis Cardinals wanted him to get ready for the 1946 season under Cardinals third-base coach Miguel Ángel González, who in the winter owned and managed the Habana team of the Cuban League. On December 11 the twenty-five-year-old Sisler debuted for Habana, clubbing two home runs and driving in three runs. Marianao's starting pitcher Charlie Cuellar, a Cuban-American native of Ybor City, Florida, also made his Cuban League debut that day. Thanks to a two-run line-drive single to center by Orestes Miñoso, Cuellar reached the bottom of the seventh inning with a 2–0 lead, having given up just one hit. But Sisler cut the lead in half with his first home run, a towering blast that cleared the fence in right field by sixteen feet. Habana tied the score in the eighth inning, and Cuellar did not make it out of the ninth. After René Monteagudo led off with a walk, Sisler crushed a high pitch from Cuellar that rolled to the scoreboard in left-center field some 447 feet from home plate and gave Habana a 4–2 victory. In chronicling Sisler's first appearance in Cuba, sportswriter René Molina wrote in the next day's *Diario de la Marina*:

> Dick Sisler's debut in Cuba will be recorded in the history of our baseball along with its indelible characters. . . . The son of the unforgettable George Sisler, who appears empowered to disprove the theory that the sons of stars never reach the glory of their

ancestors, became a central figure in Habana's victory. . . . The old students of the pastime agreed at the end of the game that never in the history of professional games played at La Tropical had a comparable feat been accomplished.[41]

The next pitcher to be victimized in dramatic fashion by Sisler was Almendares left-hander Agapito Mayor, a future Cuban Baseball Hall of Famer. In a wild 9–8 Almendares victory on January 23 that saw Habana's furious ninth-inning rally fall short, Sisler's first-inning home run—"the inhuman blast of the American Hercules"—stood out above all else, according to Molina's account of the game: "Not the sensational victory by Almendares against Habana . . . not the final and dangerous rally by the vanquished, not the spectacular developments throughout the game, exercised as much influence over those present as the huge blast by Dick Sisler."[42] It's no wonder. Sisler's titanic tater cleared a second fence at the expansive La Tropical stadium by "several meters," passing between the A and the L of the Maltina soft drink sign to lodge itself on the roof of the adjacent beer factory.

Following his game-winning hit against Almendares, Miñoso returned to the Marianao dugout to find not only appreciative teammates but also the extended hand of Jorge Pasquel. Trolling for talent for the Mexican League teams he and his brothers owned, Pasquel asked Miñoso to meet him at the Hotel Rió along El Prado, a stately European-style boulevard in the heart of Havana. Miñoso agreed. At the hotel, Pasquel greeted Miñoso with a duffle bag filled with money. "What I saw stunned me," Miñoso wrote in his autobiography. "I had never seen so much money in my life, thousands and thousands of American dollar bills."[43] Pasquel offered Miñoso $10,000 to play one season in Mexico, but Miñoso declined. His ultimate goal was to play baseball in the United States. Even after Pasquel upped the offer to $30,000 for two seasons, Miñoso didn't budge.

Landing a promising Cuban League rookie would have been a nice catch, but Pasquel was after bigger fish. He wanted to fill Mexican League rosters with major leaguers. So Pasquel approached almost any player who would listen. He offered Dick Sisler $7,500, an expensive car, a diamond watch, and a diamond pin to break his contract with the St. Louis Cardinals. Despite having no guarantee of making the big leagues after his military stint, Sisler declined.[44] Pasquel's brother Bernardo made a run at Sal Maglie. Cienfuegos manager Adolfo Luque, who had already agreed to manage in the Mexican League for the 1946 season, introduced Maglie to Bernardo at Havana's Sevilla-Biltmore hotel. The offer to Maglie: $7,500—equal to his 1946 contract with the New York Giants—plus a $3,000 bonus.[45] "The only difference was the bonus and that wasn't large enough to make me throw over the big leagues and play under conditions which I knew nothing about," Maglie would say years later. "I asked him to double the offer and he said he couldn't, but he did give me his card and asked me to get in touch with him if I changed my mind."[46] That simple gesture would cost Maglie later.

Maglie had bounced back from a bad outing before, usually with a stellar complete-game victory. So there was no reason to think he wouldn't do the same after failing to pitch past the fourth inning in a 5–3 loss to Habana on January 15. No reason, except perhaps for Dick Sisler. The St. Louis Cardinals first baseman was making quite the impression in his rookie season in the Cuban League, eliciting awe from Cuban fans and breathless prose from the island's veteran newspapermen. La Tropical was still buzzing from Sisler's mammoth home run the previous day when Cienfuegos arrived for its game against Habana. The Elephants had been in first place since Sal Maglie's complete-game 10–2 victory against Habana on December 10. Of Maglie's nine wins, seven had come against Habana. The Lions again faced Maglie, their nemesis and the league's leading pitcher. Maglie never stood a chance.

The first of Sisler's three home runs against Maglie came in the first inning. It struck the giant clock in right-center field, 426 feet from home plate, on one bounce. Four innings later, his second flew over the 385-foot mark of the first fence and bounced against the *S* on the Cristal beer ad. Sisler's final home run cleared the right-field fence, 398 feet away, by more than 30 feet. Despite Sisler's performance, Maglie left the game after 6⅓ innings with Cienfuegos holding a 7–5 lead. But Sisler's home run with one out helped trigger a four-run inning for Habana, giving the Lions an 8–7 lead.

Sisler, who had also singled in the third, came to the plate in the eighth inning against reliever Ramón Roger. Trailing by one run and not wanting to risk a fourth home run, Cienfuegos manager Adolfo Luque ordered Roger to intentionally walk Sisler with a runner on second and one out. The strategy prevented Sisler from hitting a fourth home run, but it didn't stop Habana from beating Cienfuegos 9–7. "Yesterday Sisler proclaimed himself to be the most popular and most loved man in Cuba, achieving the enormous feat of hitting three home runs in one contest,"[47] columnist Eladio Secades wrote in the following day's *Diario de la Marina*. Although Maglie wasn't charged with the loss, he was well into a slide that would see him lose four of his final five starts.

Despite Maglie's struggles in the second half of the season, Cienfuegos won the Cuban League championship, the team's first title in three seasons with Adolfo Luque at the helm. The Eternal Rivals, Habana and Almendares, finished tied for second at 30 wins and 30 losses, while Marianao was a distant fourth. Its one bright spot was Orestes Miñoso, who batted .294 and was named the league's rookie of the year by a vote of Cuban sportswriters. Sisler finished the season batting .301 with a league-leading nine home runs in 146 at-bats. "When Sisler played for Habana and started hitting home runs, if at that moment he had been nominated for president of Cuba, he would have won," said Cuban broadcaster Rafael "Felo" Ramírez, who began broadcasting baseball in Cuba in 1945 at age twenty-two. "He was one of the largest figures in Cuban baseball."[48]

On January 27, Cuba's Dirección General de Educación Física y Deportes (DGEFD), the General Directorate for Physical Education and Sports, presented Sisler with a medal and a watch. On February 3, La Tropical stadium played host to Dick Sisler Day between games of a doubleheader that featured Almendares versus Marianao and Cienfuegos versus Habana. Manuel Márquez-Sterling, professor emeritus of history at Plymouth State University in New Hampshire, explained the greater impact that Sisler, and a later appearance in Cuba by Boston Red Sox slugger Ted Williams, had on the Cuban League: "The transformation of Cuban baseball from 'Cobbean' to 'Ruthian,' which in the United States had happened in the '20s, was about to come to Cuba. A new generation of Cuban fans who had never seen [Ty] Cobb play had tasted, for the first time, and in a repeated fashion, the sudden and magical power of the long ball. The boys of the 'magical wand' had finally arrived in Cuban baseball."[49]

According to Philadelphia Phillies teammate Robin Roberts, Sisler was so popular in Cuba that "he and his wife Dot needed police protection wherever they went."[50] But perhaps no greater testimonial to Sisler's impact was provided than by author Ernest Hemingway, a "serious baseball fan" whom Sisler "became acquainted with" in Cuba.[51] In his 1952 Pulitzer Prize–winning novel *The Old Man and the Sea*, Hemingway immortalized Sisler, writing this exchange between the old fisherman, Santiago, and the boy with whom he fishes:

"... I think of Dick Sisler and those great drives in the old park."
"There was nothing ever like them. He hits the longest ball I have ever seen."
"Do you remember when he used to come to the Terrace? I wanted to take him fishing but I was too timid to ask him. Then I asked you to ask him and you were too timid."
"I know. It was a great mistake. He might have gone with us. Then we would have that for all of our lives."[52]

By almost any measure, the Cuban League's final season at La Tropical was a rousing success. With World War II ending in August 1945 and the 1946 major-league season yet to begin, the 1945–46 Cuban League season was "the first important postwar season anywhere," Cuban baseball historian Roberto González Echevarría wrote. He noted that the league was stocked with talent: Cubans with major-league experience, young major leaguers, returning war veterans, players who had already jumped to the Mexican League, and Negro league stars.[53] That collection of talent did not disappoint. The memorable exploits of Sisler, Miñoso, and Maglie would be talked about among fans and observers of the game in Cuba for decades. And La Tropical set a new attendance record with a total gate of $390,686, more than double that of the previous season,[54] as the league was about to move to a shiny new baseball cathedral in the heart of Havana.

Boxing Ernest Hemingway

By his own telling, Branch Rickey's desire to break Major League Baseball's twentieth-century color barrier was born in 1904, when he coached baseball at Ohio Wesleyan University. The team's black first baseman, Charles Thomas, had been barred from a South Bend, Indiana, hotel during a trip to play Notre Dame. But Rickey interceded and persuaded the hotel manager to allow Thomas to share Rickey's room as an unregistered guest. In the room, according to Rickey, Thomas furiously rubbed his hands, saying, "If I could only make them white."[1] It took nearly five decades, but in the spring of 1947 Rickey finally was in a position to make his desire to integrate baseball a reality.

Born in Stockdale, Ohio, on December 20, 1881, Rickey played catcher at Ohio Wesleyan before signing his first baseball contract. His professional playing career did not amount to much—just 120 games for the St. Louis Browns and New York Highlanders before an arm injury effectively ended his playing days in 1907. Rickey had two at-bats for the Browns in 1914. That's when his baseball career really took off. He served as a field manager or executive for the Browns, St. Louis Cardinals, Brooklyn Dodgers, and Pittsburgh Pirates from 1913 to 1959. Along the way, Rickey developed a contradictory and complicated reputation.

Rickey was a devout Methodist who never cursed or drank. But he was not above using underhanded tactics, such as hiding players in the Cardinals' vast farm system. He refused to play or manage on Sundays, but he never turned down the gate from games his teams played on the Sabbath.[2] He was the first high-level baseball executive willing to integrate Major League Baseball, but did he do so out of altruism or because there was talent to be plundered and a buck to be made? Rickey once described black players as "the greatest untapped reservoir of raw material in the history of our game," adding, "Negroes will make us winners for years to come."[3] One Rickey biography summed him up this way: "He was another Lincoln; he was Simon Legree; he was a saint, and he was a grievous, unrepentant sinner; he was one of baseball's best executives and innovators, or he was one of the worst of them to his bosses in St. Louis, Brooklyn, and Pittsburgh. . . . Rickey was 'The Mahatma' or 'El Cheapo,' depending on who was writing about him.'"[4]

Rickey joined the Browns as a scout in 1913 and later became the team's field manager before moving up to vice president and general manager by 1917. After joining the Cardinals in 1918, he invented the modern farm system for developing talent through minor-league teams affiliated with their big-league clubs. When Rogers Hornsby replaced Rickey as the Cardinals' field manager in 1925, Rickey remained as the team's vice president and business manager, but the acrimony between him and Cardinals owner Sam Breadon grew beyond repair by the time Rickey's contract expired in 1942, and the two parted ways. The Cardinals were $175,000 in debt when Rickey joined the team, but the players he developed went on to win six National League pennants and four World Series during his tenure.[5] Rickey brought that résumé when he joined the Dodgers as president and general manager in October 1942.

In Rickey's first three seasons at the helm, from 1943 to 1945, the Dodgers finished third, seventh, and third in the National League. He then turned his attention toward integration and identifying who would become Major League Baseball's first acknowledged black player since Moses Fleetwood Walker played with the 1884 Toledo Blue Stockings. Aside from whatever personal motivations may have driven Rickey, external forces were at work as well. Members of the "black press"—Wendell Smith of the *Pittsburgh Courier* and Sam Lacy of the

Baltimore Afro-American among the most vocal—had long championed the cause of integrating baseball. Baseball commissioner Kenesaw Mountain Landis did nothing during his twenty-one-year tenure to break baseball's color barrier. But the man the black press disdainfully referred to as the Great White Father died on November 25, 1944. And the vital role African American servicemen played in World War II prompted questions about the practice of segregation. Landis's replacement, Albert Benjamin "Happy" Chandler, gave voice to such questions, telling Wendell Smith and fellow *Pittsburgh Courier* writer Ric Roberts: "If a black boy can make it on Okinawa and Guadalcanal, hell, he can make it in baseball."[6]

The front page of the May 4, 1933, edition of the *Sporting News* carried a prominently placed article under the headline "A Worthy Offspring." It featured Fred "Dixie" Walker, son of former Washington Senators pitcher Ewart "Dixie" Walker. The younger Walker had batted .350 for the International League's Newark club, and the article trumpeted him as "the ultimate successor to one of the coveted Yankee outfield places"[7]—high praise, considering that the outfield of the 1933 New York Yankees included future Hall of Famers Babe Ruth and Earle Combs and All-Star Ben Chapman. Walker batted .274 with 15 home runs and 51 runs batted in with the Yankees in 1933, earning a spot as the right fielder on the *Sporting News*'s rookie team. But the promise of future stardom was not fulfilled in the Bronx. Shoulder and knee injuries plagued Walker's early major-league career.

The first glimpse of Walker's true potential came in his sixth major-league season. He batted .302, drove in 95 runs, and led the American League with 16 triples with the Chicago White Sox in 1937. But after a six-player trade sent Walker to Detroit for the 1938 season, injuries once again limited his effectiveness, and the Tigers released him in 1939.[8] The Brooklyn Dodgers wasted little time snapping him up, and Walker batted over .300 in seven of his nine seasons with the Dodgers. He led the National League with a .357 batting average in 1944 and drove in a league-leading 124 runs in 1945.

Walker quickly established himself as one of the most popular players in Dodgers history, earning the nickname "the People's Choice"—or "the People's Cherce" in the Brooklyn vernacular. The nickname was born in teammate Hugh Casey's Brooklyn bar. A well-lubricated fan was extolling the virtues of "Dem Bums" to *Brooklyn Eagle* sportswriter Tommy Holmes. When the discussion turned to Walker, the fan said, "Ah, Dixie. He's the people's choice," but it sounded like "peepul's cherce."[9] The moniker stuck, and other New York columnists and writers began referring to Walker as "the People's Cherce" in print. After Walker's playing days with the Dodgers concluded, his name would become synonymous with racism and bigotry, forever linked with a failed effort to prevent integration in the major leagues.

In the early 1940s, Branch Rickey began considering which player might be up to the monumental task of integrating baseball. While perhaps apocryphal, legend has it that star Cuban shortstop Silvio García was among Rickey's early candidates. Born in Limonar, Matanzas, on October 11, 1914, García entered the Cuban League for the 1931–32 season with Habana before playing four seasons with Marianao and one with Almendares. When García joined Santa Clara for the 1940–41 season, his career blossomed as he batted .314. The following season with Cienfuegos, García led the Cuban League in batting (.351), home runs (4), hits (60), and runs (24) in 46 games. He followed that up by batting .303 in 1942–43 and .329 in 1943–44.[10] It was García's performance with a Cuban all-star team during spring training games against the Dodgers in 1942 that confirmed to Rickey that García had major-league talent.[11]

A 1984 *Atlantic Monthly* article credits Cuban baseball historian Edel Casas with providing the details of a meeting between Rickey and García. According to Casas, the pair met in Havana in 1945, with Rickey entertaining the idea of signing the hard-hitting Cuban. In their interview, presumably conducted through an interpreter, Rickey asked García, "What would you do if a white American slapped your face?" García responded directly: "I kill him."[12] Given the racial epithets the first black player in the major leagues in more than six decades was bound to face, whatever consideration Rickey was giving to García surely ended with that meeting.

But it is unlikely García would have been tabbed to break baseball's color barrier even had he displayed more restraint in his answer to Rickey's question, as author Adrián Burgos Jr. notes:

> Rickey's signing of García would not have eliminated all the ambiguity that the Washington Senators, the Cincinnati Reds, and other major-league organizations had played on in justifying the signing of "mulatto" Cubans and Latinos. Players like Pedro Dibut, Roberto Estalella, and Tommy de la Cruz were Cuban and not black, organizational officials explained. García did not represent the optimal prospect through which Rickey and the Dodgers could shatter the ambiguity that long had sustained the color line's system of racial exclusion.[13]

Rickey would need an African American to break baseball's color barrier. Before he even decided who that player would be, Rickey shared his intentions with one member of the Dodgers organization who was not within Rickey's inner circle in the front office: Red Barber.

Walter Lanier Barber, known as "Red" for the color of his hair, was born on February 17, 1908, in Columbus, Mississippi. He had started his career as a baseball broadcaster with the Cincinnati Reds in 1934. Barber was brought to Brooklyn by Larry MacPhail, then president of the Dodgers, in 1938 to be the "Voice of the Dodgers." With Rickey running the Dodgers during World War II, he and Barber one day walked to Joe's Restaurant, a Brooklyn landmark around the corner from the team's offices at 215 Montague Street. During their lunch Rickey told Barber something that left the Dodgers radio play-by-play man speechless. The team's scouts who were scouring the Negro leagues and the Caribbean were not looking for talent to fill a future Negro league team owned by the Dodgers. "What I'm telling you is this: there is a Negro ballplayer coming to the Dodgers," Rickey told Barber. "I don't know who he is, and I don't know where he is, and I don't know when he's coming. But he is coming. And he is coming soon, just as soon as we can find him."[14]

Rickey explained that his family were opposed to his plan and that he was taking Barber into his confidence. Barber responded only with silence. "I have often wondered why this man told *me* about this earth-shaking project," Barber wrote in 1968. "I gave him back 100 per cent silence, because he had shaken me. He had shaken me to my heels. And I think *that* is why he told me, because he knew it would shake me." Born in Mississippi, raised in Florida, Barber was a son of the South. And suddenly he faced the possibility of having to call major-league games that included a black player. Barber went home that night to Scarsdale, New York, and told his wife, Lylah, that he would quit his job as the Dodgers' broadcaster. She assured him he didn't need to make an immediate decision and suggested, "Why don't you have a martini?" After much tortured self-examination, Barber eventually concluded that whenever baseball's first black player of the modern era arrived in Brooklyn, all he had to do was "treat him as a ballplayer, broadcast the ball."[15]

Growing up in a predominantly white section of Pasadena, California, Jack Roosevelt Robinson was used to having to stand up for himself. He had been born on January 31, 1919 in Cairo, Georgia, the young-est of sharecroppers Jerry and Mallie Robinson's five children. Before Jackie reached his first birthday, Jerry Robinson abandoned the fam-ily. In 1920 Mallie Robinson moved what remained of her family to Pasadena, where white neighbors did not always welcome them with open arms. Fights between the Robinson brothers and the neighbor-hood's white kids were common, leading to occasional run-ins with the police.[16] None of those compared to the trouble he found himself in as a young army lieutenant at Fort Hood, Texas.

After becoming UCLA's first four-sport letterman in football, bas-ketball, baseball, and track, Robinson was drafted into the U.S. Army in 1942. Eventually assigned to Fort Hood, Robinson on July 6, 1944, refused a white bus driver's demand he move to the back of the bus.[17] After a heated exchange, military police were called to the scene. Ensu-ing events led to Robinson being placed under arrest on July 24. When the case of *The United States v. 2nd Lieutenant Jack R. Robinson* began on

August 2, 1944, Robinson faced charges of "behaving with disrespect toward . . . his superior officer" and "willful disobedience of a lawful command" from a superior officer. With Robinson facing a court-martial and a possible dishonorable discharge, his defense argued that no articles of war had been violated, but that "a few individuals sought to vent their bigotry on a Negro they considered 'uppity' because he had the audacity to seek to exercise rights that belonged to him as an American and as a soldier."[18]

Whether on the streets of Pasadena or in a military trial, this was not the first or last time Robinson would fight against bigotry. He was acquitted in his legal fight by a two-thirds vote.[19] "Jackie was not the kind of man to take [it]," said Don Newcombe, who spent six seasons as Robinson's teammate with the Brooklyn Dodgers. "Jackie was a man who would always fight back. That's the way he was. He was not afraid to fight back."[20] Despite Robinson's penchant for fighting back, his baseball skills, background as a college athlete at UCLA, and military service all factored into elevating Robinson as Branch Rickey's choice to break baseball's color barrier.

Following his honorable discharge from the army, Robinson signed with the Negro American League's Kansas City Monarchs, and he batted .349 during the 1945 season. At Rickey's behest, Clyde Sukeforth had begun scouting Negro league teams under the pretense of looking for talent to fill a new black team, the Brooklyn Brown Bombers. In August of that season, Sukeforth approached Robinson before a Monarchs game at Chicago's Comiskey Park and invited him to meet with Rickey. On August 28, 1945, Sukeforth brought Robinson to Rickey's Brooklyn office at 215 Montague Street. During the three-hour meeting, Rickey revealed his plan to have Robinson join the Dodgers and grilled him about the obstacles Robinson would face from teammates, opponents, and fans alike. Then Robinson asked, "Mr. Rickey, do you want a ballplayer who's afraid to fight back?" Rickey's response: "I want a player with the guts not to fight back."[21]

The Dodgers announced the signing of Jackie Robinson on October 23, 1945. He would be assigned to the Montreal Royals, Brooklyn's

Class-AAA affiliate in the International League. An Associated Press reporter called Dixie Walker's Birmingham, Alabama, home that day seeking his comment. What did Walker think about his team signing a black player, the first such signing by a major-league team in the twentieth century? Walker tried to evade the question at first. "No, I haven't heard," he said. "I've been busy here at home since the season ended. We have a lot of work to do in the house." Walker finally relented. "Well, he's signed with Montreal," he said. "It doesn't matter to me as long as he isn't on our club."[22]

Walker's baseball pedigree included his father, Ewart "Dixie" Walker; a brother, Harry "the Hat" Walker; and an uncle, Ernie Walker. The younger Dixie had been born on September 24, 1910, in Villa Rica, Georgia, and raised in Birmingham, where Ewart owned a sporting goods and hardware store. But Ewart was an alcoholic, and the store essentially was run by Dixie and Harry, or a manager when the pair were away playing baseball. In a 1981 interview with *New York Times* writer Ira Berkow, Walker admitted he was concerned how Birmingham's citizens would react to him playing baseball with a black teammate. "I didn't know if they would spit on me or not," Walker told Berkow. "And it was no secret I was worried about my business."[23]

But Walker also made it clear his concern for the family business was not the only reason for him to be wary of Robinson's signing. He was a son of the South, with all of the prejudices that growing up below the Mason-Dixon Line entailed. "In those days, you grew up in a different manner than you do today," Walker told Berkow. "We thought blacks didn't have ice water in their veins and so couldn't take the pressures of playing big league baseball. Well, we know now that was as big a farce as there ever was. A person learns and you begin to change with the times."[24] But in 1945, Dixie Walker had no desire to have a black teammate.

In his autobiography, Leo Durocher wrote that his part in signing Robinson "was zero. I read about it in the paper like everybody else."[25] But if the Dodgers' manager had any objections, there's little doubt he would have expressed them. Born on July 27, 1905, in West Springfield,

Massachusetts, Durocher earned his "Leo the Lip" nickname with the 1928 World Series–winning New York Yankees. The diminutive short-stop didn't let his rookie status keep him from becoming a first-class bench jockey against opponents or antagonizing veteran stars on his own team. But when manager Miller Huggins died in 1929, Durocher lost his biggest ally on the team, and the Yankees sold him to the Cincinnati Reds before the 1930 season. In Cincinnati, Durocher "found his gambling appetites even more easily indulged than in New York."[26]

Traded to the St. Louis Cardinals in 1933, Durocher became the captain of the Gashouse Gang, a collection of pugs willing to scrap with teammates and opponents alike. In St. Louis, Durocher played on his second World Series championship team, divorced his first wife, Ruth Hartley, and married wife number two, successful fashion designer Grace Dozier—all in 1934.[27] But by 1937 a strained relationship with Cardinals manager Frankie Frisch prompted a trade to the Dodgers. There Durocher reunited with Larry MacPhail, who had traded him from Cincinnati to the Cardinals, who were then being run by Branch Rickey. The relationship between Durocher, MacPhail, and Rickey eventually prevented Durocher from participating in the most socially significant baseball season in modern history.

After Jackie Robinson signed his minor-league contract with the Dodgers in 1945, the first steps on his path to the majors began in Daytona Beach in the spring of 1946. The Dodgers had set up their spring training camp on the white side of the Florida resort town. The Montreal Royals, Brooklyn's farm team that included Robinson and another African American player, pitcher John Wright, trained in the town's black district. Given such divisions, what kind of reception would Robinson receive?

One answer came on March 17, when the Dodgers and Royals played an exhibition game at City Island Ballpark. Robinson's five innings came and went without incident as "widespread applause drowned out scattered boos." In other Jim Crow Florida towns, however, Robinson's presence wasn't always greeted so warmly. At a pre-training camp in the town of Sanford, Robinson and Wright were barred from the

Mayfair Hotel, where the Dodgers stayed. And after a group of local officials informed Branch Rickey that blacks and whites were not allowed on the same field, *Pittsburgh Courier* sportswriter Wendell Smith drove the pair out of town at Rickey's behest. In Jacksonville the city's parks commission cancelled a game between the Royals and Jersey City on March 23 rather than let Robinson become the first African American to play baseball against whites in the city's ballpark. The Royals arrived in DeLand for a March 25 game only to find a lighting system malfunction had forced the game's cancellation. Later in the week, the Royals found the stadium in Jacksonville padlocked.[28]

These were the kinds of incidents Rickey wanted to avoid when he decided to relocate the organization's spring training camp from Florida to Cuba for 1947. In Havana, "Jackie Robinson and other Negro candidates," Wendell Smith predicted, "will be able to try out for the team in complete freedom."[29] Smith's assertion did not play out exactly as predicted.

The Dodgers were no strangers to Havana. Under Larry MacPhail as president, the team had held spring training at the Cuban League's home stadium, La Tropical, in 1941 and 1942. Those visits were part of what became known in Cuba as the American Series, games played on Cuban soil by major-league teams or barnstorming Negro leaguers before and after the Cuban League season. The Series dated to 1891, when an All-Americans team, led by future New York Giants manager and future Hall of Famer John McGraw, went 5–0 in games against four Cuban squads: Habana, Fe, Almendares, and All-Cubans.[30]

In 1941 the Dodgers were one of five major-league teams—along with the New York Giants, Cleveland Indians, Cincinnati Reds, and Boston Red Sox—to hit the field at La Tropical that spring. Brooklyn swept a pair of three-game series against the Giants and Indians but split four games against a Cuban all-star team (one game ended in a 7–7 tie). Cuban pitcher Gilberto Torres beat the Dodgers' Hugh Casey 9–1, and Adrián Zabala was a 4–3 winner against Brooklyn.[31] Some of the real action, however, took place away from La Tropical.

One Sunday exhibition game between the Dodgers and Indians was to feature Bob Feller against Van Lingle Mungo. Feller led the American League with 27 wins, a 2.61 earned run average, and 261 strikeouts in 1940. Mungo was on his last legs, but earlier in his career the Dodgers right-hander had won 16, 18, 16, and 18 games in consecutive seasons from 1933 to 1936. Mungo seemed uninterested in regaining his playing form of previous seasons in the spring of 1941. He was more focused on two women—Lady Ruth Vine, a hostess at Havana's Hotel Nacional, and the female half of the husband-and-wife dance team of Carreño and Carreño. That became apparent on the eve of Mungo's scheduled start against Feller.

Dodgers manager Leo Durocher had been ejected from Saturday's game for arguing an umpire's call and Cuban soldiers had to surround the manager and escort him "the whole 600 feet to the clubhouse." Afterward, Durocher and MacPhail went to the International Casino for dinner and roulette. Durocher eventually returned to the Hotel Nacional, where the Dodgers were staying, to check on Mungo. Durocher had granted Mungo permission to stay out late the previous two nights and suddenly felt uneasy about what the pitcher might be up to that night. When Durocher reached the Nacional around 12:30 in the morning, he came across Mungo, who bumped into walls as he stumbled out of the hotel bar. "That's how drunk he was," Durocher wrote in his autobiography, saying Mungo was "almost impossible to understand." For the third consecutive night, Mungo asked Durocher for late leave. Durocher couldn't believe it and threatened to fine him $200. "You've got five minutes to get up those stairs and get to your room," Durocher yelled, and a grumbling Mungo obliged. Not long afterward, however, from the window of his suite, Durocher saw Mungo leave the hotel with Lady Ruth on one arm and dancer Cristina Carreño, formerly Miriam Morgan of Wilkes-Barre, Pennsylvania, on the other. "What the hell do they see in him, either of them?" Durocher thought. "As drunk as that, both of them?"[32]

Not surprisingly, Mungo didn't make it on time to La Tropical the following day. He staggered into the Dodgers clubhouse complaining that the team bus had left without him. Durocher slapped him with a $200 fine for breaking training rules and another $200 for not showing up on time. Realizing Mungo was still drunk, Durocher fined Mungo another $200 and ordered him to leave the ballpark and return to the hotel. When Mungo tried to threaten Durocher, the manager encouraged the player to take his best shot: "Go ahead. It's me and you. I'm going to sink this Coca-Cola bottle into that numbskull of yours." Even in his condition, Mungo wasn't foolish enough to take on his pugnacious manager. But on his way out of the stadium, Mungo punched a cabdriver, incurring another fine, $400 from MacPhail, who ordered the pitcher to return to the States on the seven-o'clock boat to Miami that night.[33]

Did Mungo follow orders and leave? Of course not. At six the next morning, the hotel manager summoned Durocher to room 273, where he found policemen, soldiers with bayonets, and Cristina's husband, Francisco Collada Carreño, a former bullfighter turned conga dancer, carrying a butcher knife. Señor Carreño had found his wife in bed with Mungo and Lady Ruth. The ensuing scuffle had required police intervention. While soldiers restrained Carreño, Dodgers executive Babe Hamberger dragged Mungo away and hid him in the hotel's basement. Hamberger eventually delivered Mungo to the Havana Harbor wharf where a Pan-Am seaplane was waiting to get him off the island. "Police came running down the wharf after him, blowing whistles," Durocher wrote. "Somebody threw a rope out of the plane, Mungo grabbed it. They pulled him aboard and he got out of Cuba."[34]

The following spring, the Dodgers again sojourned in Cuba, where they split two games with the Giants but lost three of five against a Cuban all-star team. Tomás de la Cruz, Agapito Mayor, and Rodolfo Fernández limited Brooklyn to six runs in the local nine's three victories. But once again, the most interesting action took place off the field, this time at Finca Vigía, Ernest Hemingway's farm in San Francisco de Paula, about ten miles outside Havana. Hemingway's interest in baseball, particularly in Cuba, eventually seeped into his writings. His 1952 Pulitzer Prize-winning novel *The Old Man and the Sea*, includes references not only to Cuban League player Dick Sisler but to legendary managers Adolfo Luque and Miguel Ángel González.[35]

Norberto Fuentes's 1984 biography *Hemingway in Cuba* describes

Hemingway's allegiance to the Cuban League while the writer was recovering from hepatitis in November of 1955:

> It was in these days, during his convalescence, that Hemingway enjoyed a rare indulgence. He would settle himself for hours in front of the TV set to watch the outcome of Cuba's championship baseball games. He was a fan of the "Havana" club, a professional team whose red uniforms bore the figure of a lion. His impassioned TV viewing and his heated arguments in defense of the "Havana" made [Doctor Herrera] Sotolongo at times fear for Ernest's health. There was a certain American pitcher, Wilmer Mizell (whom the Cubans called "Vinagre" Maicel) who was his special favorite and who broke a record that year, much to Hemingway's delight.[36]

In the 1955–56 Cuban League season, Wilmer "Vinegar Bend" Mizell, who pitched nine major-league seasons mostly with the St. Louis Cardinals, set a Cuban League record by striking out 206 batters in 179 innings. But Hemingway's interest in and connection to baseball in Cuba began more than a decade earlier.

During the Dodgers' 1942 spring training in Cuba, Hemingway attended games at La Tropical and shot dice at the Nacional Casino with Dodgers players such as Kirby Higbe and Hugh Casey. One day the writer invited Casey, Higbe, Billy Herman, Larry French, and Augie Galan to his farm for skeet shooting, dinner, and drinks—many drinks. After dinner Hemingway's then-wife, Martha Gellhorn, turned in for the night as the men continued enjoying libations. "Hemingway was really loaded," Herman told author Peter Golenbock for a 2002 oral history on the Brooklyn Dodgers. "Hemingway was looking at Hugh Casey, kind of sizing him up." That's when Hemingway insisted the two of them lace up boxing gloves. Herman told Golenbock that as a hesitant Casey was pulling on his gloves, Hemingway sucker-punched the Dodgers pitcher, knocking him into a bookshelf and bringing a tray of booze, glasses, and ice crashing to the marble floor. That quelled whatever reluctance Casey might have had about engaging in fisticuffs with the famous writer. "He just got up and finished putting on his gloves," Herman said. "Without saying a single word, Casey started hitting him, really belting him."[37]

Twice the ruckus brought Martha downstairs, and twice Hemingway waved her back to bed, insisting it was all in good fun. The fun ended when Hemingway kicked Casey in the crotch. The other players had seen enough, made the two combatants take off the gloves, and decided it was time to the head back to the Hotel Nacional. But before the players were driven back to their hotel, according to Herman, Hemingway pulled Casey aside and asked him to spend the night so they could take part in another challenge the next morning: "You got the best of me," Hemingway told Casey. "You beat the hell out of me. I was real drunk, but tomorrow morning we'll both be sober and we'll duel. You pick it. Knives, guns, swords, anything you want. You pick the weapon." Before Casey had time to accept, his teammates dragged him out of the house.[38]

At the ballpark the next day, an embarrassed Hemingway apologized. "I don't know what got into me," he told the players. "I knew exactly what got into him—about a quart, that's what," Herman told Golenbock. Despite the sucker punch and the kick to the groin during their pugilistic encounter, Higbe concluded, "Ernest and Casey just hit it off. Those were two of a kind, really."[39] Years later, Casey and Hemingway met similar fates. On July 3, 1951, with his estranged wife listening on the telephone as he sat in an Atlanta hotel room, Casey put a 16-gauge shotgun to his throat and pulled the trigger, ending his life at age thirty-eight. Kathleen Casey, who pleaded with Hugh not to take his life, said his last words were: "I'm innocent of those charges"— accusations of paternity that had been leveled by another woman.[40] Almost ten years later to the day, on July 2, 1961, Hemingway was found dead in his Ketchum, Idaho, home, a shotgun wound to his head and a 12-gauge shotgun at his side.

After the eventful visits in 1941 and 1942, Durocher once again led the Dodgers to Cuba for spring training in 1947. His flight from Los Angeles arrived at New York's La Guardia Airport on Monday, February

17, 1947. At the airport, reporters peppered him with questions: about the Dodgers, about his recent marriage to Hollywood actress Laraine Day, about Robinson's prospects of joining his team. Durocher extolled the virtues of Brooklyn's outfield, refused to comment on his marriage, and was reticent about Robinson. He pointed out that Robinson would be on Montreal's roster and not Brooklyn's. "I don't see how I can pay much attention to him since I will be plenty occupied with my own players," Durocher said. "We are scheduled to play several games against Montreal in Havana and Panama and I will probably get a better look at him then."[41] Durocher later became far more vocal about his intentions for Robinson—just not with the press.

Durocher wouldn't have to worry about keeping Van Lingle Mungo sober and away from Havana showgirls on this visit. Mungo's escapades had gotten him run out of Brooklyn in 1941, and his playing career ended in 1945. Hugh Casey and Kirby Higbe were still on the roster, presumably wiser after the drunken bout at Ernest Hemingway's ranch in 1942. But Casey and Higbe would find themselves at the center of a very different situation in 1947, one that purportedly sought to derail Robinson's ascension to the major leagues. The episode would prompt a tongue-lashing from Durocher more severe than anything he had ever unleashed on Mungo in 1941.

And Durocher would have his own issues to deal with in Cuba. After failed marriages to Ruth Hartley and Grace Dozier, Durocher was ensconced in a scandalous relationship with Day. Durocher married her in January of 1947 while she was still mired in divorce proceedings against her husband, singer Ray Hendricks.[42] Durocher's relationship with Day would tangentially affect spring training, but his other associations would have a more devastating impact upon his 1947 season. He had been living at the home of actor George Raft, who was friends with gangster Bugsy Siegel. Worried about the implications of such an association, Dodgers president Branch Rickey sent team executive Arthur Mann to Happy Chandler's office to ask the baseball commissioner to scare Durocher.[43]

According to longtime Dodgers broadcaster Red Barber, Chandler ordered Durocher to "sever connections with all kinds of people regarded as undesirables by baseball—gangsters, known gamblers, companions of known gamblers and racketeers,"[44] such as Memphis Engelberg and Connie Immerman. Engelberg worked as a horse-racing bookmaker, and Immerman ran the Cotton Club in New York and a casino in Havana. Durocher agreed. Chandler also instructed Durocher to move out of Raft's house. Again, Durocher agreed. But in Cuba, a chance sighting of Engelberg and Immerman—not with Durocher but with Larry MacPhail, now the New York Yankees president—would undo Durocher's season.

In a letter dated February 4, 1947, *Pittsburgh Courier* sportswriter Wendell Smith wrote Jackie Robinson. Smith expressed his expectations for the Brooklyn Dodgers' upcoming spring-training camp, which would be based in Havana, Cuba, and include trips to Venezuela and Panama. "I doubt seriously that you will have to make the trip to South America," Smith wrote. "I was talking to Rickey on the telephone the other day and from what I could gather he intends to keep you with Montreal. I would not be surprised, however, if you and [Robinson's Montreal Royals teammate Roy] Campanella are assigned to the Dodgers before the regular season opens."[45]

Smith also tried to assuage any anxiety Robinson might have been feeling heading into spring training. "You should not worry about the plans they have for you," Smith wrote. "As I see it you are definitely going to get a chance. All you have to do is keep a cool head, play the kind of ball you are capable of playing and don't worry about anything. As you know, Rickey is no dummy. He is a very methodical man and will see to it that you are treated right. All you have to do is take care of Jackie Robinson on the playing field and he will do the rest."[46] In mid-February of 1947, Robinson and Dixie Walker each boarded trains, Walker in Alabama and Robinson in Los Angeles. They were bound for Miami, where members of the Dodgers and their Montreal farm team would gather before continuing on to Havana.[47]

Aside from Robinson, the Royals roster included three other African American players whom the Dodgers had signed from their respective Negro league teams—Campanella, Don Newcombe, and Roy Partlow. Forgoing Jim Crow Florida, where the Dodgers had trained the previous spring, team president Branch Rickey chose as the staging ground for his great experiment the island of Cuba, which had played host to interracial baseball since 1900. Rickey hoped that after seeing Robinson's performance in the tropics—the Dodgers had also scheduled games against the Royals in Panama—Dodgers players would willingly accept Robinson as the first African American player in the majors since before the turn of the twentieth century. But the trip to Cuba would not unfold nearly as smoothly as Rickey had envisioned.

Opening Day, Havana

More than 2,000 people attended as Monsignor Alfredo Muller, the Catholic bishop of Havana, blessed El Gran Stadium on Thursday, October 25, 1946. The new steel-and-concrete stadium was the product of La Compañía Operadora de Stadiums, the company formed by wealthy Cubans Bobby Maduro and Miguelito Suárez to build a more modern baseball stadium close to the heart of Havana, one to accommodate growing attendance. El Gran Stadium "represents a great bit of dreaming" by Maduro and Suárez, J. G. Taylor Spink wrote in the *Sporting News*. "Construction difficulties, labor troubles, and mounting costs hiked their expenditure to $1,800,000, when they had figured to spend one million."[1] Havana's new baseball cathedral was only three-quarters complete for the monsignor's benediction. And the start of the 1946–47 Cuban League season was a day away. No matter. The season would start on schedule in its new home.

Construction issues and an incomplete stadium were far from the only potential hurdles leading up to opening day. For months, Mexican League president Jorge Pasquel had been luring major-league players to jump their contracts for the monetarily greener pastures of Mexico. Many of those players had been stalwarts in Cuba's winter league. And Cuban League managers and coaches also had participated in the Mexican League. For them, stints in Mexico meant banishment from organized baseball—Major League Baseball and its affiliated professional minor leagues—if they did not desist. For the Cuban League, having those players, managers, and coaches on their rosters could mean excommunication from organized baseball. Aside from outside threats—sanctions imposed by baseball commissioner Happy Chandler for jumping to Mexico—the Cuban League faced a threat from within as well: a rival league made up of players in good standing with organized baseball. The alternate league would play at La Tropical, the stadium that had been home to the Cuban League from 1930 to 1946. How would such a schism impact a sport that had become so ingrained in Cuban culture since the 1870s?

Albert Benjamin "Happy" Chandler turned his attention to politics not long after graduating from law school at the University of Kentucky in 1924. Born in Corydon, Kentucky, on July 14, 1898, the jovial Chandler earned his nickname while playing baseball at Transylvania College in Lexington, Kentucky. He served as a senator in the Kentucky state legislature, as the state's lieutenant governor, and then as governor before representing his home state in the U.S. Senate from October 10, 1939, until November 1, 1945. That's when Chandler, who had advocated for the game to continue operating during World War II, resigned to become commissioner of baseball. After baseball's first commissioner, Kenesaw Mountain Landis, died on November 25, 1944, Major League Baseball's sixteen owners unanimously elected Chandler on April 24, 1945.[2]

Almost from his first day as commissioner, Chandler found himself dealing with history-altering events. The month he was officially installed, Dodgers president Branch Rickey signed Jackie Robinson with the intention of having him break baseball's color barrier—a plan opposed by baseball's other fifteen team owners. And not long after Chandler took office, Major League Baseball faced perhaps its biggest outside challenge since the rival Federal League of 1914–15 tried luring major-league players with more lucrative contracts. Perpetrating the raids this time was Pasquel. By February of 1946 he had already started throwing around the $30 million he had at his disposal for the Mexican

League "so as to make it as good, or better than, baseball in the United States."[3]

As far as Pasquel was concerned, he was giving organized baseball a taste of its own medicine. And he and his brothers were more than willing to engage in a little saber rattling. Pasquel argued that, for years, major-league teams had raided players under Mexican League contracts, specifically accusing Washington Senators scout Joe Cambria of the tactic. Cambria was a ubiquitous presence in Cuba, where he became affectionately known as Papa Joe. The native of Messina, Italy, began signing Cuban players for Senators owner Clark Griffith in 1932 with the purchase of Ysmael "Mulo" Morales from Alex Pompez's New York Cubans of the Negro National League. During his three decades as a scout, Papa Joe signed more than four hundred Cuban players, many of them for Griffith, who had managed the Cincinnati Reds in 1911 when Armando Marsans and Rafael Almeida became the first Cuban-born players in the majors of the modern era. But because he signed players cheaply, not everyone in Cuba was enamored of Cambria. Cuban sportswriter Jess Losada of *Carteles* "acidly referred to him as the Christopher Columbus of baseball, denoting his thirst for and taking of the island's treasures."[4]

Pasquel's accusation that Cambria had raided the Mexican League of players under contract was the same complaint leveled by those inside organized baseball against the Pasquel brothers. But Pasquel had no intention of apologizing for or backing down from using his considerable wealth as payback. He insisted he needed big-name players and managers "to prove to the baseball world at large that we're not fooling when we say the Mexican League is going big time."[5] With the Mexican newspaper *Excelsior* proclaiming that baseball in the United States "is like a slave market," Gerardo Pasquel, one of the five brothers, agreed: "We treat the players right here. We don't treat them like slaves."[6] The headline and quote were part of a story that featured an interview with former New York Giants outfielder Danny Gardella, who was among the Pasquel brothers' early major-league recruits. "I do not intend to let the New York Giants enrich themselves any further, at my expense," Gardella said when he informed baseball writers on February 18 that he had accepted a five-year contract to play in Mexico after the Giants were only willing to pay him $500 more than the $4,500 he had earned in 1945.[7]

Gardella was but the first domino to fall. The same day as Gardella's announcement, Puerto Rican–born Dodgers outfielder/infielder Luis Rodríguez Olmo jumped his contract for a reported three-year, $40,000 deal in Mexico. Ten days later, Chicago White Sox pitcher Alejandro "Patón" Carrasquel bolted for a reported three-year, $10,000 offer. But the Mexican League had it sights set much higher than the Danny Gardellas, Luis Olmos, and Alejandro Carrasquels of the major-league world. On March 9, Boston Red Sox slugger Ted Williams rejected a $500,000 offer from Bernardo Pasquel. Two days later, Cleveland Indians ace Bob Feller confirmed he too had rejected an offer from the Pasquels, who also had taken an unsuccessful run at Detroit Tigers slugger Hank Greenberg.[8]

With such brazen efforts to abscond with contractually obligated, top-notch major-league talent, Chandler had no choice but to act to stop the raids. At a March 1946 meeting in Havana to welcome the Havana Cubans to the Class-C Florida International League and organized baseball, Chandler "issued a flat and vigorous directive to all players who have jumped contracts." His edict was simple: These players must return to their major-league teams by the start of the 1946 season or face banishment from the majors for at least five seasons. "They may not apply for reinstatement until after five years and application may not be granted even after that passage of time."[9]

Despite Chandler's warning, Pasquel's money was too enticing for some. Cuban players Tomás de la Cruz, formerly of the Cincinnati Reds, and the brothers Oliverio and Roberto Ortiz of the Washington Senators were in Mexican League uniforms when the season opened on March 22, 1946. News of St. Louis Browns shortstop Vern Stephens signing a Mexican League contract for $100,000 for five years was reported on March 30 (he returned from Mexico after just two games). On March 31, New York Giants players Sal Maglie, George Hausmann, and Roy Zimmerman jumped their major-league contracts and headed south of the border after each received the promise of a $5,000 bonus and "at least twice as much as we would be receiving from the Giants," Maglie said.[10]

Hausmann and Zimmerman, unhappy with their limited playing time in spring training, approached Maglie one day about how to get in touch with the Pasquels. They knew their teammate had turned down an offer to join the Mexican League during the winter in Cuba, and Maglie still had the business card Bernardo Pasquel had given him. Later in the day in his hotel room, Maglie allowed Hausmann and Zimmerman to use his phone to secure contracts with the Mexican League. Even Maglie got on the phone, taking one last shot to see if he could get Pasquel to double the $7,500 salary he was set to make with the Giants. When Pasquel wouldn't up his previous offer, Maglie hung up the phone, never realizing how much trouble lay ahead. "That's what fucked me up with [Giants owner Horace] Stoneham and [manager Mel] Ott," he said years later. "I suppose the switchboard operator told somebody about the call, and since it came from my room the club figured it was me who made it."[11]

The next day, Ott summoned Maglie into the manager's office and angrily accused Maglie of working as an agent for the Pasquel brothers. A livid Ott demanded to know which other Giants players were going to jump to the Mexican League. A stunned and now equally angry Maglie told Ott to figure it out for himself. Ott stormed out of his office, lining up his players and interrogating them about the Mexican League. In that moment, Maglie had to have felt that his major-league career was over after it had barely begun. At age twenty-eight, he had played all of thirteen games in the majors for the Giants in 1945, and he was about to turn his back on his dream, knowing it would lead to at least a five-year ban under Chandler's edict. Maglie boarded a train from the Giants' spring training site in Miami for Mexico.[12]

Before the start of the 1946 major-league season, Chandler, in an interview printed in the *Sporting News*, reiterated his earlier warning. Any players who jumped their organized baseball contracts to sign with the Mexican League would be barred for at least five years if they did not return to their teams by opening day of the 1946 major-league season: "Any jumper who is barred will not have the right to appeal for reinstatement within five years," Chandler said, "and after this five-year period is finished, there may be certain cases in which I will not even then entertain a plea for reinstatement."[13] Jumpers seemed unconcerned by Chandler's threats. "I'm perfectly happy here," former Dodgers catcher Mickey Owens declared. "I have no regrets," Carrasquel said. "Who would, leaving the White Sox?" And Gardella quipped: "I assure you I'm just as happy as Ott and probably less confused."[14]

Chandler also specifically addressed Cuba, saying baseball officials there had asked him to come to the island the previous fall to "help them rectify their situation." The commissioner promised there would be no ineligible players—either those who had jumped their organized baseball contracts or those who played with or against ineligible players in Mexico—in the Cuban League for the 1946–47 season. He also said he was willing to forget previous transgressions, such as St. Louis Cardinals owner Sam Breadon sending Lou Klein, Fred Martin, and Dick Sisler to play for Miguel Ángel González's Habana team during the 1945–46 Cuban League season, but Chandler also said he was going to "see that this sort of thing does not occur again."[15]

Chandler's warnings also did nothing to prevent further incursions by the Pasquels. Despite repeated denials, New York Yankees shortstop Phil Rizzuto agreed to accept a five-year offer worth $12,000 per year, plus a $15,000 bonus, after meeting with Bernardo Pasquel at a dinner party at New York's Waldorf-Astoria hotel in early May. But the next day Rizzuto had second thoughts, and a day later the Yankees filed suit to enjoin the Mexican League from trying to sign American League players.[16] By May 23 reports surfaced that Klein, Martin, and St. Louis Cardinals teammate Max Lanier, who would go on to play significant roles in the 1946–47 Cuban League season, were preparing to jump to the Mexican League. The trio failed to show up at New York's Polo Grounds for the conclusion of a series against the Giants. Instead Bernardo Pasquel escorted them to Mexico's tourist bureau in New York to obtain permits to visit Mexico. Before the team checked out of the Hotel New Yorker, Lanier left a note telling Cardinals teammate and road roommate Red Schoendienst, "So long, Red. Keep hitting line drives. I'll see you next winter and we'll go hunting. Best of luck." Lanier reportedly was offered a five-year contract worth $30,000 a year, plus a $50,000 signing bonus. "I can make more down there in a few seasons," Lanier said, "than I could in a lifetime in St. Louis."[17] Another Pasquel brother, Alfonso, tried unsuccessfully to lure Cardinals outfielder Stan Musial, offering him $130,000 for five years during a June 6 meeting at the Fairgrounds Hotel in St. Louis.[18]

In all, twenty-three players jumped their major-league contracts to play for Pasquel. They included Cuban players Roberto Ortiz (Washington Senators), Roberto Estalella (Philadelphia Athletics), René Monteagudo (Philadelphia Phillies), and Napoleón Reyes and Adrián Zabala (New York Giants). The list also included several others who either did or would play in the Cuban League, such as Venezuela's Alejandro Carrasquel (Chicago White Sox), Puerto Rico's Luis Rodríguez Olmo and Canada's Roland Gladu (Brooklyn Dodgers); and Americans Maglie, Hausmann, and Gardella (Giants) and Klein, Lanier, and Martin (St. Louis Cardinals).[19]

To stem the tide of defections, major-league owners met in Chicago on August 28 and amended Rule 18(b), which still reads in part:

> No player shall participate in any exhibition game with or against any team, which during the current season, or within one year, has had any ineligible player or which is or has been during the current season or within one year, managed or controlled by an ineligible player . . . under an assumed name, or who otherwise has violated, or attempted to violate, any exhibition game or contract; or with or against any team which, during said season or within one year, has played against teams containing such ineligible players, or so managed or controlled. Any player violating this rule . . . shall be fined not less than fifty dollars ($50), nor more than five hundred dollars ($500).[20]

Such a guilt-by-association rule meant even Cuban League players who did not flock to the riches of Mexico faced the threat of heavy fines and banishment from the majors if they played with ineligibles in Cuba. So some Cuban players turned their backs on the Cuban League in order to protect their eligibility with organized baseball. Instead, they joined La Federación Nacional de Béisbol. This National Baseball Federation was an organized-baseball-sanctioned league set up at La Tropical stadium as an alternative to Cuba's traditional winter league.

The rival league was off limits to ineligible players. Two players who walked away from the Cuban League were Gilberto Torres and Fermín Guerra, teammates with the Washington Senators. Each had played in Cuba's winter league since 1934. But neither player's loyalty to organized baseball had been completely without question in the past.

With World War II still raging, the Selective Service on July 13, 1944, informed the Senators' four Cuban players—Guerra, Torres, Roberto Ortiz, and Preston Gómez—that they had to register to be drafted into the United States Army within ten days or return to Cuba. Guerra and Ortiz quickly opted to return to their homeland rather than subject themselves to the draft. Torres, whose wife and four-year-old son had already left for Havana, wanted to stay. "It took me eleven years of playing in American baseball to get into the big leagues," Torres said, "and I do not want to quit now."[21] But on July 16, Torres decided to join Guerra and Ortiz in returning to Cuba, saying he would try to secure a new U.S. passport. Torres's departure left only Gómez, who had announced he would register for the draft and remain with the Senators.[22] Ten days later, Torres returned from Cuba to rejoin the Senators.

Before the 1946 major-league season, rumors circulated that Torres and Guerra were about to jump to the Mexican League. On March 23, Bernardo Pasquel denied he had signed Torres. That same week, the Senators received Torres's signed contract, and Guerra confirmed he and his countryman would report to Washington's spring training camp in Orlando, Florida.[23] When the pair reported on March 27, Torres explained that he had turned down a three-year contract to join the Mexican League that would have included a $5,000 signing bonus and paid him $8,000 a year plus living and traveling expenses. "That money looked good," Torres said, "but my association in the United States looked better."[24]

Torres's and Guerra's salaries with the Senators were approximately double what they earned in the Cuban League. In 1945, for example, the Senators paid Torres $8,900, compared to the $3,500 he could make in the shorter Cuban League season.[25] Had they opted for Mexico, they would have kept their winter salaries but lost their eligibility within organized baseball. By joining the National Federation, Torres and Guerra remained in good standing with their major-league clubs and still drew a winter paycheck. Torres signed to manage the rival league's Havana Reds, and Guerra enlisted for the same position with the Oriente club. Silvio García, whom Branch Rickey purportedly considered as a candidate to break baseball's color barrier, signed to manage the league's Matanzas club.

For Miguel Ángel González, the choice didn't come down to money or his status in organized baseball. The Cuban baseball icon had played his winter career almost exclusively with Habana. He managed the team and eventually became an owner. At age fifty-six, his playing days were well behind him. And his holdings with the team were more profitable than his salary as the St. Louis Cardinals third-base coach. But because of the financial windfall Klein and Martin had gained by jumping to the Mexican League during the 1946 National League season, the man who managed them in Cuba would pay a price.

The 1946 major-league season had ended on October 15 with a thrilling seventh game of the World Series between González's Cardinals and the Boston Red Sox. With the score tied at 3–3, Enos Slaughter led off the bottom of the eighth inning with a single to center. After a popped-up bunt attempt and a flyout, Slaughter remained on first with two outs. Harry "the Hat" Walker, brother of Dodgers outfielder Dixie Walker, laced a double to left-center field. As Red Sox center fielder Leon Culberson bobbled the ball, Slaughter, who had been running on the pitch, headed for third. Shortstop Johnny Pesky hesitated with Culberson's throw, and Slaughter turned past third and raced for home. Pesky's relay arrived too late to prevent the eventual winning run.

It's a matter of contention whether González waved Slaughter home or tried to hold him up. Not that it would have mattered to Slaughter. In the fourth inning of game 1, González had held up Slaughter at third base rather than let him try for an inside-the-park home run, much to Slaughter's chagrin. The Cardinals lost the game 3–2 in ten innings. In the dugout, a furious Slaughter complained to manager Eddie Dyer, who told Slaughter, "All right, all right. If it happens again and you think you can make it, go ahead."[26] Slaughter got his chance in game 7. With it, he gave the Cardinals the sixth World Series title in franchise history. It was also the fourth title González had experienced with the Cardinals, all as a coach.

González's seventeen major-league seasons included three playing stints with the Cardinals: 1915–18, 1924–25, and 1931–32. But at age forty he did not play in the Cardinals' 1931 World Series victory. After his playing days ended, González joined the Cardinals' coaching staff under manager Frankie Frisch in 1934. The "Gashouse Gang" Cardinals captained by Leo Durocher won the World Series that season. González won three more World Series rings as a Cardinals coach, in 1942, 1944, and 1946, but the 1946 crown was bittersweet. St. Louis teammates Klein and Martin played for Habana during the 1945–46 Cuban League season. As the team's owner-manager, González faced disciplinary action for managing ineligibles in the upcoming Cuban League season. So the day after the Cardinals beat the Red Sox in game 7, González requested his release from his Cardinals contract. He "packed up all his belongings . . . and took them back to Cuba," the *Sporting News* reported on October 23, 1946. "Mike tendered his resignation to President Sam Breadon and sadly said farewell to Sportsman's Park."[27]

Even in its unfinished state, El Gran Stadium was, in almost every measurable way, superior to La Tropical stadium, which had housed the Cuban League since 1930. Built in Havana's El Cerro neighborhood, El Gran Stadium was about half the distance from La Tropical to downtown Havana. Upon completion, El Gran Stadium would seat 35,080 fans, compared to 20,000 at La Tropical. Unlike its predecessor, which also had to host track and field events and soccer games, El Gran Stadium was designed specifically for baseball, with field dimensions more in keeping with the sport: 340 feet down the left- and right-field lines and 420 feet to center field. And eight light towers— four along the outfield fence and four atop the roof covering the grandstands—would allow for night games. (It was not uncommon to have games called for darkness at La Tropical.)

Unhappy over losing the Cuban League, Julio Blanco Herrera, owner of La Tropical stadium and a longtime patron of professional baseball in Cuba, channeled his displeasure toward upgrading the stadium he built in 1930 to host the second Central American Games. Blanco spent "a tidy sum modernizing his stadium."[28] He rented the stadium to a promoter for $1 so it could host the National Federation.[29] The league would be stockpiled with Cuban and American players in good standing because they had refused overtures from the Mexican League. It would include four teams: Camagüey, Matanzas, Oriente, and Havana Reds, the latter an obvious knockoff of the Cuban League's Habana club, whose primary color was red. And the rival league would run concurrently with the traditional Cuban League in 1946–47.

On the same day that Monsignor Muller blessed El Gran Stadium, the National Federation opened its rival season at La Tropical. Gilberto Torres piloted the Havana Reds to a 9–8 victory against the Fermín Guerra–managed Oriente team. Cuba's most successful amateur pitcher, Conrado Marrero, made his professional debut at age thirty-five with Oriente. He entered the game in relief in the fifth inning but couldn't maintain Oriente's lead, surrendering eight hits, including the game winner by Jorge "Cocoliso" Torres in the tenth inning. The National Federation's opening game drew some 7,000 fans at La Tropical, a number that would be dwarfed the following day across town.[30]

After the gates to El Gran Stadium opened at noon on Friday, October 26, more than sixty uniformed ushers began escorting fans to their seats. The opening game of the 1946–47 Cuban League season between Almendares and defending league champion Cienfuegos was still three hours away. The opening ceremony began at two-thirty with Havana mayor Manuel Fernández Superviella raising the Cienfuegos team's 1945–46 championship flag. Dignitaries hoisted flags for the league's other teams: Cuba's director of sports, Luis Orlando Rodríguez, for Habana; team owner Mario Mendoza for Almendares; and the mayor of Marianao for the team bearing that city's name. Finally, Cuban prime minister Carlos Prío Socarrás threw out the ceremonial first pitch before the official three-o'clock start.[31] With the first delivery by Cienfuegos's Venezuelan-born Alejandro Carrasquel to Almendares's Avelino Cañizares, El Gran Stadium officially became the latest in a line of Cuban League stadiums, parks, and fields.

Cuba's ballpark lineage dates to December 27, 1874, when Palmar del Junco, a park in the Pueblo Nuevo neighborhood of Matanzas, hosted the first officially recorded baseball game in Cuban history. On that Sunday a team from Havana took on a team from Matanzas. Habana, featuring several Cuban baseball pioneers including Esteban Bellán, won 51–9. The drubbing might have been more severe had the game not been called on account of darkness after seven innings at 5:35 p.m.[32] Bellán, born in Havana on October 1, 1849, learned to play baseball as a student at Fordham University in 1863–68. He became the first Cuban to play in the major leagues when he donned the uniform of the Troy Haymakers of the National Association in 1871. He managed Habana when Cuba's professional baseball league formed four years later.

On December 20, 1878, Adolfo Núñez, Carlos de Zaldo, and Joaquín Franke, representing the Almendares Base Ball Club, and Beltrán Senarens, Ricardo Mora, and Manuel Landa, representing the Habana Base Ball Club, gathered at number 17 Calle de Obrapía in Havana to form the Professional League of Cuban Baseball. Almendares, Habana, and Matanzas became the league's charter members, and Leopoldo de Sola served as league president.[33] The inaugural season, played on Sundays and holidays on fields in Havana and Matanzas, lasted from December 29, 1878, to February 16, 1879. In the first league game, an eight-run eighth inning propelled Habana to a 21–20 victory against Almendares.

It was the first volley in what would become a more than eighty-year battle between the two clubs—Almendares and Habana, the Cuban League's Eternal Rivals. Founded in 1868 and reestablished by Emilio Sabourín, Alfredo Maruri, Ernesto Guilló, Enrique Canal, Juan Lavotal, Pedro Bulnes, and Ricardo Mora in 1878, Habana bore the color red as its emblem from its inception. Almendares, founded the same year as the league by players Teodoro and Carlos de Zaldo, J. Frankee, Fernando Zayas, Leonardo Ovies, Alfredo Lacazette, Antonio Alsola, Adolfo Núñez, Zacarías Barrios, and Alejando Reed, wore blue. Habana went undefeated (4–0–1) to win the Cuban League's first season. For beating Almendares and Matanzas, Habana received a white-and-red silk flag with the words "Championship 1878." Habana's players each received a silver medal with the inscription "Isla de Cuba Base Ball Championship, 1878."[34]

Over the next several decades, numerous venues served as home to Cuban League teams. Palmar del Junco, de facto "birthplace of Cuban baseball," was Matanzas's home field from the league's inception. The second Almendares Park, which opened for the 1918–19 Cuban League season, was home to the Almendares team for twelve seasons. In the city of Santa Clara, the Leopardos (Leopards) called Boulanger Park home during the early decades of the twentieth century. And Cienfuegos played its home games in Aida Park in the city of Cienfuegos during those early decades as well.[35] Then Julio Blanco Herrera built La Tropical, the stadium that hosted all Cuban League teams in one central location on the outskirts of Havana from 1930 to 1946 before the league moved to El Gran Stadium.

Anticipation soared for the inaugural season at El Gran Stadium, and the 1946–47 Cuban League season would be well chronicled. No fewer than fifteen Havana newspapers would cover the league's games. Those papers employed more than thirty beat writers, including fourteen future members of the Cuban Baseball Hall of Fame, to cover the league. Among those writers, three—Bernardo "Llillo" Jiménez, Fausto La Villa, and Fausto Miranda—worked for *Información*. Another two, Jess Losada and Galbino Delgado, wrote for *Prensa Libre*. And two others, Eladio Secades and René Molina, worked for the Havana newspaper *Diario de la Marina*.[36] Miranda—whose brother, shortstop Guillermo "Willy" Miranda, played twelve seasons in the Cuban League and nine in the majors—went on to found the sports section of *El Miami Herald*, predecessor of *El Nuevo Herald*, the Spanish-language version of the *Miami Herald*. Delgado was inducted into the Cuban Baseball Hall of Fame in 2007 for his work as a broadcaster. And Molina was enshrined as a broadcaster in 1997.

The occupants of El Gran Stadium's broadcast booths were as impressive as their press box counterparts. Five radio stations would broadcast the league's games during the 1946–47 season. Future Cuban Baseball Hall of Fame broadcaster Carlos "Cuco" Conde, who also was a writer for *Alerta*, called the games for station CMW Onda Deportiva. In 1941 it was Conde who had hung the nickname Petroleros, meaning Oilers, on Cienfuegos. The crass and racist term, used in Cuba to describe white men who liked black women,[37] stuck and was commonly used by *Diario de la Marina* in place of Elefantes. Manolo de la Reguera did play-by-play for CMBZ–Radio Salas and RHC–Cadena Azul. De la Reguera was inducted into the Cuban Baseball Hall of Fame in 1997. CMX Mil Deiz's lead announcer was Manolo Ortega. Radio station COCO boasted three future Cuban Baseball Hall of Fame broadcasters: play-by-play announcers Orlando Sánchez Diago and Rafael "Felo" Ramírez and commentator Pedro Galiana.[38] Ramírez became the first Cuban-born broadcaster to receive the National Baseball Hall of Fame's Ford C. Frick Award in 2001. Born on June 22, 1923, in Bayamo, Ramírez made his broadcast debut at age twenty-two for CMBZ–Radio Salas in 1945, calling amateur baseball games in Havana for $80 per month. An offer of $300 per month brought Ramírez to COCO, where he joined Conde to call professional games during the inaugural season at El Gran Stadium.

The writers and broadcasters were not the only key contributors to the Cuban League who had made the move from La Tropical to the new stadium. Others who had been fixtures at the previous stadium included the field arbiters: home-plate umpire Amado Maestri and base umpires Bernardino Rodríguez and Kiko Magriñat. A player with Almendares in 1897, Magriñat became an umpire in 1913 and was still working games in his seventies. Rodríguez, who had played amateur ball before becoming an umpire, was famous for getting decked during a game by Roberto Ortiz. But none was more respected than Maestri. A former amateur player, Maestri turned to umpiring in 1935 and had a low tolerance for arguments.[39] Longtime Los Angeles Dodgers manager Tommy Lasorda, who pitched in the Cuban League in the 1950s, has told a perhaps apocryphal tale attesting to that. Angered by Maestri's calls behind the plate, Lasorda started cursing the umpire, who "pulled open his jacket to show me the biggest pistol I have ever seen, tucked into this belt," Lasorda wrote in his 1985 autobiography. "That convinced me."[40]

Others who also moved from La Tropical to the new stadium included public-address announcer Luis González Moré and official scorekeeper Julio Fránquiz. Cuban baseball historian Roberto González Echevarría described Moré, who was known as El Conde, the Count, as having a "rich, deep voice and flawless diction," and said that his "voice and elocution gave the proceedings a solemn tone." Fránquiz, González Echevarría wrote, "took his job very seriously and seemed impervious to criticism," which often was leveled from the press box. Perhaps the most visible of the supporting cast who made the move to the new stadium was ballboy Faustino Zulueta, who actually was a burly, menacing, grown black man. Mockingly known as Bicicleta, or Bicycle, for the laboring way he chased balls, Zulueta looked after baseballs "as if he were defending consecrated objects," González Echevarría wrote. "With his histrionics and his often frantic and futile attempts to capture errant baseballs, he was part of the show."[41]

The radio rights to broadcast the Cuban League became a point of contention before the 1946–47 season began. RHC–Cadena Azul and CMBZ–Radio Salas, the Cuban network that had carried the World Series, had been awarded exclusive rights in Cuba for the sum of $20,000. Complaints and pressure from Cuba's other radio stations eventually allowed three more stations—COCO, CMW, and Communist Party station CMX—to purchase rights by paying the original contract holders $7,000 each.[42] With blanket coverage of the league secured on Cuba's radio airwaves, attention turned to opening day and the game's probable starters. Cienfuegos opened defense of its Cuban League championship with Alejandro Carrasquel on the mound. The Venezuelan-born right-hander had pitched with the Washington Senators since 1939 and was no stranger to the Cuban League. Playing for the Cuba team (so named, but not a national team) during the 1938–39 season, Carrasquel pitched a league-leading 26 games. In compiling an 11–7 record for a team that won only 25 games, Carrasquel was named the league's most valuable player.[43] He also played in 1944–45, splitting the season between Almendares and Marianao. Carrasquel's counterpart on Almendares for the opener would be Agapito Mayor, the league having announced the lefty as the probable starter the previous night.[44]

Mayor had been a vital pitcher for the Alacranes, or Scorpions, since joining the Almendares team for the 1938–39 season. He also had another factor in his favor. "This pitcher has a rare specialty: beating Cienfuegos," *Diario de la Marina* columnist Eladio Secades proclaimed in the newspaper's editions on the morning of October 26. "Agapito is as ugly as he is valiant and left-handed."[45] The reference to Mayor's aesthetically challenged facial features was borne out in the lefty's nickname, Triple Feo, or Triple Ugly. Mayor's appearance notwithstanding, some speculated that right-handed curve-ball specialist Jorge Comellas might start. Indeed, Almendares manager Adolfo Luque made the last-minute switch to Comellas, who had pitched seven games with the Chicago Cubs in 1945. Although Mayor missed pitching in the opener, he would play a pivotal role at the conclusion of the season.

More than 31,000 fans passed through the turnstiles at El Gran Stadium for the season opener. The crowd easily eclipsed the attendance record set the previous season at La Tropical and was, to that point, the largest to watch a sporting event in Cuban history.[46] With the stadium still incomplete, the overflow crowd spilled onto foul territory. Under special ground rules, the fans were cordoned off from the playing field along the first- and third-base lines.[47] Cienfuegos scored first. The Elephants took the early 1–0 lead off Comellas when Almendares right fielder Roberto Ortiz botched two plays in the third inning. Cienfuegos third baseman Conrado Pérez hit a line drive that became a triple when Ortiz charged the ball but backed off at the last instant and was unable to keep the ball in front of him. Napoleón Reyes followed with what appeared to be an easy out until Ortiz momentarily lost the ball in the sun. It dropped in for a Texas leaguer and allowed Pérez to score from third. With fans in the bleacher seats still taunting the misplay, Ortiz redeemed himself by making a miraculous catch to rob Roland Gladu of an extra-base hit. A groundout by Danny Gardella ended the Cienfuegos threat.

Carrasquel looked strong for the first three innings, but Almendares hung three runs on him in the fourth. Lloyd Davenport opened the inning with a line drive over third baseman Conrado Pérez's head, stole second, moved to third on Lázaro Salazar's liner over short, and scored on a wild pitch to tie the game at 1–1. Later in the inning, a line-drive base hit by Almendares third baseman Héctor Rodríguez drove home Salazar and Ortiz. Almendares scored another four runs in the sixth inning to knock Carrasquel out of the game. In the seventh Ortiz blasted a two-run homer 350 feet over the right-field fence to complete Almendares's 9–1 victory.

The triumph prompted such a reaction among Almendares fans that "Havana looked as though it were in the midst of a national celebration. There were demonstrations, music, dancing, fireworks . . . a resurgence of enthusiasm that even the owners and operators of the new stadium could not have imagined."[48] The accounts of the day were equally effusive in their review of El Gran Stadium's grand opening. "With pride it can be said that the winter league season began with a World Series atmosphere," *Diario de la Marina* columnist Eladio Secades wrote. "A beautiful page of progress has been written, not only for baseball as a pastime for all Cubans, but for Havana as an important capital."[49]

The American Series

The first wave of Brooklyn Dodgers, traveling from New York by train, arrived in Miami on Wednesday, February 19, 1946. After a two-hour layover in the Magic City, the forty-six-man traveling party boarded two Pan American Airlines Clippers bound for Havana, where they would begin setting up for spring training. Signs, billboards, and placards emblazoned with the words "¡Los Dodgers están aquí!"—The Dodgers are here!—greeted the arriving contingent in the Cuban capital that night. The Dodgers "received a rousing welcome from the extremely baseball-conscious citizenry," Roscoe McGowen wrote in the *New York Times*.[1] Despite the initial *bienvenidas*, however, "Cuban baseball fans hardly noticed" the team's presence in Havana, according to Cuban baseball historian Roberto González Echevarría.[2]

The remaining members of the team, including Leo Durocher, embarked on their flight to the Pearl of the Antilles the next night. But even Durocher's presence did not elevate the Dodgers in the consciousness of Cuban fans. This despite the scandalous marriage to actress Laraine Day that made the Brooklyn manager a household name in the gossip columns as well as on the sports pages. Durocher's celebrity status notwithstanding, the most significant members of the organization's total contingent in Cuba had not yet arrived. African American players assigned to the Dodgers' Class-AAA Montreal Royals team—Jackie Robinson, Roy Campanella, Don Newcombe, and Roy Partlow—were scheduled to arrive later in the week.

Cuban fans were aware of the impact Robinson's ascension to the Dodgers would have, not only on Major League Baseball but on Cuban players as well. If Robinson could earn a roster spot with the Dodgers, it would open the door to the majors for the first time to black Cubans. "They speculated over that, of course," broadcaster Felo Ramírez recalled years later. "Silvio García was in the group that was considered to be the first, so that was reason enough for curiosity for everyone."[3] Previously, Cubans who had played in the majors generally fell into two groups: white Cubans—Armando Marsans, Adolfo Luque, and Miguel Ángel González among them—or Cubans of distant African descent, such as Roberto "Tarzán" Estalella and Tomás de la Cruz, who had light skin and thus were "protected by American confusion over race, color, and nationality."[4] Having Robinson on the Dodgers would change that.

Robinson's delayed presence in Havana wasn't the only reason Cuban fans felt blasé about the Dodgers' arrival. The most exciting finish in Cuban League history was unfolding, with Eternal Rivals Almendares and Habana battling for the championship until their season-ending series. Adding to the Cuban fans' nonchalant attitude toward the Dodgers was the fact that they had seen it all before. The Dodgers had trained in Havana in 1913 (under the name Superbas), 1921, 1941, and 1942. In fact, major-league players and teams had been training or barnstorming in Cuba since before the turn of the twentieth century. "There was interest, but it wasn't that feverish, because Cuba had a tradition of the presence of big-league teams training in Cuba," Ramírez said. "Training is different from actual games. When there were Cuban teams playing against them, then yes, that brought more interest."[5]

The first visit to Cuba by major-league players came in 1891, when Alfred Lawson brought an all-star team for exhibition games. Its roster included a seventeen-year-old John McGraw, who went on to a Hall of Fame career as manager of the New York Giants. The son of an Irish immigrant, John Joseph McGraw was born on April 7, 1873, in Truxton, New York. By the time McGraw was eleven, his mother and four siblings had died during a diphtheria epidemic that swept the Tioughnioga Valley in upstate New York during the winter of 1884–85. In the years after the epidemic subsided, friction between McGraw and his father eventually boiled over. Still reeling from the toll the epidemic inflicted on his family, McGraw's father had little tolerance for his son's obsession with baseball. After one argument between father and son, McGraw bolted from his house, never to return, and found refuge with a neighbor who took him into her home.[6]

Out from under his father's roof, McGraw thrived. He worked various jobs, earning money to buy the annual *Spalding Base Ball Guide* and keep up with the game's yearly rules changes. His play was nearly as impressive as his baseball mind. Six days before his seventeenth birthday, McGraw signed his first professional contract on April 1, 1890, with Olean of the newly formed New York–Pennsylvania League. A short-lived, error-plagued stint resulted in his release. Undaunted, McGraw joined the Wellsville team of the fledgling Western New York League in June of 1890. In twenty-four games, McGraw batted .365 in 107 at-bats. His performance caught the eye of Lawson, a twenty-one-year-old journeyman pitcher who began the year in the majors, pitching and losing three games for the Boston Braves and Pittsburgh Pirates.[7]

Not much of a pitcher, Lawson was a master at self-promotion and persuasion. He recruited players for a series of games in Cuba over the winter. Impressed by McGraw's savvy—his knowledge of the rules produced a forfeit to Wellsville in a game at Hornell—Lawson asked McGraw to join his American All-Stars. The team arrived in Cuba in late January of 1891.[8] With the country still under Spanish rule, many of its citizens subsisted in poverty and with little education. Baseball, introduced in Cuba during the 1860s, had begun to eclipse bullfighting, horse racing, and cockfighting. The Cuban people's preference for baseball over bullfighting embodied the country's rejection of Spanish colonial rule. "Baseball . . . has contributed much to redeeming us from such degrading spectacles" as bullfights, the March 12, 1882, edition of *El Base Ball* proclaimed.[9]

In a ballpark on the outskirts of Havana, the American All-Stars swept five games against the Cubans, who to the surprise of the Americans "played not only with enthusiasm, but also . . . with considerable skill." McGraw's hustling style quickly endeared him to Cuban fans, for whom hanging nicknames on players was customary. Because of his diminutive size—five foot five and 155 pounds—and the bright yellow uniforms worn by the all-star team, the locals dubbed McGraw El Mono Amarillo, the Yellow Monkey. After one game McGraw, still in uniform, became separated from his teammates, miles from the team's hotel. As dozens of fans recognized McGraw, the ensuing furor almost prompted local police to arrest him for disturbing the peace. But a famous Havana billiards player named Alfredo de Oro intervened and sent McGraw on his way in a horse-drawn taxi.[10]

McGraw, who began his major-league playing career with the Baltimore Orioles of the American Association later in 1891, returned to Cuba years later as manager of the New York Giants, one of many teams to play exhibition or spring training games in Cuba during the first half of the twentieth century. Such games became known in Cuba as the American Series. The visits—whether by black or white teams—didn't usually involve encounters with local constables. But often they were marked by notable performances by both Cuban and American players. José Méndez turned in some of the most memorable ones during the early decades of the American Series.

Born on March 18, 1887, in Cárdenas in the province of Matanzas, José de la Caridad Méndez grew up as baseball became ingrained in Cuban culture. Raised in humble circumstances, Méndez worked at a young age as a day laborer in a carpentry workshop. He learned to play the clarinet, but his true interest lay in baseball. By age thirteen, Méndez played on men's teams, impressing teammates and opponents with "the speed of his arm and the ease with which he fielded at shortstop." Méndez's break came on Christmas Eve 1907. Players for Almendares attended a game between Remedios and Caibarién to scout a hotshot pitcher. They were unimpressed but took notice of the Remedios shortstop, who "fielded like nobody else and had an arm that inspired fear." Seeing the shortstop come in to pitch in the closing innings of the game, Carlos "Bebé" Royer informed Almendares's owner that "his name is Méndez and don't waste one minute and sign him."[11]

Despite his five-foot-nine-inch, 150-pound frame, Méndez was a force during his rookie season in the Cuban League. In his pitching debut on February 2, 1908, Méndez tossed two shutout innings in relief of star pitcher José Muñoz in a 12–0 victory against the Fe team. He followed up with a complete-game 8–3 victory against Matanzas in his first start on Wednesday, February 19. Méndez earned his first career shutout on February 23, a 2–0 victory against Fe. As Almendares won the 1908 Cuban League championship, Méndez went undefeated to earn champion-pitcher status. Accounts of his exact record vary, crediting him with between seven and nine wins. What remains unquestioned is Méndez's talent, which he displayed against visiting major-league teams during the next four Cuban winters.

The Cincinnati Reds were the first major-league team to play in Cuba after Méndez made his Cuban League debut. They had finished fifth in the National League before traveling to Havana in the fall of 1908. After knocking around the Habana team in three games, the Reds ran into a buzzsaw on November 15. Méndez struck out nine, walked two, and took a no-hitter into the ninth as Almendares won 1–0. Miller Huggins, who went on to manage the great New York Yankees teams of the 1920s, dribbled a slow roller between first and second for the Reds' only hit. "He beat us," Huggins would say. "Everybody gets beaten sometimes. Méndez must have something when only one hit is all we were able to get against him."[12]

Méndez shut out the Reds in seven innings of relief on November 25. He followed up on December 3 with a five-hit shutout of Cincinnati in which he struck out eight and walked none. The twenty-one-year-old Méndez, who became known in Cuba as El Diamante Negro, the Black Diamond, dominated Cincinnati. In twenty-five innings he allowed one run against the Reds, who limped out of Cuba with five victories in ten games. "José Méndez's rise to fame was meteoric," wrote Cuban baseball historian Severo Nieto Fernández. "Never before had anything like that occurred in Cuba. In less than a year, Méndez had become the most extraordinary pitcher ever to pass through a baseball camp on the island."[13]

The Detroit Tigers visited Cuba the following winter, but the 1909 American League champions came without AL batting champion Ty Cobb or fellow future Hall of Famer Sam Crawford. The Tigers did bring 21-game winner Ed Willett. He won the first meeting between the Tigers and Almendares as Detroit rapped out eleven hits against Méndez in a 9–3 victory. One Havana newspaper called it the "worst beating of his [Méndez's then-brief] career." In another game, Méndez battled George Mullin, who had led the majors in wins with a 29–8 record in 1909. Pitching like "the heretofore invincible Méndez," according to the *U.S. Reach Guide*, the Cuban right-hander held Detroit to six hits and one earned run, but four Almendares errors gave the Tigers a 4–0 victory. Méndez beat Detroit 2–1 for his lone victory against the Tigers that winter. The five-hit decision came on the heels of Detroit's worst loss on the trip. Méndez's teammate Eustaquio "Bombín" Pedroso had tossed an eleven-inning no-hitter as Almendares won 2–1. Exuberant Cuban fans collected 300 pesos for Pedroso, who was wined and dined to such an extent he didn't pitch again versus Detroit. Even without having to face Pedroso again, the Tigers left Cuba with a 4–8 record in games against Almendares and Habana. Cuba's *La Lucha* newspaper dubbed the Tigers' performance "disastrous," while the *Reach Guide* described it as a "disgrace." Before the winter concluded, Méndez outdueled Howie Camnitz, ace of the World Series champion Pittsburgh Pirates, who came to Cuba as a member of an all-star big-league team. Camnitz won 25 games for the Pirates in 1909 but lost 3–1 to Almendares as Méndez surrendered just two hits, struck out ten, and walked two.[14]

The Tigers returned to Cuba following the 1910 major-league season. Again they took on Cuban teams manned by those whom *Detroit Times* writer Paul Bruske described as the "dusky representatives of the fertile isle."[15] This time they brought Sam Crawford, the American League RBI champion with 120, and Ty Cobb, who led the AL with a .385 batting average. In his first two starts, Méndez held Crawford hitless. But on November 13, Méndez lost 3–0 to George Mullin, who had come off his second consecutive 20-win season for Detroit in 1910. On November 21, Méndez settled for a no-decision in a 2–2 tie.

Cobb joined the Tigers late, his boat arriving from Key West on November 26. The Georgia Peach made his debut in Cuba the next day at Almendares Park. Cobb went 3-for-4 with a home run as the Tigers beat Almendares and José Muñoz 4–0. Finally it was time for Cobb to confront Méndez. In their first encounter, Cobb singled and struck out against Méndez. Again Crawford could not reach Méndez in four at-bats, but Detroit won 6–3. The Tigers also split a pair of eleven-inning games against Pedroso, losing 2–1 and winning 3–2. The Tigers left Cuba this time feeling more satisfied, thanks to a 7–4–1 record against island teams.[16]

The series remains famous for an enduring though likely apocryphal tale about Cobb's escapades on the basepaths. The story is so ingrained in Cuban baseball folklore that decades later it was still being passed down from one generation of fans to another and has been written into several long-after-the-facts accounts. Details vary, but the basic story remains the same. In one game, Cobb was thrown out at second base on three consecutive steal attempts by Cuban team catchers Bruce Petway and Gervacio "Strike" González. After being thrown out the third time, Cobb insisted the bases had been set too far apart and demanded the distance be measured. When umpires acquiesced, they confirmed first and second base were three inches further apart than the standard ninety feet. But the umpires still declared Cobb out, much to his chagrin.[17]

It's a great legend, but a legend nonetheless, according to research by baseball historian Gary Ashwill. He correctly points out that González and Petway played for different teams in the Cuban League, González for Almendares and Petway for Habana. It is possible Cobb was thrown out on three consecutive steal attempts over the course of two games. But according to his research, La Lucha newspaper printed play-by-play accounts of three of Cobb's five games in Cuba and they included no such occurrence. And neither La Lucha nor Diario de la Marina describes Cobb stopping a game to have the basepath measured.[18]

Connie Mack's World Series champion Philadelphia Athletics

became the next major-league team to try its luck in Cuba. Winners of 102 regular-season games in 1910, the Athletics lost 6 of 10 games to Cuban teams that fall. Jack Combs, a 31-game winner, beat Bombín Pedroso 2–1 and 7–4, but 23-game winner Chief Bender lost twice. And Méndez defeated future Hall of Famer Eddie Plank twice, 5–2 and 7–5.[19] Although these were merely exhibition games, American League president Ban Johnson was not pleased to see his league champion go down to such teams, especially given their complexion. After the Athletics' embarrassing showing in Cuba, Johnson decreed, "We want no makeshift club calling themselves the Athletics to go to Cuba to be beaten by colored teams."[20]

But Johnson's prohibition did little to stop National League teams; even the Athletics returned to Cuba following the 1912 major-league season and played much better, winning ten of twelve games. During the fall of 1911, the Athletics' cross-town National League neighbors, the Phillies, fared slightly better in their visit to Cuba. The Phillies had finished fourth in the National League, but they won five and lost four against Cuban squads, losing twice to Méndez.[21] The Phillies' visit, however, was but an opening act for the arrival of the New York Giants and the bombastic return of John McGraw.

The National League champion Giants were three weeks removed from an intense six-game World Series when they ventured into Cuba in the winter of 1911. Tempers had flared—none more so than John Mc-Graw's—as the Philadelphia Athletics team beat New York four games to two to win the Series. The Giants manager had drawn a reprimand for glaring at American League president Ban Johnson during game 3 and telling him, "This is a sure-thing game. Old American League methods. . . . You've got it all framed up to rob us."[22] McGraw was no less intense as he returned to Cuba for the first time since his initial visit as a player in 1891. With each player guaranteed $500, McGraw and seventeen other members of the Giants, along with their wives, a group of sportswriters, and National League umpire Cy Rigler traveled by boat to Havana for a series against Almendares and Habana that began on November 25.

Cuba, thirteen years after gaining its independence, seemed much more prosperous than the Spanish colony McGraw remembered from his previous visit. The poverty he once witnessed was less visible.[23] Baseball, just beginning to take hold with the Cuban people during McGraw's earlier trip, had become a national obsession. And Cuban fans had perhaps no greater source of national pride than outfielder Armando Marsans and infielder Rafael Almeida. The pair had become the first Cuban-born players to reach the majors since 1871 when they debuted for the Cincinnati Reds on July 4, 1911.

McGraw's Giants were the fifth major-league team since 1908 to come to Cuba for off-season games. The previous four mostly had struggled against local teams, and the trend continued with New York. After 26-game winner Christy Mathewson won the first game 4–1, the Giants lost the next two outings. The first defeat came on November 27, a 6–4 loss to Almendares and black pitcher Bombín Pedroso. The following day, the Giants fell 3–2 to Habana and pitcher Adolfo Luque, a white Cuban who would go on to a twenty-year major-league career. The losses were more than McGraw could stomach. "You'll beat these clowns or I'll know the reason why," he ranted, directing the brunt of his ire toward outfielder Josh DeVore. Since arriving, DeVore had taken full advantage of Havana's nightlife and failed to produce at the plate, incurring a $25 fine from his manager. When DeVore protested, McGraw lashed out: "Take the next boat home. I didn't come down here to let a lot of coffee-colored Cubans show me up."[24]

The marquee pitching matchup of the series came on November 30: José Méndez versus Christy Mathewson. McGraw, still fuming over the losses, directed his venom toward Méndez. Choosing the moment that "a respectful hush" had fallen over the crowd, McGraw, in a voice loud enough to be heard in the stands, bellowed, "Who's that guy?" as Méndez took the mound.[25] McGraw's disrespectful display would have repercussions later. During the game, Méndez allowed only five hits, but one was a two-run triple, while Mathewson threw a three-hit shutout for a 4–0 victory against Almendares. Elated by the team's response to his challenge, McGraw threw a party that night at a Havana restaurant. At three in the morning, a group of Cuban fans upset by McGraw's rudeness toward Méndez confronted McGraw and umpire Cy Rigler. When one pulled a knife, the burly Rigler wrestled the weapon loose and held the fans at bay until police arrived. A local judge, however, sided against McGraw and Rigler, fining them $20 each and ordering them to publish a statement of apology in the *Havana Post*, the city's English-language daily.[26]

Almendares lost Méndez's next start, falling to Otis Crandall despite Méndez striking out eleven Giants. But on December 14, Pedroso and Méndez combined to beat the Giants 7–4, handing Mathewson his only loss of the series. Through five innings, Pedroso gave up five hits before yielding to Méndez, who held the Giants to one hit the rest of the game. The victory went to Méndez, giving him eight wins, seven losses, and a tie against major-league competition. Even as the Giants went on to win nine of the twelve games against Cuban teams, the accolades rolled in for Méndez. Mathewson, who went 3–1 with a 2.31 ERA in the series, called Méndez "a great pitcher."[27] Second baseman Larry Doyle invoked a comparison to Mathewson when he said Méndez "surely deserves the name 'Black Matty.' . . . I'm not sure that Méndez wouldn't create a terrible stir in the big leagues, were it not for his color. He has wonderful speed, a tantalizing slow ball, and perfect control. I've never seen a pitcher with better control."[28]

Even McGraw, despite berating his team for losing two games to a predominantly black team, admitted he would give $50,000 for Méndez and another $50,000 for his battery mate Gervasio "Strike" González "if only they were white."[29] Méndez, McGraw said, "is better than any pitcher except Mordecai Brown and Christy Mathewson— and sometimes, I think he's better than Matty."[30] With his experience in Cuba, McGraw came to realize that it was wrong to exclude blacks from the major leagues. "Without mincing words," McGraw's second wife Blanche Sindall McGraw later wrote, "John bemoaned the failure of baseball, himself included, to cast aside custom or unwritten law . . . and sign a player on ability alone, regardless of race or color."[31]

White major-league teams were not the only ones that traveled to Cuba to play in the so-called American Series. Negro league teams also barnstormed Cuba during the first half of the twentieth century. The first all-black team from the United States to do so was the 1900 Cuban X-Giants. Ironically, the team had no Cuban players but did include Sol White, who in 1907 published *Sol White's Official Base Ball Guide*, a valuable source of black baseball history in America before 1920. The team also included rookie pitcher Andrew "Rube" Foster. He became known as the Father of Black Baseball after founding the Negro National League in 1920. On this inaugural trip, the X-Giants won 14 of 17 games against Cuban teams. Visits to the island became an annual excursion as the X-Giants returned each winter from 1903 to 1906. Other black teams followed.

The Philadelphia Giants, with future Hall of Famer John Henry "Pop" Lloyd, played two series in the fall of 1907, winning 9 of 22 games. The Brooklyn Royal Giants split 16 games against Almendares and Habana in the winter of 1908. Foster returned with the Chicago Leland Giants in 1910. In 14 games in Cuba, the Leland Giants lost to Almendares's José Méndez three times and to Bombín Pedroso twice. In 1912 the Lincoln Giants managed only 5 wins in 13 contests against Habana and Almendares, despite the presence of future Hall of Fame pitcher Smokey Joe Williams, who went 0–4 against Cuban teams on the trip.

On it went, as Cuba welcomed Negro league teams and players with open arms and open checkbooks. Back home in the United States, baseball's "gentleman's agreement" had barred black players from playing in the majors since before the turn of the century. By 1900 no such restrictions existed in Cuba in professional baseball. Aside from barnstorming, it also was common for some of the greatest players in Negro leagues history to sign up with Cuban teams in the country's winter league. The first Negro leagues star to do so was Lloyd, often compared to Hall of Fame shortstop Honus Wagner. "You could put Wagner and Lloyd in a bag together and whichever you pulled out, you wouldn't go wrong," Philadelphia Athletics manager Connie Mack once said.[32]

Born in Palatka, Florida, on April 25, 1884, Lloyd joined Habana the winter after his 1907 barnstorming trip with the Philadelphia Giants.

According to Cuban baseball historian Jorge S. Figueredo, Lloyd batted .300 or better seven times during his career in Cuba, and his lifetime .329 average ranks fourth-best in Cuban League history.[33] Despite the Cuban League being integrated, Cuban fans were not above racial insensitivity. Known in America as "the Black Wagner," Lloyd had a more racially tinged nickname in Cuba: "Bemba de Cuchara." *Bemba* means fat lips and *cuchara* means spoon, so his nickname translated roughly as Spoon Lips. If he felt slighted by the nickname, Lloyd didn't let it stop him from returning to Cuba, where he played thirteen winter seasons between 1908 and 1930. Other Negro league stars such as Foster, Oscar Charleston, Willie Wells, Cool Papa Bell, Judy Johnson, and Ray Dandridge played multiple winters in the Cuban League.

Not every Negro-leagues star was enamored with playing in Cuba, as Satchel Paige's experience suggests. Abel Linares, the driving force behind many of the Negro-league teams' visits to Cuba, essentially owned the Cuban League. At one point Linares owned the Eternal Rivals, Almendares and Habana, as well as Santa Clara, which first joined the league for the 1923–24 season. Linares signed Paige to play for Santa Clara during the 1929–30 season, paying the flamboyant pitcher $100 per game. Buoyed by his first experience in a nonsegregated hotel, Paige strolled into the lobby of a Cuban hotel and called for "someone to mix up a snort."[34] Unfortunately for Paige, baseball players were precluded from drinking so as to maintain the game's integrity for the intense betting by Cuban fans. Paige resorted to bribing bartenders to deliver drinks to his room.

On the field, Paige pitched eleven games, recording six wins and five losses. He also incurred the ire of the locals, the reasons for which vary, even by Paige's own telling. In one account, a local mayor summoned Paige to his office after losing bets on the Santa Clara pitcher. When the mayor asked, in Spanish if he had intentionally lost one game, Paige, not understanding the question, smiled and nodded. "He almost jumped over his desk, and one of the guys standing around watching us had to hold him down," Paige would recall. "Knowing how the mayor felt, those boys got me out of town fast."[35] In another account, local displeasure involved a woman, and it was the Santa Clara owner who arranged Paige's abrupt departure from the island.[36] According to Santa Clara general manager Emilio de Armas, Paige had deflowered a young lady "from the provincial mulatto bourgeoisie," and he never returned to play in Cuba because he feared a statutory rape accusation.[37] Despite the issues with Paige, Linares had more successes than failures as a promoter. He scored his biggest coup in 1920, luring America's most prominent sporting figure to play a series of exhibition games in Cuba.

Before the New York Yankees purchased him from the Boston Red Sox for $125,000, George Herman "Babe" Ruth led the American League with a .657 slugging percentage in 1919 and hit what was at the time an astonishing 29 home runs. After joining the Yankees for the 1920 season, Ruth forever changed the game, clouting 54 home runs to go along with 137 runs batted in and a .376 batting average. That season, Ruth hit more home runs than all but one of the sixteen major-league teams. Baseball, in any country, had no higher drawing card than Ruth.

Linares offered the Babe $1,000 per game to play with a group of John McGraw's New York Giants on a tour of the island. Although McGraw would not show up in Havana until after the series, he had become something of a fixture in Cuba since the Giants' exhibition tour in 1911. Two years before the 1920 series, McGraw had bought an ownership interest in the Oriental Park Horse Racing Track in Marianao and often spent his off-season months in Cuba. If Linares could persuade Ruth to join McGraw's Giants this off-season, Cuban fans would be treated to a hitting matchup between the Sultan of Swat and their own slugger, Cristóbal Torriente.

Born on November 16, 1893, in Cienfuegos, Cristóbal Torriente joined Cuba's army at age seventeen. When he wasn't using his burly frame to lift artillery shells onto mules, Torriente played for the army's baseball team.[38] Torriente joined the Cuban League's Habana club in 1913, the first of fourteen professional seasons he played in Cuba. That same year, Cuban promoter Tinti Molina signed Torriente to play for the Cuban Stars of Havana, the first of his twelve seasons in the Negro leagues, including six with the Chicago American Giants of the

National Negro League. After batting .371 his first season with the Stars, Torriente returned to Cuba the following winter to join the Cuban League's Almendares club.

Torriente's numbers in the Cuban League vary slightly depending on the source, but he led the league in home runs in 1913–14 with a grand total of two, due likely to the first Almendares Park's distant fences. Torriente led the Cuban League in hitting in 1914–15, batting .387, according to Cuban baseball historian Jorge S. Figueredo. Torriente's second Cuban League batting title came during the 1919–20 season, when he hit .360. Figueredo credits Torriente with batting .352 over fourteen seasons in Cuba, the second-highest career average in league history. Figueredo also credits Torriente with hitting .300 or better in all but three of those seasons and leading the Cuban League in home runs five times.[39] Torriente's hitting skills were on full display for Babe Ruth's visit to Cuba.

Cuban promoter Abel Linares had already closed the deal with members of the New York Giants. They would come to Cuba in late October of 1920 to play exhibition games against Almendares and Habana. But Linares hadn't yet secured the big fish. Yankees slugger Babe Ruth wasn't there when the Giants arrived by steamer in Havana on October 15. Linares and a big crowd of fans greeted the players at the dock and escorted them to Havana's Hotel Plaza. But the best moment for Linares that day came when he received a cable from Ruth saying, "Okay, I'll play on the 30th."[40]

Cuban baseball historian Yuyo Ruiz noted that Ruth arrived in Cuba "amid the island's maturing image as a sports centre."[41] Five years before Ruth's visit, Cuba had played host to the epic world heavyweight boxing title fight between Jack Johnson and Jesse Willard, which Willard won in 26 rounds. Ruth's arrival meant a heavyweight clash of a different kind, between baseball's top power hitters, one from the United States and one from Cuba. Torriente's hitting prowess had first been on display against major-league talent the previous winter. The 1919 Pittsburgh Pirates, fresh off a third-place National League finish, were the first major-league team to tour Cuba since the St. Louis

Federals of the defunct Federal League did so in 1915. The four-year hiatus was due, in part, to World War I. As the Pirates won ten of their sixteen games against Habana and Almendares, Torriente batted .333 and clubbed a home run that one Havana newspaper called "phenomenal."[42]

Before Torriente could go against Ruth in the autumn of 1920—the Sultan of Swat's arrival was still two weeks away—the Giants played eight games against Almendares and Habana without Ruth. Ruth's influence still was felt. Committed to shelling out $10,000 for Ruth's services, Linares needed to set ticket prices at a level to assure his staying in the black. Prices at Almendares Park ranged from $5 for box seats to $1 for bleachers and grandstand seating. Some 8,000 fans crammed Almendares Park for the series opener, an eleven-inning, 3–3 tie between the Giants and Almendares. Depending on accounts, the take for the game was between $10,000 and $16,200.[43]

Either figure boded well for Linares's financial commitment to Ruth. By the time the non-Ruth games concluded on October 28, the Giants had three wins, three losses, and two ties against Cuban competition. Such an even showing against major-league talent should have been cause for pride among Cuban fans, but the Cuban press of the day questioned the Giants' commitment. Cuban baseball historian Roberto González Echevarría quoted an October 20 *Diario de la Marina* report concluding that American players traveled to Cuba to enjoy "certain freedoms that are forbidden back home," so they could not "conduct themselves with the same earnestness as when they are competing for their league championship."[44] Such criticisms did not temper fans' eagerness for seeing Babe Ruth.

Babe Ruth and his wife, Helen, barely had arrived in Havana on October 30 before they were taken to Almendares Park for his Cuban debut. At the stadium, Ruth was "received tumultuously by fans and photographers. Kids ran up to touch him, and all were awed by his corpulence."[45] The six-foot-two, 215-pound Ruth was inserted into the Giants lineup in the cleanup spot and played center field. He went 2-for-3, ripping a triple down the right-field line to drive in two runs in the first inning. He later scored on an error and doubled in the third inning as the Giants defeated Habana 4–3.

The Giants played nine more games with Ruth, going 6–2–2 against Cuban teams. But only the fifth game, on Saturday, November 6, became etched in Cuban baseball lore. First baseman George "High Pockets" Kelly started at pitcher for the Giants, while Almendares sent Isidro Fabré to the mound. After the Giants scored three runs in the first inning, Torriente began his home run barrage. In the second inning he homered off Kelly, a blast that cleared a distant fence in right field as Almendares took a 4–3 lead. Torriente added a solo home run in the third over the fence in left-center. In the fifth, Torriente didn't hit a homer but drove in two runs—both off Ruth, who had come in from the field to pitch when Almendares loaded the bases against Kelly.

Before he became baseball's most prolific power hitter, Ruth was a dominant pitcher for the Boston Red Sox. In 1916, Ruth led the American League with a 1.75 earned run average and won 23 games. The next season, he won 24 games. And Ruth had tossed a then-record 29⅔ consecutive scoreless innings in World Series play. But Torriente ripped a vicious line drive off Ruth and past Frankie Frisch. The Giants' third baseman vividly remembered the hit years later. "It wasn't in my glove. . . . And I'm glad I wasn't in front of it," Frisch recalled. "Torriente was a hell of a ball player. Christ, I'd like to whitewash him and bring him up [to the majors]."[46]

Of course Torriente, like other black players of his era, never got that opportunity. The major leagues' color barrier would last a quarter of a century longer. But against this team of white major leaguers, Torriente clubbed his third home run of the game in the seventh inning as Almendares beat the Giants 11–4. Torriente went 4-for-5, while the Sultan of Swat had gone 0-for-3. Reaction in the Cuban press varied. "Yesterday, Cristóbal Torriente elevated himself to the greatest heights of glory and popularity," historian Yuyo Ruiz quoted *El Día* newspaper. "His hitting will enter Cuban baseball history as one of its most brilliant pages."[47] But Roberto González Echevarría noted a story in *Diario de la Marina* that suggested the game was like batting practice and some of the Giants were in no shape to compete because they were drunk.[48] In its coverage of the game, the *Los Angeles Times* called Torriente "the Babe Ruth of Cuba."[49] The Babe was far less generous to his Cuban counterpart or Torriente's teammates. "Them greasers are punk ballplayers," Ruth derided. "Only a few of them are any good. The guy they calls after me because he made a few homers is as black as a ton and a half of coal in a dark cellar."[50]

Other than the Dodgers, no major-league team visited Cuba more than the Giants. They returned—this time without John McGraw, who had died in 1934—for spring training in 1937. Bill Terry was at the helm of a team that included future Hall of Famers Carl Hubbell and Mel Ott. Hubbell was no stranger to Cuba. He had helped inaugurate La Tropical stadium in 1930 as a member of the visiting Dave Bancroft All-Stars team. The Giants' roster in the winter of 1937 also included two Cuban pitchers who wore New York colors rather than their customary Cuban League uniforms: Adolfo Luque and Tomás de la Cruz. Luque played during the winter for Almendares, and De la Cruz played for Habana.

Five days after arriving in Cuba, the Giants opened their exhibition schedule on February 24, a national holiday commemorating the start of Cuba's War of Independence against Spain. With some 7,000 fans at La Tropical, the Giants sent De la Cruz to the mound against a Cuban Armed Forces team that included professional players. De la Cruz surrendered four runs before Luque came on in relief in the eighth to a rousing ovation. But two Giant errors eventually led to a 7–4 defeat for New York.[51] The Giants lost their next two games, 9–1 against Habana on February 27 and 6–1 against Almendares on February 28. Habana's Basilo "Brujo" Rosell and Almendares's Ramón Bragaña held New York to one run in their respective outings.

The Giants' first win of the spring came against the amateur Fortuna Sports Club, a 7–2 victory as future Cuban Baseball Hall of Famer Agapito Mayor surrendered seven runs. Only Hubbell, with relief help from Fred Fitzsimmons, gave the Giants a victory against Cuban professionals. In the 7–3 win, New York hitters knocked Luis Tiant Sr. out of the game with a seven-run fifth inning. But another loss came on

March 6 when Rodolfo Fernández limited the Giants to four hits in a 4–0 Almendares victory. Perhaps the highlight of that spring training came on Sunday, March 14, in the second game against the St. Louis Cardinals, who had come to Cuba for a two-game set. The game pitted Hubbell against St. Louis's Paul Dean and drew 15,000–20,000 fans at La Tropical as the Giants won 5–4.[52]

Over the next decade—with a four-year interruption because of World War II—nine different major-league teams played spring training games in Cuba: the Cincinnati Reds, St. Louis Cardinals, Brooklyn Dodgers, New York Giants, Cleveland Indians, Boston Red Sox, Washington Senators, New York Yankees, and Boston Braves. But one team stood out. On the morning of Friday, February 21, 1947, forty-six players from the Dodgers hit the field at Havana's Gran Stadium to begin the most significant spring-training session in major-league history.

For the moment, however, the attention of Cuban fans was elsewhere. Hours after the Dodgers held their first workout at El Gran Stadium, the new 35,000-seat park hosted a Cuban League game between Almendares and Cienfuegos. Almendares starting pitcher Agapito Mayor scattered seven hits over 7⅓ innings as the Scorpions defeated Cienfuegos 9–4. The victory pulled Almendares to within two games of league-leading Habana with four games left to play. A little more than two weeks earlier, Almendares had trailed in the standings by 5½ games and appeared to be out of contention, but the Scorpions had rattled off a series of victories to inject excitement into the Cuban League pennant chase.

Living Legends

The moment Miguel Ángel González stepped off a plane at Havana's airport in Rancho Boyeros on Friday, October 19, 1946, reporters peppered with him questions. The start of the Cuban League season and the inauguration of El Gran Stadium was a week away. But Cuban fans wanted to know more about the recently concluded major-league season than about the chances González's Habana team had of winning the country's winter-league championship. What became known as Enos Slaughter's Mad Dash Home had given González's St. Louis Cardinals a 4–3 victory against the Boston Red Sox in game 7 of the World Series. For his part in the Series-clinching play, González had been accorded hero status in Cuba.

González manned his usual post in the third-base coaching box on the play. With the score tied at 3–3 in the bottom of the eighth inning, Slaughter raced home from first base on Harry "the Hat" Walker's double to score the eventual winning run. Accounts vary as to González's role. Did he wave Slaughter home? Did Slaughter run through González's stop sign? It's difficult to tell from newsreel footage of the play. Years later, Slaughter said González was so shocked at Slaughter's daring on the basepaths that González froze: "I think he was flabbergasted."[1] Upon González's return to Cuba, *Diario de la Marina* columnist Eladio Secades was more than willing to credit him with sending Slaughter home. He explained how beyond the play's "three heroes"—Slaughter, Walker, and González—the key was "one fool," Red Sox shortstop Johnny Pesky, who "incredibly fell asleep with the ball in his hands" on the relay throw from the outfield. "Whenever Mike González finished telling the story," Secades wrote, "he immediately had to start telling it again" for the next inquisitor.[2]

Regardless of González's role in Slaughter's Mad Dash, few questioned his skills as a major-league coach or Cuban League player and manager. Between 1910 and 1936, González played twenty-three Cuban League seasons, almost exclusively with Habana, primarily as the Lions' catcher. He batted over .300 in seven seasons, including three over .400.[3] He also managed Habana many of those seasons, leading the team to nine Cuban League championships from 1914 to 1944. Eight other times during that thirty-year period, Habana finished second with González at the helm. By the early 1940s González had purchased a percentage of the team. Much of what González accomplished in Cuba was influenced, at least in part, by his experience during a seventeen-year career as a major-league player and thirteen years as a major-league coach.

Adolfo Luque came into the 1946–47 Cuban League season knowing full well he had coached his last major-league game. He cleared out his locker and walked out of the New York Giants clubhouse in September 1945, offering pitcher Sal Maglie a winter job with the Cienfuegos team on his way out. Luque had committed a cardinal sin as far as organized baseball was concerned after the 1945–46 Cuban League season ended. He had joined Jorge Pasquel's Mexican League as manager of Puebla for the 1946 season. It didn't matter that Luque's tenure was short-lived. Vocal in his criticism of Pasquel's management of the league, Luque was not immediately offered a contract for 1947. But the damage had been done, and he found himself ineligible in the eyes of organized baseball.

Prevented from managing ineligible players south of the border, Luque at fifty-seven had only his Cuban League career to fall back on. But what a career it had been. The pitcher who had been the first star Latino player in the majors won 106 games in twenty-four seasons in

Cuba from 1912 to 1944. Luque's win total was the second-best career mark in Cuban League history behind future Hall of Famer and fellow Cuban baseball legend Martín Dihigo. Luque also managed in his homeland even as he was playing, holding his first managerial post at age twenty-nine in 1919–20 and guiding Almendares to that season's pennant.

As a manager, Luque was every bit the "snarling, vulgar, cursing, aggressive pug" he was as a player, ready to put up his fists or reach for a firearm against anyone—whether an opposing player or one of his own.[4] Camilo Pascual, who played in the Cuban League from 1952–61 and pitched for the Washington Senators and Minnesota Twins in 1950s and 1960s, said, "If things didn't go his way, he became a maniac," while Preston Gómez, who played for Luque with Cienfuegos in 1944–45 and managed the San Diego Padres, Houston Astros, and Chicago Cubs from 1969 to 1980, described Luque as "very strict and very demanding," to the point of not allowing players to shower after a game without his permission. "If we lost we would go back out on the field and practice."[5]

Ten times over his first twenty-three seasons as a manager in Cuba, Luque led a team to a championship, the most recent coming in 1945–46 when he managed Cienfuegos to its first-ever Cuban League title. Over the years he established himself, alongside Miguel Ángel González, as one of the two greatest managers in Cuban League history. After a three-season stint with Cienfuegos, Luque was back at the helm of Almendares for the 1946–47 season. The quest for Almendares's eighth Cuban League championship under Luque's direction began auspiciously on Saturday, October 26, 1946. In the inauguration of El Gran Stadium, the Scorpions cruised to a 9–1 victory against Cienfuegos, now managed by Dihigo.

Martín Dihigo's final Cuban League season as a manager and part-time player got off to a good start in the inaugural game at Havana's gleaming new stadium. Cienfuegos's starting pitcher Alejandro Carrasquel breezed through the first three innings, and the Elephants held a 1–0 lead against Almendares. But the game began to unravel in the fourth inning as Almendares put three runs on the scoreboard against Dihigo's Venezuelan starting pitcher. Things only got worse in the sixth as Carrasquel surrendered five runs on nine hits and the Scorpions knocked him out of the game. To stem the flood, Dihigo turned first to venerable left-hander Luis Tiant Sr., then to minor-league journeyman Homer Gibson, and finally to Cuban League star Adrián Zabala, all to no avail. The final tally: Almendares 9, Cienfuegos 1.

Earlier in his career, Dihigo, who had played in the Cuban League since 1922 and managed in it since 1935, might simply have strode to the mound and taken the ball himself, ending the scoring threat and rallying his team to victory with his arm and his bat. He had won more than 100 games as pitcher and batted nearly .300 during his Cuban League career. But at age forty-one, Dihigo's considerable baseball skills had diminished. He would play in only fifteen games, recording one hit in eleven at-bats and a 1–3 record as a pitcher for the 1946–47 season. The season belonged to other teams and younger players.

It had not been so in past Cuban League seasons. From the first time Dihigo stepped onto a professional baseball field at age sixteen— whether in Cuba or the United States—his talent was obvious. Dihigo played every position except catcher at a high level. He "could do everything—pitcher, good hitter, good fielder," said former Kansas City Monarchs pitcher Hilton Smith. "And pitching, he threw everything, overhand or sidearm, good curve ball and a good fastball. . . . Had he come along today, he'd lead the major leagues in winning, would have hit .300 too, tremendous power."[6] Dihigo's talent impacted baseball in the United States and across Latin America for decades, earning him the unprecedented honor of being inducted into the Halls of Fame in the United States, Cuba, and Mexico. Cuban fans called him El Inmortal, the Immortal One. In Mexico and Venezuela he was known at El Maestro, the Master. But because of the color of his skin, Dihigo never played in a major-league game.

More than 31,000 fans—the largest crowd ever to attend a Cuban sporting event—watched Almendares's 9–1 victory against Cienfuegos to open the 1946–47 season. The next day, on October 26, even more fans packed into El Gran Stadium, with more than 36,000 attending Sunday's doubleheader. Another 5,000-plus had to be turned away. Not surprising, considering that the Eternal Rivals, Habana and Almendares, played in the nightcap for the first time that season. The first game of the day pitted Marianao against Cienfuegos. The Elephants hoped to bounce back from their opening-day drubbing, but Marianao, under manager Armando Marsans, soundly defeated Cienfuegos 14–3 as Orestes Miñoso went 4-for-5 and Roberto "Tarzán" Estalella drove in three runs.

The 1946–47 season was Marsans's ninth as a manager in the Cuban League since 1912. He had won only one Cuban League pennant, in 1917 at the helm of Orientals. Marsans was Miñoso's first manager in the Cuban League. "I liked him," said Miñoso, who played thirteen full major-league seasons. "He used to be very funny, but when you played the game, you better mind your business."[7] In his two previous seasons managing Marianao, Marsans failed to direct the Gray Monks out of last place. The Cuban baseball pioneer's playing career in Cuba had been far more distinguished.

Marsans began playing in the Cuban League in 1905 with Almendares, the team for which he played most of his career. He retired as a player after the 1927–28 season with the Cuban League career mark for most stolen bases at 135. He had batted over .300 six times, including a .400 mark in 1913. Marsans and countryman Rafael Almeida became the first Cubans to play in the major leagues in the modern era (since 1900) when they debuted for the Cincinnati Reds on July 4, 1911. Despite being white, Marsans and Almeida—as well as other early Cubans in the majors such as Adolfo Luque and Miguel Ángel González—were dogged by questions and speculation about their racial heritage.

Armando Marsans was born on October 3, 1885, in Matanzas to a first-generation Cuban merchant father and a Cuban mother of Spanish descent. As Marsans and other Cuban players began reaching the majors in the early part of the twentieth century, questions arose as to their racial lineage. Much of what is known—or, perhaps more accurately, was written—about Marsans's youth came as American newspapers rushed to assure fans that Marsans and Rafael Almeida, as they began playing in the majors, were not of African descent. A *Philadelphia Inquirer* story described Marsans and Almeida as "raised in the lap of luxury," while another writer toasted "these two Cuban aristocrats of the diamond."[8]

Marsans's family reportedly fled Cuba in the years before the Spanish-American War, relocating to the United States, where Armando learned to play baseball in New York's Central Park. The reason for the Marsans family's exile: a young Armando was caught by Spanish authorities plotting to arm Cuban rebels. If the story is true, he and a friend entered a Spanish barracks, where they traded rationed cigarettes for ammunition that would be smuggled to supply the local insurgency.[9] Among the few details of Marsans's youth attributed to Marsans himself was his work as a newsboy for the English-language *Havana Post*. Marsans told the newspaper's sports editor of his desire to play baseball in America. Eventually the editor helped Marsans sign in 1905 with the Havana-based All-Cubans, who barnstormed the United States.[10]

At that time it was not uncommon for white Cubans to play on black barnstorming teams in the U.S. No doubt Marsans's participation on black teams, such as the All-Cubans and the Cuban Stars of Havana, helped feed the concerns some had about his race. Those concerns came to a head when Marsans, Almeida, and fellow Cubans Alfredo Cabrera and Luis Padrón signed with the New Britain Mountaineers of the Class-B Connecticut League in 1908. The Cuban players were hindered by a "widespread inability . . . of American ballplayers to differentiate between Cubans and Negro athletes," columnist Bob Considine wrote in a 1940 article in *Collier's*.[11]

The Cuban players' presence in New Britain caused enough of an uproar to prompt the league to officially ban its teams from signing black players in 1908. To protect the team's investment, New Britain manager Billy Hanna traveled to Cuba, securing sufficient documentation to show that the players, except Padrón, were "real Cubans."[12] Cincinnati Reds president Garry Herrmann first dipped his toe into this pool of racial unrest, asking New England sportswriters about

Marsans and Almeida. J. F. Sullivan, sports editor of the *Springfield (Mass.) Union*, responded to Herrmann's inquiry about Marsans: "He is Cuban, all right, not a nigger. But I find the presence of these Cubans breed [sic] discontent here, and I think it would do so even more on a major league club."[13] Sullivan's less-than-ringing endorsement did not dissuade Herrmann from signing Marsans and Almeida for the Reds in 1911.

Even at birth, Miguel Ángel González and Adolfo Luque were in proximity to each other, born into modest circumstances less than two months apart in towns separated by the Port of Havana. Luque was born in Havana on August 4, 1890. González came into the world the following month on September 24 in Regla. Their lives and careers were intertwined in the decades that followed. The Republic of Cuba, barely a decade removed from Spanish colonial rule, was still in its infancy when a young Luque enlisted in the Cuban army as an artilleryman. He also became a hard-hitting third baseman with the army's baseball team.

Luque's baseball skills impressed the exclusive Vedado Tennis Club enough to overlook Luque's humble upbringing and recruit him for its baseball team, one of the best amateur clubs in Cuba. Taking advantage of his strong arm, Vedado converted Luque into a pitcher. By 1912 he signed with the Cuban League's Fe team. There he joined González, who had already been in the league since 1910. This was the first of many times González and Luque would cross paths during their parallel careers. Each became an iconic figure with the Cuban League's most iconic teams—Luque the Almendares pitcher, González the Habana catcher.

Both were equally revered as managers, so much so that Ernest Hemingway mentioned them in his 1952 novel *The Old Man and The Sea*. "Who is the greatest manager, really, Luque or Mike Gonzalez?" Hemingway's Cuban fisherman character, Santiago, is asked. His response: "I think they are equal."[14] Perhaps they were equal as managers, but certainly not in personality. Luque was a gun-toting, drunken womanizer with a volatile temper. González was a level-headed student of the game. While Luque played for the Reds in 1926, the woman he married in Cincinnati accused him of abandoning her and the child she was carrying. He was plagued by money problems throughout his career, regularly sending cables to the Reds during the off-season requesting advances on his salary. In contrast, González's frugality allowed him to amass enough of a fortune to eventually buy the Habana Base Ball Club.

Aside from his protruding ears, young González's most distinguishing physical features were his height and weight. Tall and skinny, like a loaf of Cuban bread, González actually delivered bread in Regla before turning to baseball. He was known in Cuba as Pan de Flauta, Spanish for the baguette-shaped bread.[15] But González's gangly frame belied his athletic talents: a powerful arm and nimble defensive skills. He began his Cuban League career as an infielder before switching to catcher. González's and Luque's presence did not keep Fe from finishing third in the three-team Cuban League in 1912. Luque was winless in seven outings, while González batted .428 but played in only ten games.

Luque and González found themselves as teammates again the following year, this time in the United States. They played for the Long Branch (New Jersey) Cubans of the Class-D New York–New Jersey League. It was the first all-Cuban squad in U.S. baseball history, fielded by team owner Dr. Carlos Henríquez. The battery of González and Luque was outstanding, propelling Long Branch to the league pennant by 18½ games. González batted .333, while Luque went 22–5, winning one-third of the Cubans' games. During one particularly dominant stretch on the mound between June 4 and July 12, Luque pitched in thirteen games, winning all but one. He also played multiple positions and finished the season batting over .300.

Years later, González credited his season with Long Branch as launching his career. "If I had remained in Cuba, no doubt I would have stayed at the bank," he said of the job he had held as a teller at age seventeen. "I had no idea at the time that I would make good in the big leagues."[16] González made it to the majors to stay in 1914, playing 95 games with the Cincinnati Reds. When he returned to play in the Cuban League that winter, he rejoined Habana, where he had been traded from Fe in 1913. But no longer was he just Habana's catcher. After Cuban baseball promoter Abel Linares bought the team from Manuel Azoy in 1914, he installed the twenty-five-year-old González as manager in one of his first moves as owner.[17]

━

Martín Dihigo made his Cuban League debut at age sixteen with Habana during the 1922–23 season. By then Miguel Ángel González had already been Habana's manager for five seasons, winning four Cuban League pennants. Habana was losing to Marianao on January 21, 1923, at Almendares Park. It didn't matter that Cristóbal Torriente homered, tripled, and stole two bases. Marianao pitcher Ben Tincup, a full-blooded Cherokee who had played parts of three seasons with the Philadelphia Phillies, shut down Habana in relief. He also homered, and Marianao took the lead for good with four runs in the seventh inning. In the ninth, González sent in Dihigo to pinch-hit for José "Cheo" Hernández. Dihigo failed to get a hit in his only at-bat in the game, and Habana lost 8–5. Thus began the professional baseball career that would culminate with Dihigo's induction into Halls of Fame in three countries.

Martín Magdaleno Dihigo was born on May 25, 1906, in the city of Matanzas. He was the firstborn son to Benito Dihigo, a sergeant in the Cuban Liberation Army during the country's War of Independence, and Margarita Llanes. When he was three or four, his family moved to Pueblo Nuevo, a neighborhood of Matanzas. Their modest home was within walking distance of Palmar de Junco, site of the first recorded professional baseball game in Cuban history. Benito tried to discourage Martín from playing baseball—the father saw no future in the game—but there was no tempering his son's interest. In 1918 at age twelve, Dihigo slipped through a loose plank along the outfield fence at Palmar de Junco and snuck onto the field where a local amateur team, Bellamar, practiced with a contingent from Havana that included Miguel Ángel González. Dihigo grabbed González's glove to try to insinuate his way into the practice. Discovering the ploy, Dihigo's future manager—González would later sign Dihigo to his first Cuban League contract—demanded the return of his glove.[18]

Bellamar, which was based in Dihigo's home province of Matanzas, became the national amateur champion that year. Because Dihigo was black, however, amateur baseball in Cuba—the province of exclusive, whites-only social clubs—was off limits to him. Instead Dihigo played for various semipro teams while growing up in Matanzas, then joined the Cuban League's Habana club. The major leagues were equally off limits to Dihigo because of his skin color. So he played baseball in the United States with the Cuban Stars of the Negro leagues. Even as a youngster, the tall, graceful Dihigo made an impression. "Dihigo, the rookie infielder for Alex Pompez's Cuban Stars," *Chicago Defender* sports editor Fay Young wrote, "is, in this writer's opinion, the best youngster to come off the island since pitcher José Méndez."[19]

News of Marsans and Almeida signing with the Reds broke on June 23, 1911. A headline in the *Cincinnati Tribune* asked, "Is baseball to lower color line?" and wondered if the Reds signing two Cuban players was a "step towards letting in the Negro." The body of the story was equally damning: "These particular Cubans may be of Spanish descent and they may be of African."[20] The June 22 edition of the *Sporting News* speculated that neither player would be "permitted to perform in the big leagues if it is found that either has African blood in his veins," while the *Cincinnati Enquirer* on June 23, citing Cuban sportswriter Víctor Muñoz, countered that "both of these men are pure Spaniards, without a trace of colored blood."[21]

After the Reds paid New Britain $3,500 for Almeida and $2,500 for Marsans, team president Gerry Herrmann met his latest acquisitions at a local train station on June 28, declaring them "perfect gentlemen," while the *Philadelphia Enquirer* judged them to be "quiet and inoffensive players."[22] Marsans and Almeida quickly signed their major-league contracts but remained on the Reds' bench for their first few games in uniform. On Tuesday, July 4, 1911, the temperature in Chicago climbed past 100 degrees, topping out at 102. As had been the case since they joined the team, Almeida and Marsans were not in the starting lineup when the Reds began the second game of a three-game series against the Cubs. Almeida officially became the first Cuban-born player to make his major-league debut in the modern era when he entered the game as a pinch hitter in the seventh inning. He struck out, but Marsans, who entered as a pinch hitter in the eighth, recorded a single for his first major-league hit.

Now that both Cubans officially were major leaguers, newspaper reporters rushed to paint them as fully white. *Chicago Daily News* sports writer Bill Phelon defended Almeida and Marsans—"The Cubans . . . are a proud race, the sort of people who can show pedigrees of purest Spanish strain, and a Negro cross is regarded with the same sentiment as in the United States"—and one *Cincinnati Enquirer* sportswriter proclaimed, "We have in our midst two descendants of a noble Spanish race, with no ignoble African blood. . . . Permit me to introduce two of the purest bars of Castilian soap that ever floated to these shores."[23]

Major-league teams took notice of Adolfo Luque's dominating performance with the Long Branch Cubans in 1913, so the New York Yankees and others began scouting the Cuban right-hander. "Luque is a very light-skinned Cuban . . . and looks more like an Italian than a full-blooded Cuban," one New York newspaper wrote,[24] apparently to justify the team's interest in Luque. Long Branch eventually sold the pitcher to the Boston Braves, who signed "the Pride of Havana" to a contract that paid him $250 per month. Luque made his major-league debut on May 20, 1914, becoming the first Latino to pitch a major-league game. He held the Pittsburgh Pirates to five hits but lost 4–1. The next day's *New York Times* wrote, "Luque, a Cuban, pitched a good game but was accorded poor run support,"[25] a plaint that became a theme of Luque's career.

Despite his notable debut, Luque bounced around the minors for several years before signing in 1918 with the Reds, managed by future Hall of Fame pitcher Christy Mathewson. As a teenager, Luque saw Mathewson pitch in Cuba and studied the former New York Giants star. But Luque's tutelage under Mathewson in Cincinnati was short lived. With World War I raging, Matty enlisted in the army late in the 1918 season. Exposed to mustard gas during a training exercise, Mathewson contracted tuberculosis and never returned to the Reds. Luque went 10–3 with a 2.63 earned run average while starting 9 games and relieving in 21 others during the 1919 season. On October 3 he became the first Latino to appear in a World Series, pitching one inning in game 3, the first game the Chicago "Black Sox" tried to win during their plot to throw the best-of-nine Series. Luque also pitched four innings in game 7, which the White Sox won. Altogether he pitched five innings, struck out six, and allowed no runs as the Reds won the Series.

With Major League Baseball in 1921 outlawing trick pitches that created deceptive movement—the spitball, shine ball, and emery ball—Luque became one of the few pitchers to successfully navigate the transition out of the dead-ball era. Author Nick C. Wilson noted that from 1910 to 1919, seventy-six pitchers recorded an ERA under 2.00 for a season. But from 1920 to 1929, only two did so.[26] One was Luque, who registered one of the finest single-season performances by a pitcher in baseball history during the 1923 season. He went 27–8 with a 1.93 earned run average while throwing six shutouts to lead the National League. He was second in strikeouts with 151 and third in complete games with 28. Luque allowed only two home runs and held opposing hitters to a .235 average, the lowest by a National League pitcher that season. Aside from Luque, only future Hall of Famer Grover Cleveland Alexander recorded an ERA under 2.00 during the 1920s. After Luque's spectacular season, some 30,000 fans greeted Papa Montero at Havana Harbor in October. His return to Cuba was cause for a parade through Havana's streets that included Luque's former artillery division, popular music groups, and a contingent of Cuba's baseball players. The next day Luque appeared at the Martí Theatre to reenact his famous fight with New York Giants outfielder Casey Stengel.[27]

Despite once again leading the National League with a 2.63 earned run average in 1925 and finishing with a 3.24 career ERA in the majors, Luque never came close to matching his 1923 performance. But Luque, whose career major-league record was 194–179, had one last hurrah in the majors, winning the decisive game 5 of the 1933 World Series for the New York Giants. The score was tied 3–3 and runners were on first and third when Luque relieved starter Hal Schumacher in the sixth inning. With two outs, Luque got Washington Senators catcher Luke

Sewell to ground out to end the threat. After Luque breezed through the next three innings, Mel Ott homered in the tenth to break the tie.

With a toe bleeding from a broken nail he sustained in the ninth inning, Luque got the first two outs of the bottom of the tenth before Joe Cronin singled. Then Fred Schulte worked the count to three balls and two strikes against Luque. As future Hall of Famer and game 4 winner Carl Hubbell warmed up in the bullpen, Giants manager Bill Terry went out to the mound, but Luque insisted he could close out the game. "I peetch," Terry said in what the *New York Times* described as a "hilarious" impersonation of Luque.[28] Facing Joe Kuhel, who batted .322 for the season, Luque struck out the Senators first baseman on three straight curve balls. At age forty, Luque gave the Giants the World Series title. It would be twenty-one years before another Latino (Puerto Rican pitcher Rubén Gómez with the New York Giants in 1954) appeared in a World Series. Throughout his twenty seasons in the majors, Luque left an indelible mark. "When Luque got out on the mound, his blue eyes blazed malevolently at each hitter and he defied them," *New York Times* sportswriter Arthur Daley once wrote. "He was a mean cuss at times and they said he never threw a beanball by accident."[29]

What Miguel Ángel González lacked in fiery charisma—an attribute Adolfo Luque had in abundance—he more than made up for with his mind. González was "steady, smart, conservative, and loyal and came to be regarded as the most knowledgeable baseball man in Cuba."[30] As manager, he led Habana to fourteen Cuban League championships and eventually became the winningest manager in league history with 846 victories.[31] As a player in the majors, González's skills were apparent as well. After 83 games with the Reds in 1914, he was traded to the St. Louis Cardinals prior to spring training in 1915. For the next four seasons, González was the Cardinals' primary catcher. But his association with the team continued in one form or another for much of the next three decades. After a stint with the New York Giants, González returned to the Cardinals in 1924, leading National League catchers in games caught, putouts, and double plays while hitting 27 doubles. The next season, he led National League catchers in fielding percentage and made just four errors, while splitting the year between the Cardinals and the Chicago Cubs.

In his seventeen-year major-league career, González had played eight seasons with the Cardinals (1915–18, 1924–25, and 1931–32). Retiring as a player in 1932, González eventually became a coach with St. Louis, beginning in 1934. The subdued González may have seemed an awkward fit with the raucous Gashouse Gang. But "we considered him as one of us," said Don Gutteridge, an infielder with the Cardinals from 1936 to 1940.[32] González made history in St. Louis four years later. With seventeen games remaining in the 1938 season, the Cardinals fired Frisch on September 11, handing the reins of the team to González. As the first Cuban-born—and Latino—manager in major-league history, González guided St. Louis to an 8–8 record to finish the season.

The following season, González remained on the Cardinals' coaching staff under new manager Ray Blades and got a second stint as interim manager when St. Louis fired Blades 38 games into the 1940 season. This time the Cardinals went 1–5 with González at the helm, running his career managerial record to 9–13. "He was a really good coach," Gutteridge said. "I admired him."[33] González also is credited with coining a terse scouting evaluation, in broken English, of a specific type of player: "Good field, no hit."[34] Unfortunately, that well-known phrase hurt González's reputation as a coach, but Hall of Fame Cuban broadcaster Felo Ramírez described González as "very intelligent and very scientific."[35]

When they debuted in 1911, Rafael Almeida was the more highly touted of the first two Cuban-born major-league players of the modern era. The Cincinnati Reds paid more for Almeida than they had for his New Britain teammate Armando Marsans. Almeida batted .313 his rookie season in the majors, while Marsans hit just .261. But Marsans had the longer big-league career; Almeida's was done by 1913, while Marsans played until 1918.

Aside from the questions surrounding his race, Marsans's major-league career also was marked by contract disputes and lawsuits. After batting .317 and .297 in back-to-back seasons with the Reds, Marsans demanded—without success—a $7,000 salary for the 1914 season. So in June he jumped to the St. Louis Terriers of the Federal League for a three-year, $21,000 contract. The move prompted Reds president Gerry Herrmann to suspend Marsans on June 14 and file suit to prevent the Cuban outfielder from playing in the Federal League. "I made a serious mistake when I joined the Feds and I want to come back," Marsans told a friend, according to a January 1915 report by New York writer Joe Vila.[36]

Despite the acrimony between them, Herrmann enlisted John McGraw and Miller Huggins, who managed the New York Giants and St. Louis Cardinals respectively, to visit Marsans in Cuba and attempt to arrange some sort of reconciliation with Major League Baseball. Marsans rebuffed McGraw's overtures, saying he wouldn't play for the Giants manager "for $20,000." He also blasted New York baseball writers because "they have always thought it funny to poke jokes at me."[37] On August 19, 1915, a U.S. federal district court judge lifted an injunction and allowed Marsans to play for the Terriers in the rival major league. He returned to the National League in 1916, joining the St. Louis Browns and stealing a career-high 46 bases. But by 1918 he played in just 37 games with the New York Yankees.

Marsans's Cuban League playing career—mostly with Almendares—lasted until 1928. He retired as the top base stealer in league history, batted over .300 in six different seasons and led the league with a .400 batting average in 1913. Marsans and Almeida were among the first ten players inducted into the Cuban Baseball Hall of Fame in 1939, joining such other luminaries as José Méndez and Cristóbal Torriente. As a manager in the Cuban League, Marsans had directed Orientals to the pennant in 1917 and four other times managed teams to second-place finishes. But his first two seasons managing Marianao had not gone well, with the Gray Monks finishing fourth (out of four teams) each season. Marsans would not complete the 1946–47 Cuban League season in a Marianao uniform.

Marsans's major-league career may have lasted only eight seasons, but that was a lifetime compared to Martín Dihigo's. The first Cuban-born player who would be enshrined in the National Baseball Hall of Fame in Cooperstown, New York, never set foot on a major-league diamond, because he was black. Trying to quantify Dihigo's talent as a baseball player through statistics is difficult. In the Negro leagues, given their barnstorming nature, record keeping often was incomplete. But the firsthand testimonials from those who played with or against him paint a picture of Dihigo as the most versatile player in baseball history. Perhaps no player was more emphatic in his assessment than fellow Hall of Famer Buck Leonard: "I say he was the best ballplayer of all time, black or white. He could do it all. . . . You take your Ruths, Cobbs, and DiMaggios. Give me Dihigo. I bet I would beat you almost every time."[38]

Dihigo began his Negro leagues career with Cuban American Alex Pompez's Cuban Stars of the Eastern Colored League, playing with the team in 1923–27 and again in 1930. As a teenager traveling across the United States, Dihigo was exposed to a racism he had not known in Cuba. "I began to experience the hatred of 'gringos,'" Dihigo once said. "Those gringos were such cretins that in many hotels, if they, by chance, admitted us, they would go to the extreme of denying us water to bathe," he wrote in an autobiography, *Primeros Pasos en el Profesionalismo*, published in Cuba.[39] But Dihigo was undaunted, continuing to play in the United States, with the Homestead Grays (1928), Hilldale Daisies (1929–31), Baltimore Black Sox (1931), and Pompez's New York Cubans (1935–36 and 1945).[40]

Whether it was on the mound or at the plate, Dihigo flourished in the Cuban League. Baseball historian Jorge S. Figueredo credits Dihigo with a long list of accomplishments during his twenty-one seasons in Cuba: four Cuban League MVP awards, two seasons batting over .400, most victories in professional Cuban history (107), twice leading the Cuban League in victories. He played for Habana, Almendares, Cienfuegos, Marianao, and Santa Clara. In 1935–36, his first Cuban League season as a player-manager, Dihigo led Santa Clara to the Cuban League title. He led the league in batting average (.358), runs, hits, triples, and runs batted in, and went a league-best 11–2 as pitcher to earn MVP honors.

The following season he took Marianao to the championship. Dihigo's former team, Santa Clara, led Marianao by three games in the standings with three games remaining between the two teams. Marianao swept the regular season-ending series to force a three-game playoff at La Tropical stadium. In the first game, Negro leagues star Raymond Brown beat Dihigo 6–1, but Marianao bounced back in the second game with a 4–2 victory as Silvio García "pitched the best game of his career to even the series."[41] On two days' rest, Dihigo started the decisive game and shut out the Leopards for eight innings as Marianao won the Cuban League title with a 7–3 victory. Having compiled a 14–10 record to go along with a .323 average, Dihigo won his second consecutive MVP award. The 1946–47 Cuban League season would finish in similarly exciting fashion, but this time Dihigo would only play the role of spectator.

Figure 1. Miguel Ángel González as a catcher for Habana during the 1915–16 Cuban League season. *Bohemia* magazine, author's collection.

Figure 2. Armando Marsans, who joined Rafael Almeida as the first Cuban-born major-league players of the modern era when they debuted with the Cincinnati Reds on July 4, 1911. Courtesy of Library of Congress, Prints & Photographs Division.

Figure 3. Silvio García, purportedly considered in 1945 by Dodgers president Branch Rickey to break the major-league color barrier. Propagandas Montiel Los Reyes del Deporte card, 1946–47, author's collection.

Figure 4. José Méndez, "El Diamante Negro" (the Black Diamond), who dominated the barnstorming Cincinnati Reds during their 1908 visit to Cuba, allowing one run in 25 innings. Courtesy of the National Pastime Museum.

Figure 5. Adolfo Luque, second from left, Alacranes manager during the 1947–48 Liga Nacional season at La Tropical stadium. *Bohemia* magazine, author's collection.

Figure 6. The 1946–47 Habana team. Francisco Caulfield/Brillantina Sol de Oro postcard, author's collection.

Above: Figure 7. Aerial view of El Gran Stadium of Havana, which opened on October 26, 1946. Courtesy of Cuban Heritage Collection of the University of Miami Libraries.

Left: Figure 8. Bobby Maduro, whose Compañia Operadora de Stadiums completed construction of El Gran Stadium in time for the 1946–47 Cuban League season. *Bohemia* magazine, author's collection.

Above: Figure 9. Almendares pitchers Max Lanier and Agapito Mayor, who combined to win nine of the Scorpions' final thirteen victories at the end of the 1946–47 season. *Bohemia* magazine, author's collection.

Right: Figure 10. Almendares catcher Andrés Fleitas, most valuable player of the 1946–47 Cuban League season. *Carteles* magazine, author's collection.

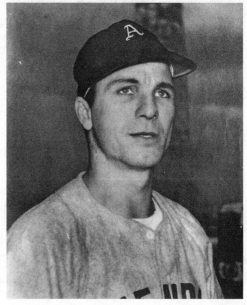

Above: Figure 11. Brothers Heberto and Carlos Blanco in the Habana dugout on November 3, 1946. *Bohemia* magazine, author's collection.

Left: Figure 12. Agapito Mayor, who recorded six of Almendares's 14 victories during the final month of the 1946–74 Cuban League season, shown in a 1943–44 La Campaña Cubana card, author's collection.

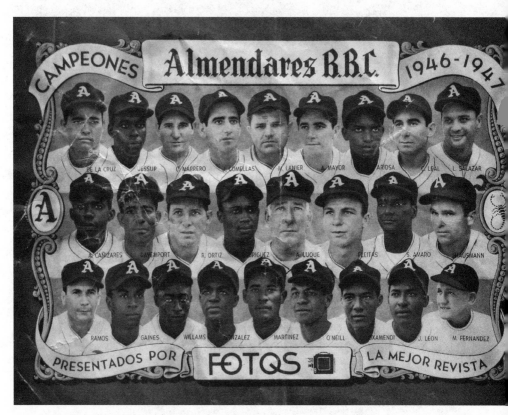

Figure 13. The 1946–47 Cuban League champion Almendares team.
Fotos premium, Álvarez y Saurina/Editorial Neptuno, author's collection.

Figure 14. Max Lanier, who pitched for Alacranes in the rival Liga Nacional during the winter of 1947–48. Francisco Caulfield/Brillantina Sol de Oro card, author's collection.

Figure 15. Roberto Ortiz, 1946–47 Cuban League leader with eleven home runs, shown in an Alacranes uniform. Francisco Caulfield/Brillantina Sol de Oro postcard, 1947–48, author's collection.

Figure 16. Cristóbal
Torriente, who blast-
ed three home runs
in a game against a
barnstorming New
York Giants team that
featured Babe Ruth
during a 1920 visit
to Cuba. Courtesy of
the National Pastime
Museum.

Figure 17. Martín Dihigo, winning pitcher in 104 career games in the Cuban League, who also won two pennants as a manager but managed Cienfuegos to a last-place tie during the 1946–47 season. Courtesy of the National Pastime Museum.

Figure 18. Fermín Guerra, manager of Oriente during the 1946–47 National Federation season, here shown with Almendares. 1949–50 card, author's collection.

Figure 19. Brooklyn Dodgers manager Leo Durocher shaking hands with Montreal Royals infielder Jackie Robinson at El Gran Stadium during a series of exhibition games in Havana in March 1947. Courtesy of the Rucker Archive.

Figure 20. René Cañizares, who wrote about the Cuban League for the *Sporting News*, with Brooklyn Dodgers broadcaster Red Barber during spring training. Courtesy of University of Florida George A. Smathers Library.

Figure 21. Napoleón Reyes, one of the players who jumped to the Mexican League and were ruled ineligible by organized baseball, shown here with Cuba of the Liga Nacional. Francisco Caulfield/Brillantina Sol de Oro postcard, 1947–48, author's collection.

Figure 22. Salvador Hernández, who managed Leones of the Liga Nacional. Francisco Caulfield/Brillantina Sol de Oro postcard, 1947–48, author's collection.

Right: Figure 23. Danny Gardella, one of the first players to jump his major-league contract to sign with the Mexican League, here shown in the uniform of National Federation team Santiago on November 30, 1947. *Bohemia* magazine, author's collection.

Left: Figure 24. Habana pitcher Fred Martin, who went 1–4 in the final two months of the season against Almendares as Habana won only two of its ten games against the Scorpions in January and February of 1947. Francisco Caulfield/Brillantina Sol de Oro postcard, 1947–48, author's collection.

Separate and Unequal

Pittsburgh Courier sports columnist Wendell Smith sat next to Dodgers manager Leo Durocher as the four-engine Pan American Clipper traversed the 200 miles from Miami to Havana. Before leaving New York for Miami, Leo the Lip had been uncharacteristically reticent when Gotham's newspaper reporters asked about Jackie Robinson's prospects for making Brooklyn's roster. As the plane's engines rumbled above the blue expanse of the Florida Straits, a relaxed Durocher opened up to Smith, who had championed the cause of integrating Major League Baseball as a member of the black press and would be in Cuba to cover Robinson.

Heading into spring training and the 1947 major-league season, Durocher seemed far more willing to discuss the hot topic with Smith than he had been with the reporters he regularly dealt with back in New York. "He's my type of ball player," Smith quoted Durocher in his column. "Jackie can hit, run, and field. What more can a manager ask of a ball player? . . . Jackie Robinson is a damn good ball player."[1] He also engaged Smith about the other three black players on the Montreal Royals roster—catcher Roy Campanella and pitchers Don Newcombe and Roy Partlow—who would train in Cuba. Durocher had not seen Campanella, but "I understand he has a rifle arm and can really hit."[2]

But Durocher had seen Robinson, in exhibitions on the West Coast the previous October. And the fact Robinson didn't register a hit off Bob Feller in those exhibitions didn't dissuade the Dodgers manager. As the plane began its descent and the Morro Castle at Havana Harbor came into view, Smith asked Durocher if he thought Robinson would make the Dodgers. "I honestly don't know," Durocher told Smith in a "confidential" tone. Then, referring to Dodgers president Branch Rickey, he said, "I don't think he's definitely made up his mind about Jackie and the Dodgers. . . . If he says Robinson's a Dodger, that's what he'll be."[3]

El Malecón, a wide, four-mile roadway from Havana Bay to the Vedado neighborhood, snakes along Havana's north coast. On a high bluff overlooking the road sits the Hotel Nacional. Designed by McKim, Mead & White and built by the New York firm of Purdy & Henderson, the fourteen-story, twin-towered landmark was built in fourteen months on a promontory known as the Loma de Taganana. Centuries earlier, the site had been home to the Spanish shore battery of Santa Clara. Constructed in response to attacks from pirates and privateers and the capture of Havana by British naval forces in 1762, the fortification defended Havana into the late eighteenth century, and two cannons still decorate the hotel gardens.[4]

An eclectic melding of Moorish-Andalusian, art deco, neoclassical, and neocolonial architectural styles, the Hotel Nacional opened on the night of December 30, 1930. Less than three years later the Nacional—like the battery upon which it was built—found itself under siege. Political unrest had precluded a decisive playoff series being played after Habana and Almendares finished the 1932–33 season tied in the standings with 13–9 records. In September of 1933 a popular uprising overthrew Gerardo Machado, Cuba's brutal U.S.-backed dictator, and Cuban army sergeant Fulgencio Batista seized power. Amid the turmoil, the Nacional came under artillery fire on October 2, 1933.[5] Some three hundred military leaders under the deposed Machado had taken refuge in the hotel, which was bombarded for several days. Cut off from supplies and running out of ammunition, the displaced officers eventually surrendered. Cuba's political upheaval continued into the following year, forcing cancellation of the 1933–34 Cuban League season. It was the first time the league had failed to play a season since Cuba's War of Independence from Spain wiped out the 1895–96 and 1896–97 seasons and forced truncation in 1897–98.

The military assault of 1933 apparently did little to tarnish the appeal of the Nacional. Whatever damage had been sustained by the palatial hotel was repaired, and the rich and famous from Cuba and elsewhere flocked to Havana's flagship hotel. During the 1930s the hotel's guest list included an eclectic roster of names: actors Johnny Weissmuller, Errol Flynn, Buster Keaton, and Tom Mix, boxer Jack Dempsey, and mobsters Meyer Lansky and Santo Trafficante Jr.[6] In the 1940s the hotel's guest book included the names of future members of the National Baseball Hall of Fame: Leo Durocher, Pee Wee Reese, Joe Medwick, Billy Herman, and Arky Vaughn. The Dodgers made Havana their spring training home in 1941 and 1942. Each time, they domiciled in the exclusive Nacional. And when the Dodgers returned to Cuba in 1947, they would stay there again.

As the Dodgers began checking into the Hotel Nacional on the night of February 19, 1947, they could not have imagined some of the shenanigans that had taken place at the stately resort in the months and weeks prior to their arrival in Cuba. During Christmas week of 1946, nearly a dozen high-ranking mobsters had convened on the hotel's upper floors to discuss their plans for Havana, a gathering that had sinister overtones. Lansky, a partner in the corporation that owned the Nacional, organized the conference, which included such mobsters as Charles "Lucky" Luciano, Albert Anastasia, Frank Costello, and Trafficante. From December 22 to 26, the top two floors of the Nacional were closed to the public, the hotel grounds were guarded by a private security force, and no journalists, police, or Cuban bureaucrats were allowed on the premises.[7]

The primary item on the agenda was Lansky's proposal for turning Havana into the capital of the mob's Caribbean gambling empire, away from the prying eye of American law enforcement. Another major topic of discussion: a solution to the mob's problem with Bugsy Siegel. The building of the Flamingo Hotel and Casino in Las Vegas had been plagued by cost overruns, and Lansky was convinced his boyhood friend had been skimming.[8] Years later, Luciano quoted Lansky as saying during the meeting at the Nacional that "Benny's got to be hit."[9] Lansky vehemently denied giving that order, but on June 29, 1947, bullets riddled Siegel as he sat in the living room of girlfriend Virginia Hill's Beverly Hills home.

Before the mobsters got down to their serious business, they opened their conference with a lavish feast in a special banquet room in the lower level of the Nacional. After dinner, showgirls from the Tropicana, Montmartre, and Sans Souci nightclubs and prostitutes from the Casa Marina bordello entertained the guests.[10]

More shocking might have been revelations about actor/singer Frank Sinatra's activities. The week before the Dodgers arrived, the crooner and Luciano participated in a drunken orgy in Sinatra's hotel suite. Sinatra, a mob groupie, landed at the Havana airport the morning of February 11 and headed for the Nacional, where he was to perform for the gathering of mobsters. He brought with him a suitcase filled with $2 million he allegedly delivered to Luciano's suite at the hotel.[11] Luciano had been in Havana since October 29, 1946. After having his 30-to-50-year prison sentence on prostitution charges commuted for helping in the war effort against Nazi Germany, Luciano was deported from the United States to his native Sicily.[12] But fellow mobster and longtime friend Meyer Lansky arranged to bring him to Havana. Lucky had been living the high life at the Nacional ever since.

Referencing files from the U.S. Narcotics Bureau, author T. J. English described a "ribald bacchanalia" in Sinatra's suite that included "a planeload of call girls" and Al Capone's younger brother, Ralph, among the guests.[13]

Somehow a contingent of Cuban Girl Scouts escorted by a Catholic nun were allowed to visit Sinatra's suite. According to an account preserved in the files of the Narcotics Bureau, the Girl Scouts were there to present Sinatra with an award of some sort and had been allowed past security "through a series of disastrous mistakes by various personnel." The call girls were quickly hidden away in a back bedroom. When the Girl Scouts entered the suite, there were bottles on the floor, lingerie was hanging from lampshades, and the air was filled with the stench of stale perfume. Sinatra entered the front room in a robe and silk scarf as if nothing were wrong. The ruse was exposed when four naked bodies fell giggling into the front room. The nun and her charges quickly left the suite in a state of shock.[14]

The Dodgers themselves were no strangers to scandalous events at the Nacional, having contributed their own brand during past visits to Havana. On this trip, however, they avoided such dalliances, or at least were more discreet about them.

Dodgers president Branch Rickey and Mexican League owner Jorge Pasquel flew into Havana within hours of each other on Thursday, February 20. Rickey flew the Dodgers' private plane from the organization's minor-league camp in Pensacola, Florida. Pasquel arrived from Mexico aboard his private plane, *El Mexicano*. Approached at the airport by reporters, Pasquel said, "I don't want you to talk to me about baseball."[15] He was not nearly so reticent with players in the Dodgers organization. Members of the Montreal Royals, including Roy Campanella and Don Newcombe, arrived the next day. Jackie Robinson flew in on Saturday. Even before Robinson arrived at the Royals' camp, Pasquel reached the Royals infielder via messenger with an offer to play south of the border. Robinson responded that he "wasn't the least bit interested."[16]

Undeterred by Robinson's rebuff, Pasquel approached Campanella on a Havana street with an offer to join the Mexico City team for $10,000 over five seasons. "Lookee Campy, you will never be on Brookleen team," Wendell Smith phonetically quoted Pasquel. "Come to Mexico and play for me. I weel pay you good."[17] According to the *Sporting News*, Campanella, who had played with Monterrey in 1942 and 1943, told Pasquel he would consider his offer, only to report the encounter to Royals manager Clay Hopper, who then informed Rickey.[18] Five days after arriving in Havana, Pasquel held court with forty Brooklyn Dodgers players in the lobby of the Hotel Nacional. The players were arrayed five and six deep around the Mexican League president. Despite the threat of player holdouts and the prospect of league teams folding, Pasquel boasted, "My league will be stronger than ever. I will take players [from] anywhere."[19] Rickey was not pleased with Pasquel's public wooing of his players. He had wanted to meet Pasquel to "talk seriously with him about the possibility of his legally joining organized baseball," Rickey said, "but I'm not so sure now."[20]

Pasquel was not alone in socializing with the Dodgers in Cuba. During the closing days of the Cuban League season, Almendares pitcher Max Lanier, who had jumped his contract with the St. Louis Cardinals to play in Mexico, spent his down time at the Hotel Nacional visiting Dixie Walker, Rube Melton, and Bobby Bragan to gossip about baseball. "There is no doubt," New York Journal-American writer Michael Gaven wrote, "that Lanier misses the American way of living and playing baseball."[21] Lanier admitted to the writer that he would like to be back in the majors. "Who wouldn't?" he said. "Still, I have no regrets."[22] Lanier's profession of contentment, however, was belied by his decision to hold out against the Mexican League's Veracruz team. He refused to accept a 50 percent cut from his 1946 salary of $14,000 for the 1947 season.[23]

Lanier also had expressed his frustration that Pasquel seemed willing to talk to plenty of other players in Cuba but not him. "Pasquel came to New York to sign me before," Lanier told Lester Bromberg of the New York World-Telegram. "Now he's in Havana and won't walk across the street. I don't care. I'll wait. I can sit on the bench here until he's ready."[24] Rickey, who had signed Lanier when he ran the Cardinals, seemed to empathize with the lefty pitcher. "Poor Lanier!" Rickey lamented. "There is nothing Lanier can say now except that he is not sorry he jumped. Well, he would return twice what he got if he could wipe out the stigma of the contract breaking, and return to the Cardinals."[25]

Rickey had been busy since he arrived in Cuba. As the Dodgers president made the rounds of the Havana camp sites, one of his outfielders became an inventor. After seeing teammate Lou Ruchser smacked in the jaw by a line drive on the first day of practice, Dixie Walker created a contraption to protect first basemen during infield drills. His idea was simple. He fashioned a wire screen in a frame nine feet high by six feet wide positioned in front of the first-base bag. Durocher hailed it as the "greatest idea in the world. . . . I'll bet everybody in the league will be using it during batting practice this season."[26] In fact, Walker's innovation would be used by baseball teams for decades to come.

Another potentially groundbreaking development during the early days of training camp came on Monday, February 24. When heavy rains limited the Dodgers' workout at El Gran Stadium to an hour of running and throwing, Rickey left the Dodgers camp to visit the Havana Military Academy, a fancy school for the sons of rich Cubans located about fifteen miles outside the capital, where the Royals had their training facility. Clay Hopper had been less than pleased with Montreal's camp, where the finishing touches were still incomplete. Three days prior to Rickey's inspection, trees and bushes and rocks still littered the "field," but "Now there is a freshly sodded diamond," *New York Times* sportswriter Roscoe McGowen wrote, "and half the outfield has been cleared of stones."[27]

After visiting the Academy, Rickey returned to Havana, where he put Mexican second baseman Beto Ávila through a workout at El Gran Stadium. A native of Veracruz, Ávila was playing for Cuba's Marianao team and challenging for the league batting title in the closing days of the 1946–47 Cuban League season. Monchy de Arcos, a lawyer friend of Leo Durocher, described Ávila as "crazy about Brooklyn baseball. He . . . likes to play rough, and so he likes Brooklyn."[28] In the Mexican League, Ávila had played for Puebla, finishing second for the batting title with a .359 average during the 1946 season. Despite playing in Mexico, he was not subject to commissioner Happy Chandler's ban, because he had never been under contract with any American team in organized baseball. Speculation among the writers focused on whether the Dodgers "were watching player reaction to the use of a dark-complexioned second baseman in the Dodgers lineup," *Baltimore*

Afro-American writer Sam Lacy wrote of the tryout. "Ávila is one of the swarthier Mexicans."[29]

Like Wendell Smith, Lacy had traveled to Cuba to cover Robinson's efforts to make the Dodgers roster. Not long after his arrival, Lacy described his initial impressions of the island. "I had heard the Cubans are a deeply religious people," he wrote. "In two days here, I have learned that baseball is their religion."[30] According to Lacy, the Dodgers urged their players to see as many Cuban League games as possible, going so far as to provide transportation for them to the park from the Hotel Nacional. He speculated the tactic was another way to demonstrate how interracial teams could compete "with not the slightest sign of friction."[31]

To Lacy, one interesting observation from the Cuban League series was seeing two white former major-league players, each playing "in an otherwise all-colored infield."[32] Former Cardinal Lou Klein played third base for Habana with first baseman Lennie Pearson, second baseman Carlos Blanco, and shortstop Hank Thompson, each of whom had played in the Negro leagues. Almendares second baseman George Hausmann, a former Giant, played with Negro leaguers Buck O'Neil (first base), Avelino Cañizares (shortstop), and Héctor Rodríguez (third base). On Tuesday, February 25, players from the Royals and Dodgers—including Robinson and Brooklyn stalwarts Eddie Stanky, Pee Wee Reese, and Pete Reiser—attended the decisive game of the Cuban League season between Almendares and Habana at El Gran Stadium. The game was interrupted as Robinson was introduced over the public-address system. "He took bows to the wild shouting of 38,000 jabbering fans," wrote Lacy, who noted that the Brooklyn players sitting in the same section "were hardly noticed."[33]

The glow didn't last long before it turned to disappointment. Unlike the Dodgers, none of the minor-league Royals enjoyed the opulent accommodations of the Hotel Nacional. Instead, they all stayed and trained on the grounds of the Havana Military Academy near Marianao. All, that is, except for the team's four African American players, Robinson, Campanella, Newcombe, and Partlow. While he chose to use Cuba's less volatile racial climate as the springboard for Robinson's ascension to the majors, "the ever-cautious Rickey, fearing disruptive racial incidents in the Royals camp, had opted for separate facilities" for the Royals' black and white players.[34]

It was an odd choice. The Royals already had played the entire 1946 International League season with Robinson on the roster. Manager Clay Hopper, Mississippi born and bred, initially objected to Robinson's presence during spring training in 1946, asking Rickey, "Do you really think a nigger's a human being?"[35] But as the season wore on, Robinson earned Hopper's respect with his play. The racial strife the Royals experienced largely came from outside the team as it went on the road. Most notably, a riot broke out during a June series in Baltimore, when fans swarmed the field after a 5–2 victory by the Royals. Rickey's decision to segregate the Royals' black players from the rest of the team meant housing them at the Hotel Los Angeles in Old Havana. They "live in a musty, third-rate hotel in the heart of town," wrote the *New York Sun*'s Herbert Goren. "The place looks like a movie version of a water-front hostelry in Singapore."[36] Every day a car shuttled the black players fifteen miles so they could join their white teammates for practice and drove them back to Havana after workouts were completed. "I thought we left Florida to train in Cuba," Robinson complained, "so we could get away from Jim Crow."[37]

Campanella and Newcombe had each played in Havana before coming to Cuba for spring training in 1947, but they had vastly different opinions of playing on the island. Born in Philadelphia on November 19, 1921, Campanella had played for the Baltimore Elite Giants of the Negro National League from 1937 to 1942 before spending two seasons in the Mexican League. During the 1943–44 Cuban League season, Campanella played for Marianao, batting .266 and driving in 27 runs in 31 games. "I enjoyed every day of it," Campanella wrote years later, "and reached the point where my Spanish was almost as good as my English."[38] Signed by the Dodgers in 1946, Campanella batted .290 with 13 home runs as Newcombe's teammate with the Nashua Dodgers of the Class-B New England League. Campanella took in stride the issues surrounding his return to Cuba. "I tried not to notice the things that bothered Jackie," Campanella wrote. "Not that I didn't mind them. It's just that some men can have the same problems and yet face them differently."[39]

Years later, Newcombe was more vocal than Robinson had been in airing his grievances with their accommodations in Havana in the spring of 1947. "That damn hotel," he said. "It was full of cockroaches. It was so hot you couldn't sleep; no air conditioning. I remember one day, and I'll never forget it as long as I live. During this process of losing weight that [Dodgers farm director] Branch Rickey Jr. made me do, for my conditioning in spring training, I ate a lot of soup down there. One day, I stirred up a bowl of vegetable soup, and a big cockroach came out. I puked up my insides. This was the hotel coffee shop. I never ate there again. Nor did I eat very much more the next three or four days."[40]

Newcombe was born on June 14, 1926, in Madison, New Jersey. After a successful season with Nashua—14 wins, 4 losses, and a 2.21 earned run average—he got his first taste of Cuba after the 1946 New England League season. He joined the Matanzas club of Cuba's short-lived Federación Nacional. Newcombe played in only two games before the league folded. But his view of Cuba never changed the three times he played there. "I saw what happened to black people, especially American blacks," Newcombe said. "We couldn't go into nightclubs, we couldn't go into restaurants. We had only special places we could go. It was almost as bad as being in Miami or being in Jackson, Mississippi."[41]

Newcombe's impressions of Cuba stand in sharp contrast with those of many other Negro league players who have said they experienced far more freedom playing in Cuba and other Latin American countries than they had in the United States. Perhaps Newcombe's opinion was tainted, at least in part, by being segregated from the other Royals players during spring training in 1946. That separation played out in a particularly distasteful manner when he tried to meet with Dodgers president Branch Rickey at the Hotel Nacional. Although Cuba didn't have the legalized discrimination of the United States, it's not surprising that an exclusive hotel catering to American tourists, such as the Nacional, would practice its own brand of restrictions. "I wasn't even allowed to go in the lobby of the Nacional hotel to see Mr. Rickey on baseball business one day," Newcombe said. "I had to get permission from the bellhop. In fact, one [white] bellhop put me out of the lobby. I told him I had to see Mr. Rickey with the Dodgers. I was allowed to go to the house telephone and call Mr. Rickey to get permission to go up to his room to see him."[42]

Since 1945, Pasquel had made himself the scourge of organized baseball by convincing major-league players to jump their contracts to play in the Mexican League. And now that he was in Havana, he didn't stop his attempts to lure members of the Dodgers organization after his failed efforts with Robinson and Campanella. Even with the Mexican League struggling financially—Pasquel not only was trying to cut former major-league pitcher Max Lanier's contract from $14,000 to $7,000 but reportedly set a league salary limit of $5,000 per season[43]—the Mexican millionaire arrived in Havana during spring training to continue his recruiting efforts. At the Hotel Nacional, he wandered the lobby to see which Dodgers he might lure to Mexico.

Pasquel first approached Dixie Walker. The *Sporting News* described this exchange between the Mexican League owner and the Dodgers outfielder:

"How about Mexico," Pasquel said.

"Oh, you scouted me last year and said I was too old," Walker responded.

"No, no, not so," Pasquel countered.

"Well, you want pitchers and I am only a broken down outfielder," Walker said as he walked away.[44]

Pasquel's pitch to Dodgers players didn't end with Walker. "If any of you boys want to play in Mexico, write me a letter," Pasquel said. "We will operate this year. I will bet $2,000,000 on it and deposit the money in a New York bank."[45]

Because of Pasquel's overtures toward his players and other major leaguers, Branch Rickey concluded Pasquel was an "assassin of base-ball careers" and an "adolescent who believes he can twist baseball's tail with the use of money," but he still tried to meet with Pasquel in Havana, saying it would be to everyone's advantage "if he stopped being illegal and made his peace with Organized Baseball."[46] Pasquel left Havana without convincing any of the Dodgers or Royals to bolt. That didn't quell his bravado. Pasquel refused to talk to Rickey and boasted to the Mexican press about hanging up on the Dodgers president. "After that I went down to the hotel lobby and told newspapermen just what I thought of Rickey," Pasquel said, "and I also advised his players to come see me if they were interested in playing in Mexico." But he also took the chance to take a swipe at Rickey's team, saying "the Brooklyn club has very few players who could make the grade in Mexico."[47]

Robinson and the Royals' other black players had company in dealing with the accommodations at the Hotel Los Angeles. Sam Lacy and Wendell Smith, who were in Havana to cover Robinson's spring training, also were housed at the Los Angeles so they could more easily chronicle his progress. Born on April 10, 1904, in Mystic, Connecticut, Sam Lacy grew up in Washington, D.C., where in high school he lettered in three sports, including baseball. After graduating from Howard University, Lacy worked at several Washington radio stations and in 1934 became the *Washington Tribune*'s sports editor. In 1936 Lacy floated the idea of signing Negro league players as a way for Washington Senators owner Clark Griffith to improve his ball club—to no avail.[48] But what would become Lacy's calling—pushing for the integration of Major League Baseball—had begun. He devoted many of his columns during the 1930s and 1940s to that cause. After a stint at the *Chicago Defender*, Lacy joined the *Baltimore Afro-American* in 1943.

Integrating baseball was just as much Wendell Smith's calling. Born on March 23, 1914, in Detroit, Smith, whose father worked as a chef for Henry Ford, was the only black student at Detroit's Southeastern High School. Like Lacy, he played baseball and was one of the top pitchers on his American Legion team. After watching Smith throw a shutout, a major-league scout signed one of Smith's teammates, saying, "I wish I could sign you but I can't." The incident shaped Smith as a journalist. "That's when I decided that if I ever got into a position to do anything," he said, "I'd dedicate my life to getting Negro players into the big leagues."[49] Smith played baseball at West Virginia State College, and joined the *Pittsburgh Courier* after graduating in 1937. Smith used his position at the newspaper to push for baseball's integration and recommended Robinson to Rickey.

The Dodgers president had put Smith on the team's payroll to room with Robinson on the road as Robinson began his quest to reach the major leagues. Given that goal, the accommodations Rickey set up for Robinson in Cuba made no sense. "It was a fleabag hotel where we slept on heavy spreads that we used for mattresses," Lacy said years later. "The springs were coming up—pressing into our bodies—which shows you just the type of hotel we were in. That was where we had to stay during that period. . . . The conditions were actually miserable."[50] The separate accommodations confused and angered Robinson. "He hated it. He hated it with a passion, as did all of us," Newcombe said. "Jackie was more outspoken about it, but he knew there wasn't anything he could do about it. He was trying to get to the big club. He had to keep his cool and be quiet."[51]

While the Royals' black players were relegated to substandard accommodations, the Dodgers were living in the Cuban lap of luxury at the Nacional. "At the swank Hotel Nacional de Cuba," the *Sporting News* described, "the Brooklyn players have been sleeping in golden beds and eating off platinum plates."[52] Sportswriter Dan Daniel wrote "the rumba band is playing native music" and "the spirit of inflation is in the air" as he satirically described the scene at the Hotel Nacional's dining room. "The planked filet mignon en Bordeau was a bit tough last evening," Daniel quoted one unnamed Dodger at dinner as saying. "I went for the frog legs, Provencale, and crepe suzette. The crepes here are delicious, and so reasonable." At the hotel's cabana club, another unnamed Dodger mused how he wished "the boys back in the pool hall . . . could see me right now; hobbing with the rich, and nobbing with millionaires."[53]

Tale of Two Leagues

On the day Marianao beat Cienfuegos 14–3 to open its 1946–47 Cuban League season schedule, manager Armando Marsans received a cable from Max Lanier. The former St. Louis Cardinals All-Star pitcher said he would arrive in Cuba soon. Marianao had signed Lanier hoping he might help the Gray Monks reverse their fortunes. Marianao had debuted in the Cuban League in 1922–23 under Baldomero "Merito" Acosta. The rookie manager played for the Washington Senators and Philadelphia Athletics from 1913 to 1918 and was a Cuban League star in the early decades of the twentieth century. He batted over .300 three times in twelve Cuban League seasons from 1913 to 1925 and in 1918 became the only outfielder in league history to complete an unassisted triple play.[1] Acosta's fledgling Marianao team shocked the established Habana and Almendares clubs by winning the championship. (Another first-year team, Santa Clara, withdrew in mid-January 1923 after a league decision vacated a victory against Marianao.) Acosta became Marianao's part owner, but over the next twenty-one seasons, the team won only one Cuban League pennant, in 1936–37. Perhaps Lanier could change that.

A native of Denton, North Carolina, Hubert Max Lanier was a natural right-hander. But after twice breaking his right arm as a child, he learned to throw left-handed.[2] Lanier's left arm eventually carried him to the majors, where he debuted with the Cardinals on April 30, 1938.

By 1943 Lanier achieved All-Star status, finishing the season with a 15–7 record and a National League–leading 1.90 earned run average. In 1944 he won a career-high seventeen games with a 2.65 ERA. After an arm injury limited him to four games in 1945, Lanier won his first six starts to open the 1946 season while compiling a 1.93 ERA. But just when it appeared he was on his way to his best season in the majors, Lanier bolted for the Mexican League.

News that Lanier and fellow Cardinals Lou Klein and Fred Martin were preparing to jump first broke on May 23 when the trio failed to show up at the Polo Grounds, where St. Louis was winding up a series with the New York Giants. Pasquel offered Lanier a five-year contract paying him $30,000, along with a $50,000 signing bonus. "We ain't mad at no one," Lanier said in St. Louis on May 25, admitting it was "an awful lot of money to go to Mexico, a sum a North Carolina farm boy couldn't refuse."[3] Lanier arrived in Mexico on May 31 and made his first appearance for Veracruz on June 2, entering a game against the Mexico City Reds in relief. He struck out four, allowed one hit, and walked one batter in 3⅔ innings to earn the victory, an 11–9 win in twelve innings.[4] On June 15 baseball commissioner Happy Chandler barred Lanier, Klein, and Martin from organized baseball for at least five years. With limited options, all three players set their sights on playing in Cuba following the conclusion of the 1946 Mexican League season. Klein and Martin signed with Habana, Lanier with Marianao.

In Habana's third game of the season on October 31, first baseman Lennie Pearson's eighth-inning home run lifted the Lions to a 1–0 victory over Marianao. Pearson had been a standout with the Negro National League's Newark Eagles since 1937, and his home run handed teammate Manuel García the victory. The Lions' starting pitcher was less than two months shy of his forty-first birthday. The victory was García's first in a string of wins that would propel Habana to the top of the Cuban League standings by the start of December. Born in Manacas, Las Villas, Cuba, on December 28, 1905, García began his Negro league career in 1926 with Abel Linares's Cuban Stars (West) team that was based out of Chicago. He then joined Almendares for the 1926–27 Cuban League season. Over his career, the short, stocky, junkball-throwing left-hander developed a repertoire of pitches—"a big curve, a good drop, and a fastball that was described as being like 'lightning'"[5]—that helped earn him his nickname, "Cocaína," Spanish for cocaine. Buck O'Neil, the longtime Kansas City Monarchs first baseman and manager who played for Almendares in 1946–47 and became famous for his appearance in the 1994 Ken Burns documentary *Baseball*, described García in his 1996 book *I Was Right On Time*. "Cocaína, whom I used to face down in Cuba," wrote O'Neil, "got his name from his wicked curve ball, which made all us hitters go numb."[6]

García played for the Cuban Stars of the Negro National League from 1926 to 1931. After the league broke up following the 1931 season, he returned in 1933 to the Cuban Stars, now an independent team. With the formation of a new Negro National League that year, García signed with Alex Pompez's New York Cubans in 1935. After struggling in the first half of the league's split season, the Cubans won the second-half title but lost a closely fought seven-game playoff against the Pittsburgh Crawfords. García's 1936 season with the Cubans was his last in the United States. In 1937 he played with Estrellas Orientales in Santo Domingo, Dominican Republic, losing to Ciudad Trujillo, the powerhouse team put together by the country's ruthless dictator, Rafael Trujillo. That team included Negro-league stars Satchel Paige, Josh Gibson, and Cool Papa Bell, along with Cuban standouts Rodolfo Fernández and Silvio García, and was managed by Cuban star Lázaro Salazar. Cocaína García also played nine seasons in the Mexican League, where historian James A. Riley credits him with compiling a 96–68 record and a 3.82 earned run average between 1941 and 1949.[7] According to Riley, García's best seasons in Mexico came between 1942 and 1946, when he went 19–14, 16–12, 13–10, 18–11, and 14–10 in consecutive seasons.[8]

Although García was a mainstay of the Cuban League, he didn't become a dominant force in Cuba until the second half of his career. García registered eleven victories against just four defeats during the 1938–39 season to help Santa Clara to its second consecutive Cuban league title. The team included Negro leagues stars Josh Gibson, who batted .356, and Ray "Jabao" Brown, who also won 11 games.[9]

Switching allegiances to Habana for the 1941–42 season, García twice went on to lead the league in victories. In 1942–43 he went 10–3, and he followed that up the next winter by going 12–4.[10] The mark included the fifth no-hitter in Cuban League history. On December 11, 1943, García shut down Marianao 5–0 for the first no-hitter at La Tropical stadium.[11] Although he would not match such a feat in the 1946–47 season, García dominated the season's first two months, winning nine games and losing only once.

Although La Tropical no longer hosted Cuban League games for the winter of 1946, it was not abandoned. The stadium on the outskirts of Havana housed the Federación Nacional de Béisbol. In the organized-baseball-approved league set up to compete against the Cuban League, the National Federation's counterpart to Habana started well. The Havana Reds opened the season with a ten-inning, 9–8 victory against Oriente on October 25. The next day, the Reds beat Matanzas 4–1, and they followed that up with a 2–1 victory against the same team on October 29. The 7,000 fans who attended the opener saw familiar names in the teams' lineups, names that until that winter had dotted the rosters of the traditional Cuban League. Oriente starting pitcher Luis "Witto" Alomá, who was knocked out of the opener in the second inning, had played for Marianao and Almendares over the three previous winters. Havana Reds starter Julio Moreno began his professional career with Marianao in 1945–46. Reds first baseman Regino Otero had been a veteran of the Cuban League since 1936. But the most recognizable names associated with the National Federation were the player-managers of the three founding teams: Gilberto Torres with the Reds, Fermín Guerra with Oriente, and Silvio García with Matanzas.

The trio did not have quite the cachet of the Cuban League managers that season—Miguel Ángel González, Adolfo Luque, Martín Dihigo, and Armando Marsans—but they had been league stars in their own right. Because of baseball commissioner Happy Chandler's ban on even those who played with or against ineligible players, Torres and Guerra had no choice but to bolt the Cuban League if they wished to continue their major-league careers.

Born in the Havana suburb of Regla on August 23, 1915, Gilberto Torres had been a pitcher and infielder in the Cuban League, mostly with Habana, since 1934. Early in his career Torres was stricken with yellow fever, which weakened him to the point he became a junk-ball pitcher.[12] Yet he was twice named most valuable player of the Cuban League. In 1940–41 Torres led the league in winning percentage (.769) with a 10–3 record, and in 1943–44 he batted .333. His father, Ricardo Torres, played thirteen Cuban League seasons, all but one with Habana, between 1913 and 1928. Ricardo also played three seasons with the Washington Senators, from 1920 to 1922. Like his father, Gilberto also played with the Senators, joining Washington in 1944. They were the first Cuban father-son combination in major-league history.[13] By opting for the National Federation instead of the Cuban League, Torres, like Guerra, maintained his standing in organized baseball.

Fermín Guerra was born in Havana on October 11, 1912, the son of Canary Island natives who had migrated to Cuba. Guerra grew up poor and illiterate. As a boy, he sold fruits and vegetables at a large Havana marketplace. Later he worked as a batboy for Almendares at La Tropical Stadium.[14] After playing semipro ball, Guerra signed with Habana in 1934, but in 1938–39 he joined Almendares, the team with whom he was associated for most of his career in Cuba. Although he had no formal education, Guerra was smart, and he was a terrific defensive catcher. In 1936 Guerra was signed by scout Joe Cambria, who signed dozens of Cuban players for the Senators during the 1930s and 1940s. Having played with the Washington Senators in 1944–46, Guerra remained in good standing with organized baseball by taking the helm of Oriente rather than returning to Almendares.

As a black player, Silvio García didn't have to worry about protecting his status in organized baseball. Jackie Robinson was still six months away from breaking baseball's color barrier. García's motivation for jumping to the National Federation after twelve stellar seasons in the Cuban League was largely financial. In previous seasons, monthly salaries between $200 and $300 were common for players in the Cuban League. But Jorge Pasquel's Mexican League had driven up salaries in leagues throughout Latin America. A star in the Mexican League, where he batted .366, .364, .301, .314, and .350 with Mexico City from

1941 to 1945, García secured a monthly salary of $1,200 as Matanzas's player-manager for the 1946–47 National Federation season.[15]

Born in Limonar, Matanzas, on October 11, 1914, García played baseball in Cuba's armed forces and with the independent Toros de Paredes team before joining the Cuban League with Habana for the 1931–32 season.[16] The strong-armed infielder is considered perhaps the greatest shortstop in Cuban League history. García also was a decent pitcher earlier in his career, compiling a 10–2 record for Marianao in 1936–37.[17] García led the Cuban League with a .351 batting average during the 1941–42 season, one of four consecutive seasons from 1940–41 to 1943–44 during which he batted over .300.[18] But García bolted the Cienfuegos team he had played for the previous five seasons to join the National Federation.

Conrado Marrero was charged with the loss in the National Federation season opener. But his inauspicious professional debut was no indication of how Cuba's most popular amateur pitcher would fare in the pro ranks, despite his advanced age of thirty-five. Marrero was born on a farm called El Laberinto in Sagua la Grande, Villaclara, on April 25, 1911. His humble origin earned him the nickname El Guajiro de Laberinto, the Peasant of Laberinto. Marrero bore little resemblance to the prototypically tall, strong-armed pitchers of today. He was short and squat, carrying 158 pounds on a frame that barely measured five foot five. Instead of blowing away batters with a lightning bolt of an arm, he got by on guile and command of a late-breaking curve ball. In Cuba's amateur ranks, that was more than enough. Marrero debuted in 1938 with Cienfuegos Sport Club of La Liga de la Unión Atlética, Cuba's national amateur baseball league, and compiled a 10–7 record with a 2.54 earned run average. For the next seven seasons, Marrero never recorded an ERA above 2.00. He led the Athletic Union in victories in 1939 (13–4 with a 1.92 ERA) and in 1940 (15–4 with a league-leading 1.67 ERA). Three times Marrero won at least 20 games: a league-leading 22 in 1942, 21 in 1944, and 22 in 1945.[19]

But Marrero's time in the Athletic Union was not without its downside. In 1943 Cienfuegos suspended him for six months for playing with another team in Camagüey. In 1945 he again drew his team's ire for pitching in a benefit game for the Colored Society in Santo Domingo, near Santa Clara. This time the suspension was indefinite. "I said enough is enough," Marrero recalled years later, "I'm going to turn pro."[20] So after winning 128 games in seven amateur seasons, Marrero signed with Oriente of the National Federation. Despite losing the season opener, he went 8–5 with a 2.24 earned run average. His eight victories led the league. But Marrero accounted for more than one-third of Oriente's victories, and the club failed to top the league's standings in either half of the season. In the first half, Oriente would finish second, one-half game behind the Havana Reds (Oriente and Matanzas each played one game fewer than Havana). The team would come up one-half game short again in the second half, this time behind Matanzas, as the season ended prematurely.

On Wednesday, November 6, 1946, residents of Villaclara read of the passing of one of their own. The funeral notice spoke in glowing terms of Alejando Oms, who had died a pauper's death the previous day. "The distinguished Villaclara native who was a marvelous baseball player and who gave so many glorious days to Cuba and this city, the marvelous athlete who by his personal style deserved the title of Gentleman Oms," the obituary stated, "died yesterday in the city of Havana." Born on March 13, 1895, in Santa Clara in the province of Las Villas, Oms was one of the great Cuban League stars of the 1920s and 1930s. He earned the moniker El Caballero, the Gentleman, by never losing his temper and never arguing with an umpire.[21] According to Cuban baseball historian Jorge S. Figueredo, Oms finished his Cuban League career with a batting average of .345, third highest in league history. He led the league in hitting four times, including a .432 mark with Habana during the 1928–29 season, in which he was the circuit's most valuable player.[22]

Oms combined with Negro leagues star Oscar Charleston and Cuban-born Pablo "Champion" Mesa to form what is considered the greatest outfield in Cuban League history for his hometown Santa Clara Leopards, who won the pennant in 1923–24. In 1944 Oms was inducted into the Cuban Baseball Hall of Fame. He was fifty years old when Cienfuegos manager Adolfo Luque took pity on the destitute Oms and granted him a roster spot in the 1945–46 season. In his final Cuban League at-bat, Oms struck out against Habana's Fred Martin. With a funeral procession through the streets of Villaclara scheduled to begin at 8:30 on the morning of November 7, Oms's body arrived in town the evening of Wednesday, November 6. The funeral notice invited Villaclara residents to pay their respects to a "brilliant but modest athlete" and an "outstanding citizen."

That same day on the outskirts of Havana, a twenty-year-old Don Newcombe, fresh off a 14–4 season with the minor-league Nashua Dodgers, made his National Federation season debut at La Tropical stadium with Matanzas. Newcombe was one of a handful of African American players in the Dodgers organization as Rickey prepared to integrate Major League Baseball. The Havana Reds knocked the six-foot-four right-handed starting pitcher out of the game in the sixth inning en route to a 3–1 victory. The Reds continued to roll through the first month of the National Federation season, leading the standings with a 12–4 record—four games ahead of Matanzas—through the games of November 18. As the Havana Reds beat Newcombe on November 6 at La Tropical, the other team bearing the Cuban capital's name also won at Havana's Gran Stadium.

Habana had dropped two games against Almendares before the Lions won eight of the next ten decisions between the Eternal Rivals during the first two months of the season. Fred Martin, who had jumped to the Mexican League from the St. Louis Cardinals in 1946, gave Habana its first victory of the Cuban League season against the Scorpions. Martin drove in the decisive run in the 3–2 win with a single. The Williams, Oklahoma, native had returned from World War II for the 1946 major-league season as a thirty-one-year-old rookie. A sinkerball pitcher, Martin had impressed with the Class A-1 Texas League's Houston Buffalos in 1941, going 23–6 with a 1.44 earned run average before going off to war. He pitched in only six games with the Cardinals in 1946—going 2–1 with a 4.08 ERA—before jumping to the Mexican League along with Cardinals teammates Max Lanier and Lou Klein in late May. Lanier and Klein joined Veracruz; Martin signed with Mexico City. In Cuba in 1946–47, Martin became a driving force in Habana's early success as well as a factor in the team's late struggles. Only Cocaína García would win more games for Habana during the season, but no other pitcher on the Lions would lose as many.

Max Lanier made his delayed Cuban League debut with Marianao on Friday, November 8. He came to Cuba having put up impressive numbers during abbreviated seasons in the United States and Mexico. After opening the 1946 major-league season with a 6–0 record and 1.93 ERA with the Cardinals, Lanier joined Veracruz of the Mexican League. Despite lingering arm problems—the lefty had injured his throwing arm pitching against a team of major leaguers at Fort Bragg, North Carolina, before returning to the Cardinals[23]—Lanier went 8–3 with a league-leading 1.93 ERA with Veracruz. The elbow bothered Lanier enough that he left Mexico on August 6 to receive treatment back home in St. Petersburg, Florida.[24] Because Lanier arrived late for the Cuban League season, speculation about the health of his pitching arm grew. "I think my arm is going to be fine after I have this rest of more than a month,"[25] Lanier had said from Florida between the Mexican and Cuban league seasons. In his debut against Habana, Lanier gave up two hits and struck out seven through 5⅔ innings. But after tiring, he surrendered five hits and four runs, and the game concluded in a 7–7 tie.

In his first three appearances with Marianao, Lanier failed to register a victory and took the loss in an 11–1 drubbing by Habana on November 16. After giving up two runs in the third inning, Lanier kept the Lions off the scoreboard in the fourth and fifth. But he couldn't get out of the sixth inning, when Habana scored four runs. Habana starter Cocaína García tossed a complete game, striking out six and walking three. Habana teammate Sagüita Hernández drove in three runs on a pair of singles in three at-bats. Lanier did not pick up his first victory of the season until November 30. Limiting Cienfuegos to three hits while striking out six batters and walking just one, Lanier beat the Elephants 7–0 as third baseman Orestes Miñoso drove in three runs. But Lanier's next start ended in a 4–0 loss to Habana on December 6, when the lefty surrendered ten hits while striking out three and walking four in eight innings. Perhaps Lanier's arm had not fully healed.

Beyond Lanier's struggles, the game was punctuated by pregame intrigue and marred by a tragic aftermath. In late November, more than one hundred Cuban League players, including several major leaguers who had jumped to the Mexican League, formed a union to demand increased pay. The Asociación de Jugadores Profesionales de Baseball de Cuba, the Cuban Professional Baseball Players' Association, was headed by Almendares pitcher Tomás de la Cruz. The right-hander had gone 9–9 with a 3.25 earned run average in his only major-league season in 1944 with the Cincinnati Reds. Before Habana and Marianao took the field on December 6, the organization staged a fifteen-minute strike. Cuban League owners failed to respond to demands presented by De la Cruz a few days earlier: recognition of the union by the Cuban League, 25–50 percent salary increases, the staging of a game from which all proceeds would go to the union, increasing rosters to twenty-two players, and a minimum salary of $350 per month.[26]

The Cuban League relented on some of the demands: a 40 percent salary increase for players making less than $500; a 25 percent increase for those making more than $500; setting the minimum salary at $200 per month; and holding a Players' Day on January 20.[27] Although the players as a whole benefited from the strike, one player suffered greatly because of it. Habana catcher Salvador Hernández had played for the Chicago Cubs in 1942 and 1943. His mother was a regular attendee at his games at El Gran Stadium, but she died of a heart attack after this contest. As fans protested the game-delaying strike, Hernández's mother got into an argument with spectators near her box seats. During the bickering, she "suffered a shock and was taken home, where she died the next day."[28]

Marianao finished a distant fourth among the Cuban League's four teams during the 1945–46 season, fourteen games behind champion Cienfuegos. But the Gray Monks' season was not without its bright spots. Third baseman Orestes Miñoso batted .294 and was named the league's most valuable player. Shortstop Ray "Talúa" Dandridge, a

Negro leagues star with the Newark Eagles, hit .318. And right-handed starting pitcher Booker McDaniels, who played for the Negro American League's Kansas City Monarchs, led the team with nine victories. All three returned for the 1946–47 season, but only Miñoso made it past November with Marianao. By the middle of the month, both Dandridge and McDaniels had jumped to the National Federation for more money. It was a risk. Earlier in the season, the Cuban League, mimicking organized baseball's tactics, passed a rule banning for three years any player who jumped to the National Federation.[29] Depending on whether the Cuban League or the National Federation won this baseball civil war, Dandridge and McDaniels could have one option fewer for playing, and earning a living, during the winter months.

Dandridge, a native of Richmond, Virginia, had played in the Cuban League since the 1937–38 season, batting .299 and leading the league with eleven stolen bases for Almendares. The following winter he batted .319 for the Cuba team, then joined Cienfuegos for the 1940–41 season and batted .310. Throughout the 1940s, Dandridge also played in the Mexican League, including the summer of 1946. He arrived late for the 1946–47 Cuban League season, playing his first game on November 16, and batted just eight times in two games. After going 1-for-4 in Marianao's 7–5 loss to Almendares, Dandridge jumped his Cuban League contract, which paid him $750 per month plus expenses, to join the rival circuit's Oriente team for a monthly salary of $1,400.[30] After six seasons with the Monarchs, McDaniels joined the Mexican League in 1946, going 14–8 with a 3.01 earned run average with San Luis Potosí. Like Dandridge, McDaniels began the Cuban League season late, losing the only two games he started with Marianao before he jumped to the National Federation. McDaniels walked away from his $550 monthly salary for a $1,200-per-month deal with Oriente.[31] The defections drew a swift response on November 20 from Marianao owner Eloy García, who "declared he will take the matter to the courts, because of written contracts with the jumpers."[32]

The first half of the National Baseball Federation season concluded on Friday, December 7. The Havana Reds led the standings with a 14–12 record. Oriente was second at 13–12 and Matanzas was third at 12–15. A fourth team, Camagüey, managed by Tony "Pollo" Rodríguez, joined the league on December 8 and opened the second half of the season by splitting a doubleheader with the first-half champion, losing the first game 3–1 and winning the nightcap 4–3. But as the league, which had been set up to provide a winter haven for organized-baseball-eligible players, embarked on its second half, the seeds of its demise already were being sown. Cuban sports officials believed some major-league stars would help fill out the league's rosters and provide drawing cards unavailable to the Cuban League. That did not happen.

So while the Cuban League was drawing an average of 20,000 fans at El Gran Stadium, National Federation games at La Tropical barely were pulling in 1,000 fans. Cuban fans viewed the new league "as the outlaw," Cuban sportswriter René Cañizares wrote in the *Sporting News*, "and the small crowds going to Tropical Park indicate the fans do not approve of the players deserting their old teams."[33] And La Tropical could not match the atmosphere of games at El Gran Stadium: shouting, dancing fans waving bright banners bearing the colors of the four traditional teams, hawkers wearing large placards with lottery numbers for sale, and fans placing bets on everything from who would record the game's first hit to which player would boot the first play for an error. "We have nothing in the major leagues," the *Sporting News*'s Dan Daniel wrote, "to outdo the Cubans in wild enthusiasm."[34]

The addition of lights at El Gran Stadium only boosted the Cuban League's superior attendance over the rival league's games at La Tropical. On November 20, El Gran Stadium hosted its first night game, a 4–1 victory by Cienfuegos against Marianao. Two nights later, 15,000 fans had to be turned away at the gates. Businesses such as theaters, movies, jai alai, and cafés felt sufficiently threatened, Cañizares wrote, "that there is an effort to have the mayor forbid night games, as other places of entertainment are deserted when the games are on."[35] Games at La Tropical were having no such impact. The rival league was being operated as a nonprofit organization, with players drawing salaries from funds provided by stockholders of the Julio Blanco Herrera-owned Tropical Brewery. And profits—assuming there were any—were to be divided among the players as bonuses. As the second half of the season opened, the prospect of any such profits seemed highly unlikely. "Organized baseball here appears doomed, unless some help is quickly given the league at Tropical Park," Cañizares wrote, "and some of the diamond performers may leap to the rival winter league."[36]

Seeing little hope for the National Federation's long-term survival, Cuban sports commissioner Luis Orlando Rodríguez flew to Los Angeles for baseball's winter meetings in an attempt to persuade baseball commissioner Happy Chandler to reinstate Cuba's ineligible players in organized baseball. Rebuffed, Rodríguez lashed out: "I told Chandler I speak for all baseball in Cuba and could be party to no deal that excluded the Cuban League. . . . Since baseball has turned its back on us here, there seems to be no alternative but for us to form a Latin-American federation and compete as best we can against the American monopoly."[37] On December 20, Rodríguez reached the same conclusion Cañizares had. The National Federation was indeed doomed. So Rodríguez decided to cancel the Cuban Sports Commission's contract, which had been footing the bill at La Tropical stadium as of December 31. If the league was to survive, it would be up to Julio Blanco Herrera to make it happen.

By the time Miguel Ángel González bought the remaining interest in the Habana Base Ball Club in early December, his fate in organized baseball had already been sealed. At the baseball winter meetings in Los Angeles, Chandler concluded that by walking away from his position as the St. Louis Cardinals' third-base coach in favor of his ownership interests in the Cuban League, González had earned himself a five-year suspension. "González was not fooling anyone but himself," Chandler said, "when he requested his unconditional release or his free agency from the Cardinals to join his Cuban club."[38] Chandler also described the Habana manager as "indentifying himself with ineligibles."[39] González knew the potential consequences of turning his back on organized baseball, but he never wavered. "I told the owners of the St. Louis club that I had to manage my club," González told *Diario de la Marina* columnist Eladio Secades. "My decision was unchangeable."[40] Perhaps that was because his connection to Habana was destined almost from the moment he first became affiliated with the team as a player in 1910.

According to the Cuban League's official programs, Habana had as its emblem the color red since the team's founding in 1868. And because of its players' aggressive style, fans "baptized them with the name Lions."[41] Reestablished in 1878 by Cuban baseball luminaries such as Emilio Sabourín, who fought for Cuba's independence from Spain and died in prison in 1896, the team was bought from Manuel Azoy in 1914 by Cuban baseball promoter Abel Linares, who named twenty-four-year-old González its manager. After building a small fortune by saving up the money he earned as a player, coach, and manager in Cuba and the United States, González bought controlling interest in the team from Linares's widow in the early 1940s. By paying her $30,000 in December of 1946 to become sole owner,[42] González was now in complete control, and he was directing the team with which he had filled nearly every role to what appeared to be another Cuban League championship.

As González finished establishing himself as Habana's sole owner, Almendares manager Adolfo Luque began the process of dissolving his marriage to the woman from whom he had been separated since 1941. Claiming that his wife, with whom he shared a daughter, had abandoned him, Luque petitioned for divorce in early December. It was not his first failed marriage. Back when he was pitching in the majors with the Reds, Luque had married a Cincinnati woman in 1926, only to have her walk into a local law office on October 28 of that year seeking legal action against the Cuban pitcher. The letter sent to Reds owner Garry Herrmann was telling. In it, attorney Author C. Fricke said Luque's wife was about to give birth, but the pitcher "has abandoned her and he sent a cablegram stating that he has left the country."[43] Off the field, Luque lacked the stability, personal and financial, that had defined his Habana counterpart. And now he was beginning to lose control of matters on the field as well.

After jostling with Habana for first place during the first month of the season, Almendares started to slide in the standings. Help was coming for Luque and Almendares in the form of a new starting pitcher. Max Lanier surrendered twelve hits in eight-plus innings against Cienfuegos on December 12—a game that ended after ten innings in a 9–9 tie—and his record stood at 1–2. Aside from Lanier's struggles, Marianao needed a catcher. An injury to Gilberto "Chino" Valdivia had forced the Gray Monks to use pitcher Aristónico Correoso behind the plate for a few innings against Cienfuegos on December 12. Marianao had seen enough. On December 18 the Gray Monks traded Lanier to Almendares for catcher Lloyd Basset, who once had been touted as another Josh Gibson when he joined the Pittsburgh Crawfords of the Negro National League in 1937.

Basset never met those lofty expectations, but he did make two East-West All-Star Game appearances while with the Chicago American Giants of the Negro American League from 1939 to 1941. The trade proved to be a bad one for Marianao. Basset batted .164 after the deal. Lanier would finish with an 8–4 record, 7–2 with Almendares, including some of the Scorpions' most important victories down the stretch. Perhaps sensing this, Cuban baseball pioneer Armando Marsans resigned as Marianao's manager not long after the trade was completed. The Monks replaced Marsans with amateur manager Tomás "Pipo" de la Noval. He fared no better than Marsans as Marianao's manager.

Since his dominant complete-game, three-hit shutout of Marianao on October 31, Cocaína García continued to roll through Cuban League hitters—or at least hitters from two of the league's other three teams. On November 16 he again limited Marianao, this time to four hits, in a complete-game 11–1 victory as Salvador Hernández drove in three runs. In the month of December, García rattled off three victories in consecutive starts against Cienfuegos. The first came on December 4, an 11–7 victory as he went 3-for-4 as a hitter, scored two runs, and drove in another. In his next start on December 10, García struck out seven Cienfuegos batters in a complete-game 9–1 victory. His fifth consecutive victory, a 3–0 complete-game shutout of the Elephants, gave Habana a 4½-game lead in the standings. He followed up with another shutout against Marianao on December 22, a complete-game 10–0 victory that put the Lions up by four games over Almendares.

Noticeably absent from the list of the vanquished among García's six consecutive wins to open the season was Almendares. Habana manager Miguel Ángel Gonzalez had held out the lefty against the Scorpions' predominantly right-handed lineup.

García's teammate Fred Martin had no such restrictions, and he thrived against Almendares. The right-hander won four of five starts against the Scorpions through the first two months of the Cuban League season (he was tagged with a loss in a relief appearance two days after a complete-game victory against Almendares). After beating the Scorpions 3–2 in his first start on November 6, Martin picked up another complete-game win versus Almendares, outdueling Agapito Mayor for a 4–0 victory on November 18. Martin's next start against the Scorpions produced a 7–6 complete-game victory for Habana. His only loss in a start against Almendares in the season's first two months came December 13, as Martin lasted three-plus innings in losing 7–1.

In that game Almendares starter Gentry Jessup, who had played with the Chicago American Giants since 1940, took a no-hitter into the ninth inning. But after getting one out, Jessup surrendered the first Habana hit of the game, a single by Sagüita Hernández. Habana's Hank Thompson and Lou Klein followed with singles of their own, costing Jessup his shot at a shutout. Hernández's hit cost Jessup $1,000, the prize for tossing a no-hitter in the Cuban League.[44] Awarding players cash prizes for certain accomplishments was common in the Cuban League: $250 for hitting the first home run of the game, $25 for pitching a shutout. "That would happen," said Almendares first baseman Buck O'Neil. "You'd hit a home run to win a ball game and they would take up [a collection for] money. Let me hit one."[45]

After the loss to Almendares, Martin rebounded nicely in his next start, going the distance to beat the Scorpions and Mayor 5–2 on Christmas Day. Habana had moved into first place on November 29, an off day for the team. With Martin and Cocaína García leading the way, the Lions rode a 12–5 streak in December to a comfortable lead in the standings. While Habana was surging, Almendares was stumbling badly, losing 14 of 20 games from November 24 to December 31. García got his first chance against Almendares on December 30 and delivered a complete-game 6–1 victory, his seventh in a row, stretching Habana's lead to 5½ games.

Like the Cuban League, the National Federation was no stranger to labor strife, and its issues manifested in the closing days of the second half of the season. On the morning of December 29, Camagüey players refused to take the field for a game against the Havana Reds unless they were advanced a week's salary. When efforts to negotiate a settlement failed, Havana was awarded the victory by forfeit and fans were refunded their money. Meanwhile the National Federation, plagued by dwindling attendance and dripping in red ink, was unraveling. Despite the episode, the league pressed ahead with plans for a premature conclusion to its inaugural season.

Originally the league's 90-game schedule was to last 75 days. Instead the teams played fewer than 40 games and the season lasted little more than two months. The league scheduled a three-game championship to be played at La Tropical stadium. It would pit the first-half champion Havana Reds against second-half champion Matanzas, beginning on December 31. In the first—and what became the only—game played, Silvio García's Matanzas team beat Gilberto Torres's Havana Reds 4–3 in ten innings as the Reds committed five errors. The next two scheduled games were never played. According to Cuban sportswriter René Cañizares, "the players decided not to continue" playing beyond the first contest.[46]

Havana Reds outfielder Claro Duany led the league with a .368 batting average. Torres, his manager, was the third-leading hitter with a .318 batting average. García, Matanzas manager, was second with a .344 average. He also led the league with 23 stolen bases and finished second in runs batted in with 25, one behind the league leader, Oriente shortstop Tony Zardón. Oriente's Conrado Marrero led the league with eight victories, but Matanzas's Eddie Chandler was the league's champion pitcher based on his winning percentage (.857) after posting a 6–1 record. Those superlatives notwithstanding, the National Federation, in almost every measurable way, was a failure.

While Cuban League games at El Gran Stadium were averaging 20,000 spectators per game, National Federation games seldom drew 1,000 fans at La Tropical. The numbers were no better financially. According to a statement released by Cuba's National Sports Commission after the conclusion of the season, more than $81,100 was spent on the league, including $30,000 by the Sports Commission. The league took in only $38,300 to offset more than $119,600 in total expenses. Each individual team lost money as well. Oriente lost more than $19,400, the Havana Reds lost more than $14,900, and Matanzas lost more than $19,800. Camagüey, which joined the league for the final month of play, lost more than $4,600. The 52 games played at La Tropical stadium brought in average receipts of just $500.[47] Enrique Novellas, the National Federation's president, vowed that "that the Federation would start its championship next winter under better conditions."[48] That promise was never fulfilled.

Hermit in Havana

Before returning to Monterrey to play in the 1947 Mexican League season, Andrés Fleitas had time on his hands. The Cuban League season had just concluded, and Fleitas spent some of that free time taking in the latest baseball attraction to come to the island. "I saw some practices when he [Jackie Robinson] was in Cuba," Fleitas recalled years later. "There should be a monument to Robinson in every ballpark. . . . To take [the abuse] on the field and off the field, only Jackie Robinson did that. I don't think many athletes could take what Robinson had to take." Fleitas's admiration wasn't limited to Robinson's fortitude. "When Robinson dove into the bases," Fleitas said, "he looked like an assassin. He was a great athlete."[1]

Having joined the Cuban League in 1942, Fleitas, like other Cuban players, was very comfortable having black teammates. But that was a relatively new experience for his Almendares teammate Max Lanier. His first such opportunity came when he jumped his St. Louis Cardinals contract to play in the Mexican League during the 1946 season. In the recently completed 1946–47 Cuban League season, Lanier once again competed with and against black players, something that was not possible during his time in the majors with the Cardinals. Lanier was playing the final games of the Cuban League season when Robinson and the Dodgers began spring training. Asked by *Baltimore*

League from 1915 to 1943, also managed the Negro National League's New York Cubans. Miñoso's rookie performance prompted Fernández to recommend him to New York Cubans owner Alex Pompez.

The son of Cuban immigrants, Pompez was born in Key West, Florida, on May 14, 1890, grew up in Tampa, and found success in baseball in New York, where he first owned the Cuban Stars of the Eastern Colored League in 1922–29. Pompez also rose to become king of the numbers racket in Harlem, only to see Dutch Schultz muscle in on his illegal lottery operation in 1931. Pompez got out from under Schultz's control when the mobster was taken out in a gangland killing in 1935.[17] He eventually gave up the numbers racket, turning state's evidence in 1939. Pompez formed the New York Cubans the same year Schultz was gunned down in a Newark, New Jersey, tavern. But Pompez was done running numbers long before Fernández brought Miñoso to his attention. When the Cubans owner gave his permission, Miñoso signed for $300 per month, which included a salary of $150 and a $5 per diem for meal money.[18] Miñoso joined countrymen such as Alejandro Crespo, Silvio García, Rafael Noble, Luis Tiant Sr., Armando Vázquez, Rogelio Linares, and Fernando Díaz with the Cubans for the 1946 season.

Negro leagues historian James Riley credits Miñoso with batting .309 in his first season in New York.[19] After his initial season in the Negro leagues, Miñoso batted .249 as Ávila's Marianao teammate during the 1946–47 Cuban League season. Branch Rickey saw Miñoso for himself on Friday, March 7. Playing for a Cuban all-star team, Miñoso went 2-for-5 as the Royals won 7–4. That was enough for Rickey, who gave Sukeforth permission to approach Miñoso with a contract offer. "I'd rather play with the Cubans," Miñoso told Sukeforth. A disappointed Sukeforth told Sam Lacy, "I'm sorry. He's a good player with a lot of hustle and savvy."[20]

The Yankees arrived in Havana on Friday, March 7, some six hours ahead of the Dodgers. They carried with them a "giant silver cup only a little less impressive than the Empire State Building," Roscoe McGowen wrote, "emblematic of winning the Venezuelan championship from the Brooks."[21] The teams continued their series on Saturday at El

Gran Stadium in a game twice interrupted by rain. Despite a persistent drizzle, 6,000 fans watched three Dodgers pitchers—Kirby Higbe, Joe Hatten, and Rube Melton—throw a no-hitter for nine frames before the Dodgers beat the Yankees 1–0 in ten innings. Pete Reiser doubled to score the winning run after George Stirnweiss broke up the no-hitter with a single in the tenth inning.

During that game, gamblers Memphis Engelberg and Connie Immerman were observed sitting in Yankees president Larry MacPhail's box. This did not sit well with Branch Rickey, who fumed as he stormed into the lobby of the Hotel Nacional. "Did you see those two men out there today, those two gamblers sitting in MacPhail's box?" Rickey asked Herbert Goren of the *New York Sun* and Arch Murray of the *New York Post*. Given Chandler's admonishment to Durocher about consorting with gamblers, Rickey wondered aloud what fate would have befallen his manager if those two men had been spotted at the Dodgers' Ebbets Field.[22]

On Sunday, as the Yankees won 4–1, Engelberg and Immerman were among the crowd of 7,000. Once again they sat in MacPhail's box, prompting reporters to get Durocher's reaction to their presence. "Are there two sets of rules, one applying to the managers and one applying to the club owners?" Dick Young of the *New York Daily News* quoted Durocher as saying. "Where does MacPhail come off, flaunting his company with known gamblers right in front of the players' faces? If I ever said hello to one of those guys, I'd be called before Commissioner Chandler and probably barred." Told what Durocher had said, MacPhail fired back: "In the first place, it is none of Durocher's business who I have in my box. In the second place, if Durocher was quoted correctly, he's a liar. I understand that in the box next to me were two gentlemen later identified as alleged gamblers. I had nothing to do with their being there. And you can quote me as saying it is none of Durocher's business."[23]

The same weekend Rickey and Durocher questioned MacPhail's alleged choice of guests at the ballpark, Jackie Robinson received a far less controversial guest at the Royals' spring training camp. On Friday, March 7, heavyweight champion Joe Louis flew into Havana, his latest stop on a two-month tour of Latin America. Before Louis participated in a pair of exhibition bouts on Sunday night at El Gran Stadium, the champ drove fifteen miles outside the city on Saturday to visit Robinson at the Havana Military Academy, where the Royals trained. Robinson had previously visited Louis at his Pompton Lakes, New Jersey, training camp, and now Louis showed up at Royals camp to reciprocate. When Louis stepped out of the car that had been provided to drive him around Cuba, Montreal manager Clay Hopper stopped practice so the Royals could gather around Louis and Robinson on the academy's veranda.

Pittsburgh Courier writer Wendell Smith chronicled the meeting between the defending heavyweight champ and the International League's reigning batting champion, whose conversation quickly turned to golf. With an impromptu gallery of Royals looking on, Louis and Robinson took turns swinging imaginary clubs. With each swing, Robinson's teammates stared into the distance as if trying to keep an eye on a golf ball sailing down a fairway. "I think Jackie out-drove you," quipped Roy Campanella, eliciting laughter from the giddy spectators. "Naw, Robinson hit a long slice," Louis fired back. "His ball is probably in the ocean by now." Louis asked Campanella about his prospects. "They're giving me a chance," the Royals catcher said, "and that's all a guy can ask for."[24]

As photographers and autograph seekers joined the growing crowd, Louis asked Robinson about his chances to make the Dodgers. Robinson had started off slowly as the Royals began exhibition play on Tuesday, March 4, at El Gran Stadium. In the opening game against the Class-C Florida International League's Havana Cubans, Robinson went 1-for-3 with a stolen base. But he also committed an error at second base as the Cubans won 6–5. A former shortstop with the Negro American League's Kansas City Monarchs, Robinson switched to second base with the Royals in 1946. In his second spring game, Robinson went 1-for-6 with another error as the Royals and Cubans played to a twelve-inning, 5–5 tie. "Cubans have soured on him," Sam Lacy wrote of Robinson's start, which had been "something less than sensational

[and] . . . the natives don't like it." He noted that the Havana newspapers "of both languages [had] built Jackie up to the skies."[25]

By the time of Louis's visit, Robinson had begun to turn things around. He went 2-for-2 with a run scored and keyed a five-run inning as the Royals beat the Cubans 7–0 on Thursday. The next day, Robinson scored a run and drove in another while going 2-for-3 in a 7–4 Royals victory against a Cuban all-star team. Still, Robinson was reserved when answering Louis's inquiry about his prospects of making the Dodgers: "It's all up to Mr. Rickey and Leo Durocher." After Louis and Robinson finished signing autographs, the Brown Bomber climbed into a waiting car to leave for his exhibition bout in Havana with these words of encouragement for Robinson: "See you opening day at Ebbets Field with the Dodgers." Robinson yelled back: "I hope so. I sure hope so."[26]

After his visit to the Royals' camp, Joe Louis stepped into a boxing ring at El Gran Stadium on Sunday, March 9. Promoters paid the heavyweight champion of the world $30,000 to engage in a pair of three-round exhibition bouts, one against Walter Haffer and another against Art Ramsey.[27] Attendance estimates varied wildly, between 10,000 and 25,000. Among the crowd were Robinson and his Montreal teammates, as well as members of the Yankees and Dodgers. The teams had played an exhibition game at the stadium hours earlier, with New York defeating Brooklyn 4–1. The Dodgers would fly out of Havana for a series of games in Panama following the champ's exhibition. Prior to the bouts, dignitaries presented Louis with a key to the city of Havana and a Cuban flag, and they designated the champ an honorary Cuban athlete.

At El Gran Stadium, the Brown Bomber thrilled the crowd when he sent Haffer to the canvas for a nine count in the second round of their bout. Louis's second sparring partner, Ramsey, "took a fancy lacing."[28] The exhibition was Louis's final stop on a tour of South America and the Caribbean in which he traveled more than 10,000 miles over two months and pulled in an estimated $200,000.[29] Louis's exhibition complete, the Dodgers left for Panama. The Yankees remained in

Havana one more day for their final exhibition game on the island. On Monday a Cuban all-star team beat the Bronx Bombers 2–1 in front of 12,000 fans. Conrado Marrero pitched all seven innings of the rain-shortened game for the all-star squad.

Robinson and the Royals would join the Dodgers in the Canal Zone the following week but stayed behind in Cuba after Louis's exhibition. They were scheduled to play a series of games against the Class-C Florida International League's Havana Cubans. Before Robinson could return to the field for those games, however, he had to go under a doctor's knife. The toe on Robinson's left foot had been bothering him, so Royals manager Clay Hopper and team business manager Mel Jones called in Dr. Julio Sanguily, a renowned Cuban physician who was one of the owners of the Almendares Base Ball Club. In 1944 Sanguily became the club's vice president and treasurer after he and other members of Havana's prestigious Vedado Tennis Club bought the team.

Sanguily examined Robinson on Sunday before Louis's exhibition and scheduled surgery to remove an irritating callus on Robinson's toe for the next day. It was a minor procedure, but *Pittsburgh Courier* sportswriter Wendell Smith reported that Robinson's "training camp drills will be interrupted for at least a week, and maybe longer."[30] Fortunately for his bid to join the Dodgers, Robinson returned quickly to the field. He was in the lineup by Wednesday as the Royals rode a sixteen-hit barrage to a 13–2 victory against the Cubans at El Gran Stadium. He went 2-for-3 with a double, a run scored, and one RBI. Robinson's suddenly hot hitting continued. In Thursday's game, he went 2-for-5 with two runs as the Royals beat the Cubans 11–1. On Friday, Robinson went 3-for-4, doubled, scored once, and drove in two runs in a 7–3 Royals victory against the Cubans.

After the game, the Royals flew to Panama for their own tour of the Canal Zone. It would include games against the Dodgers and Robinson's potential future teammates. "Well-informed sources believe the Panama trip is of tremendous importance to Robinson," Smith wrote. "If he performs in his usual style he may cinch himself a job on the big league club."[31] In assessing Robinson's chances, Sam Lacy expressed his doubt that Robinson would be promoted to the Dodgers unless he earned a starting spot. "Rickey will not wish to risk a destruction of the

Dodger morale by placing Robinson in the clubhouse with men who may be resentful," Lacy wrote, "UNLESS Robinson is good enough to be a regular."[32]

The Dodgers' twelve-day excursion to Panama did little to distance them from the incident at El Gran Stadium. The presence of gamblers Memphis Engelberg and Connie Immerman next to Larry MacPhail's box during the weekend series in Cuba rekindled an ongoing war of words between the Yankees president and the Dodgers' Branch Rickey and Leo Durocher. The flap dated back to the off-season. MacPhail said Durocher had pursued the Yankees' managerial job, while Durocher insisted MacPhail had offered him the post. Each publicly questioned the other's honesty. MacPhail went so far as to use a November 25 news conference to give reporters a day-by-day accounting of discussions he said took place between him and Durocher throughout the month of October. "If Durocher used us with his negotiations with Rickey," MacPhail told the writers, "well that's okay with me."[33]

Durocher eventually signed a one-year contract reportedly worth at least $60,000 to return as the Dodgers' manager. But he could not let go of his animosity toward MacPhail. Durocher often used a column in the *Brooklyn Eagle* to air his grievances against MacPhail. Under Durocher's name, the column was penned by Dodgers traveling secretary and former *Eagle* staff writer Harold Parrott. The March 3 column featured Durocher's typical vitriol: "When MacPhail found I couldn't be induced to manage his Yankees for any of his inducements, he resolved to knock me, and to make life as hard as possible for me. He has added his blowhard voice to the criticism which I have been catching lately, trying to make it into a gale."[34]

With Durocher living under Happy Chandler's edict to avoid gamblers, it's no wonder he and Rickey reacted as they did to the sight of Engelberg and Immerman at El Gran Stadium, Rickey bemoaning the presence of gamblers next to MacPhail's box and wondering what such a transgression would have meant for his manager, while Durocher questioned, in print, whether different rules existed for him and the Yankees' president. The fallout from their incendiary words followed

Durocher and Rickey to the Canal Zone. The irony is that, as he had in Havana, Durocher continued to maintain a monastic lifestyle in Panama.

In the Canal Zone, Durocher bunked with four reporters in the officers' quarters at the U.S. Army barracks at Fort Gillick. He was in bed by ten and up by seven, "always squawking about the late hour in which the newspaper men called it a night," wrote Herbert Goren of the *New York Sun*. Goren painted a portrait of a pepper-pot-turned-bookworm Durocher, who had joined the Book-of-the-Month Club and was reading *Lydia Bailey*, a historical novel by popular author Kenneth Roberts. This reformed Durocher "has quit gambling . . . doesn't imbibe much, if at all," Goren wrote. "He has not lit a cigarette in four or five months. He shuns dances, parties, and even dinners."[35] Instead Durocher spent his time racking up average tolls of $100 per day to call Santa Monica, California, and talk to his actress wife Laraine Day—he affectionately called her Rainey—at least twice a day. Before Durocher briefly rejoined Day in California, the Dodgers manager discovered a storm brewing in Panama.

9

New Year's Resurrection

The final day of 1946 brought with it the same result that so many other days in December had—an Almendares defeat. The month had seen the Scorpions lose eleven of their fifteen games—the final one, appropriately enough, a 5–3 loss to Habana. Winning pitcher Pedro "Natilla" Jiménez surrendered eight walks, but Almendares, unable to muster a single hit through the first six innings, failed to capitalize on Jiménez's wildness. The Scorpions managed only three hits in the game, including Roberto Ortiz's seventh-inning home run. With recently acquired pitcher Max Lanier spending New Year's Eve back home with his family in St. Petersburg, Florida, Almendares manager Adolfo Luque opted to start Tomás de la Cruz on the mound. De la Cruz could not get past the fourth inning as Habana outfielder Pedro Formental, third baseman Lou Klein, and shortstop Hank Thompson each contributed a pair of hits. Thompson, having gone 2-for-2, overtook Almendares catcher Andrés Fleitas as the Cuban League's leading hitter, .348 to .343. More important, by the time Cuba rang in the New Year, Habana held a 6½-game lead over Almendares. "Fortunately for Almendares, 1946 ended last night," *Diario de la Marina* sportswriter René Molina wrote. "The symbolic ritual of the new year should have surprised the ten Almendares owners who were hoisting cups in unison toward the heavens in prayer for a resurrection miracle."[1]

The New Year opened for Habana much as 1946 had ended, with a victory, as the Lions defeated Marianao 6–2. Habana's flamboyant Terris McDuffie, referred to in the Cuban press as the team's "clown pitcher," pitched masterfully and "for the first time this season . . . showed good form and without his usual antics."[2] The Negro leagues star, who had pitched in the Mexican League since 1940, struck out seven and allowed just one hit—a double to Beto Ávila in the first inning—before he had to be carried off the field. McDuffie injured his ankle running to first base during his fifth-inning at-bat. Perhaps the only thing more surprising than McDuffie's performance that day was how Almendares kicked off the New Year.

After its horrid December, the Scorpions opened 1947 by beating Cienfuegos 5–2 on January 1. Starting pitcher Lázaro Salazar scattered eight hits and struck out four batters in seven innings. He also went 3-for-4 at the plate. Salazar's victory was the first of nine consecutive wins Almendares reeled off to start January. Of those nine victories, Salazar and Jorge Comellas each won two and Max Lanier won three. The game that kicked off that stretch also saw Fleitas go 3-for-5 at the plate to regain the lead in batting average over Thompson, .352 to .347. The back-and-forth battle for the batting title would continue throughout the remainder of the season, with Fleitas and Thompson always among the contenders.

Born on November 8, 1916, in Central Constancia in Abreu in the province of Las Villas, Andrés Fleitas was one of nine siblings, five brothers and four sisters. He followed his brother Ángel into baseball and began playing in 1936 with Casa Stany, a local team in Cienfuegos, at age twenty.[3] After three seasons there, he joined Hershey Sport Club of Cuba's national amateur league in 1938. In five seasons with Hershey, Fleitas played on three consecutive amateur championship teams from 1938 to 1940. His squad finished second to Conrado Marrero's Cienfuegos Sport Club team in 1941. In 1939 Fleitas finished fourth in the league in batting with a .384 average.[4]

Fleitas also played in the Amateur World Series in 1939, 1941, and 1942. His Cuban team went undefeated (6–0) and won the 1939 series, played at La Tropical stadium, beating Nicaragua and the United States for the title. The hosting Cuba team lost to Venezuela in the 1941 series as Fleitas batted .378 (14-for-37). The two teams had matching 7–1 records, forcing an extra game to determine the title. Venezuela's Daniel Conónico defeated Cuba's Conrado Marrero 3–1. In 1942 Fleitas led all hitters with a .405 batting average (15-for-37) and was named the series's most valuable player. Cuba went 10–2 to beat the Dominican Republic, Venezuela, Mexico, and the United States to win the championship, also held at La Tropical.[5]

After the Amateur World Series concluded on October 20, Fleitas made the jump to the professional ranks. Almendares manager Adolfo Luque signed Fleitas for the 1942–43 Cuban League season. After an undistinguished rookie season, Fleitas began to show the hitting prowess that would mark his Cuban League career. He batted .299 in his second season and followed that up by batting .291 in 1944–45 while leading the league with 10 doubles and 29 RBI in 53 games. In 1945–46 Fleitas batted .313 and again led the league with 14 doubles in 56 games.[6] As he excelled in Cuba, Fleitas also began his minor-league career in the United States, signing with the New York Giants' International League team in Jersey City in 1943. Luque, still coaching with the Giants at the time, facilitated Fleitas's signing.

But after the 1944 International League season, Fleitas joined Monterrey of the Mexican League. Lázaro Salazar, who had been Fleitas's Almendares teammate during the 1942–43 winter season and had played summers for Monterrey since 1942, introduced Fleitas to Jorge Pasquel. Fleitas's monthly salary with Jersey City was $350, but the Mexican League president offered to pay Fleitas $20,000 plus expenses for two seasons, so Fleitas turned his back on Jersey City. He batted .333, .275, and .304 in three Mexican League seasons from 1945 to 1947.[7] Fleitas opened the 1946–47 Cuban League season in typical fashion at the plate, hitting safely in ten of his first eleven contests. Through the games of November 19, the Almendares catcher was hitting .407, which left him behind Habana's Hank Thompson, who was batting .412. "Fleitas only got to Triple-A," battery mate Max Lanier said, "but he was a great catcher as far as I'm concerned."[8]

▰

Known among Cuban fans as Ametralladora, or Machine Gun, Hank Thompson came from what Negro leagues historian James A. Riley described as a "tough home environment" in Dallas.[9] As a teenager, the Oklahoma City native was arrested twice. Acquitted of jewelry theft, Thompson served four months in the Gatesville (Texas) Reform School for truancy.[10] After he began playing baseball, according to Riley, Thompson shot to death a man who was "trying to force his affections on Thompson's sister."[11] When he wasn't in trouble with the law or drinking, the teenaged Thompson excelled on the baseball diamond as a speedy outfielder and line-drive hitter.

In 1943 he signed with the Kansas City Monarchs of the Negro American League. As a seventeen-year-old rookie, Thompson batted .314 with a .514 slugging percentage, according to Riley.[12] His Monarchs teammates—who included future Hall of Famers Satchel Paige, Willard Brown, and Hilton Smith, as well as Buck O'Neil—gave him the nickname Youngblood. "He had a lot of kid in him," catcher Sammie Haynes said. "But he had a temper and liked to play rough."[13] World War II interrupted Thompson's baseball career in 1944, and he served as a machine gunner with the army's all-black 1695th Combat Engineers in the Battle of the Bulge.

Discharged from the army as a sergeant on June 29, 1946, Thompson rejoined the Monarchs and teammates Paige, Brown, Smith, and O'Neil in the middle of their season. Batting leadoff and playing second base, Thompson hit .287 as Kansas City won the Negro American League pennant. In the Negro World Series against the Negro National League pennant-winning Newark Eagles, he batted .296 as the Monarchs lost in seven games.[14] Coming off Kansas City's series loss, Thompson was late arriving for his first Cuban League season, which began on October 26. The Habana shortstop did not play his first game until November 2, but he eventually established himself as one of the best hitters in the league for the 1946–47 season.

Thompson's batting average stood at .133 after his first five games. But beginning with Habana's 6–0 victory against Marianao on November 11, Thompson went on a ten-game hitting streak. His average climbed as high as .412, and he still led the league with a .400 average after the games of November 23, with Almendares's Andrés Fleitas in second at .397. The next day, Fleitas raised his average to .400 to regain the lead. So it went for much of the first two months of the season, Fleitas often at the top of the league's batting leaders, with Thompson, Habana teammates Lou Klein and Alberto Hernández, and Marianao's Tony Castaño challenging him for the lead.

With the National Federation season abruptly ending on December 31, several Cuban players found themselves in an unfamiliar situation. They were in Cuba for the winter but had no place to play. Having cast their lots with the organized-baseball-sanctioned league, players such as Gilberto Torres, Fermín Guerra, and Silvio García could only watch as the final two months of the 1946–47 Cuban League season played out. Since 1931, García had spent all but three winters playing in the Cuban League. Torres and Guerra had participated in every winter season since 1934.

As a black player, García didn't have to worry about any repercussions from organized baseball if he were to return to the Cuban League. The same wasn't true for Torres and Guerra. Trying to rejoin the league would have made both players ineligible to return to their respective major-league teams. Torres had played for the Washington Senators since 1944. After playing for the Senators since 1937, Guerra had been purchased by the Philadelphia Athletics on December 3. In assessing Torres's situation, the *Sporting News*'s Frank "Buck" O'Neill wrote in January of 1947 that Torres "stands at the fork of baseball's trails. . . . Will he give up his home, his country, and his friends to stand with a game that soon may shuffle him off into the ranks of men who have outlived their usefulness?"[15] Torres and Fleitas had to watch and wait to find out what their baseball futures held—in Cuba and the United States.

On Thursday, January 2, Marianao's Sandalio Consuegra had held Cienfuegos hitless through seven innings. But his attempt to record the sixth no-hitter in Cuban history ended in the eighth when Myron "Red" Hayworth hit a roller over second base. Consuegra surrendered another hit in the ninth, but he still completed his best outing as a professional. After leading Deportivo Matanzas to the 1945 championship of Cuba's amateur league, Consuegra had signed with Marianao and gone 2–0 with a 2.86 earned run average as a Cuban League rookie in 1945–46. He was following up his first pro season with a fine sophomore campaign. Consuegra's two-hitter against Cienfuegos gave Marianao a 2–1 victory in a battle of two teams whose only goal was avoiding a last-place finish. At 14–20, Marianao was 9½ games behind league-leading Habana on January 2, while Cienfuegos was 10 games back.

Almendares, which began the next day trailing Habana by 6½ games, beat Marianao 5–0 on Friday behind the pitching of Jorge Comellas. The veteran right-hander, who had led the Cuban League with a 2.30 earned run average in 1944–45 and thrown a league-leading four shutouts in 1945–46, limited Marianao to four hits. It was the first of three victories Comellas recorded as Almendares won its first nine games in January. On Saturday, lowly Cienfuegos toppled league-leading Habana 12–9. Habana lefty Manuel "Cocaína" García failed to get out of the first inning, surrendering a single, home run, and triple to the only three batters he faced. García was able to escape with a no-decision and retain his unblemished 7–0 record—at least for the time being—because the Lions rapped out sixteen hits to out-slug the Elephants.

Almendares and Habana faced off on Sunday, January 5. Almendares lefty Max Lanier scattered seven hits to earn his first victory against his team's archrival, 6–1. Habana starter Fred Martin was knocked out in the seventh inning after allowing eight hits and four runs. The Lions' lone run came on a home run by Lou Klein. The former Cardinals infielder had hit his way among the league's batting leaders. By going 2-for-4, Klein raised his average to .321, fourth behind teammate Hank Thompson (.347), Almendares's Fleitas (.341), and Marianao's Tony Castaño (.336). The victory pulled Almendares to within 5½ games of league-leading Habana, a lead that shrank the next day.

After failing to get out of the first inning in his previous start two days earlier, Habana's Cocaína García once again took the mound on January 6, against Marianao. García held the Gray Monks scoreless through four innings, but Marianao's fourteen-hit attack—led by Beto Ávila's 4-for-6 performance—proved too much. Marianao handed García his first loss of the season, a 5–3 defeat. Although he had started the season with a 7–0 record, his first six victories came against the league's two weak teams, Marianao and Cienfuegos. Habana manager Miguel Ángel González declined to pitch García against Almendares's predominantly right-handed lineup.[16] But the seventh victory in García's streak came against the Scorpions, a 6–1 victory on December 30. After that fleeting deviation—and the January 6 loss to Marianao—García went on to beat Cienfuegos in his next two starts, 11–5 on January 10 and 6–1 on January 15.

Since joining the Cuban League with Santa Clara in 1930, Lázaro Salazar had been one of its best hitters. Six times he batted over .300, including a league-leading .407 average during the 1934–35 season, when he was named most valuable player.[17] Salazar earned the honor not only for his hitting but for his first serious foray into pitching. Early in that season Almendares manager Adolfo Luque had obtained Salazar, who was 1–0 with a 1.00 earned run average in his only start with Marianao. In 1934–35 the lefty went 5–1 with a 1.64 ERA with Almendares as the Scorpions won the pennant in the Cuban League's first season since political turmoil put play on hold for almost two years.[18]

Back with Santa Clara in 1937–38, Salazar once again was named the league's MVP, batting .318 and going 3–0 as a pitcher while leading the Leopards to the championship in his managerial debut.[19] Salazar repeated his managerial feat the following season, directing a Santa Clara team that included Josh Gibson to the league title. Salazar didn't lead the team in victories—that distinction belonged to Cocaína García and Negro leagues star Ray Brown with eleven victories each—but he did compile an impressive 6–2 record as the team's third starter.

Salazar spent the next seven Cuban League seasons bouncing between Almendares and Marianao and was back with the Scorpions for the 1946–47 season. But by then El Príncipe de Belén, the Prince of Belén—nicknamed for the Havana neighborhood from which he hailed—no longer was the hitter he had been earlier in his career. By January 1, Salazar had only 11 hits in 80 at-bats for a meager .138 batting average. Since late November the thirty-four-year-old had been losing playing time at first base to teammate Santos Amaro, whose son Rubén would play eleven major-league seasons from 1958 to 1969 with the St. Louis Cardinals, Philadelphia Phillies, New York Yankees, and California Angels. (Santos's grandson Rubén Amaro Jr. would play for the Angels, Phillies, and Cleveland Indians from 1991 to 1998 before becoming the Phillies' general manager.) By mid-December, Kansas City Monarchs star Buck O'Neil had taken over first base. And Salazar wasn't faring much better on the mound.

Pitching in relief of Agapito Mayor, the veteran lefty was tagged with the loss in a 3–2 defeat by Habana on November 6 and pitched sparingly until earning a 5–2 victory against Cienfuegos on January 1. But that was nothing compared to his performance on January 7. With Jorge Comellas sick and Jesse Jessup nursing a sore pitching arm, Almendares manager Adolfo Luque turned to Salazar. He outdueled Cienfuegos's Jean Roy for ten innings, striking out seven batters and walking four while surrendering four hits. Salazar earned the 2–1 victory when Almendares scored on a squeeze play in the tenth. *Diario de la Marina*'s René Molina described Salazar's resurgence as a "Phoenix rising from the ashes."[20] Almendares was rising from the ashes of a disastrous December as well. The victory pulled the Scorpions to within 4½ games of league-leading Habana, which had lost a pair of games the previous two days.

It wasn't until December 9 that John Jordan "Buck" O'Neil made his Cuban League debut with Almendares, pinch-hitting in a 4–1 loss to Cienfuegos. Two days later the slick-fielding Negro leagues first baseman started his first game, going 0-for-3. It may have been an unremarkable start to his winter-league campaign, but it didn't feel unremarkable to O'Neil. While he had played against white players in barnstorming exhibition games, he "never played *with* them until Cuba," O'Neil recalled years later. "With Max Lanier and a couple of guys out of the major leagues, we had a couple of white guys on [Almendares]. In Cuba, whites and blacks played on the same team. One thing I liked about Cuba was the fact that you were a baseball player, and a Cuban was a Cuban, whether he was black, green, gray. . . . You were a Cuban, regardless of what color you were, and that really stuck out with me. I liked that."[21]

Almendares liked—and, more important, needed—O'Neil. With Salazar a shadow of the hitter he once was and manager Adolfo Luque preferring to use Santos Amaro in left field, O'Neil became the Scorpions' starting first baseman. Before playing in Cuba, O'Neil had helped lead the Kansas City Monarchs to four consecutive Negro American League pennants from 1939 to 1942. He batted .353 as the Monarchs won the inaugural Negro World Series in 1942, sweeping the Negro National League's Homestead Grays.[22] After serving in a construction battalion with the U.S. Navy during World War II, O'Neil rejoined the Monarchs and led the 1946 Negro American League season in hitting with a .353 average. He also led Kansas City once more to an NAL pennant, but O'Neil was unable to deliver another championship, as the Monarchs fell to the Newark Eagles in seven games in the 1946 Negro World Series.[23]

Once he became a starter with Almendares, O'Neil started paying dividends almost immediately. After his initial hitless performances, he racked up six hits in fifteen at-bats over four games while driving in three runs and scoring four others. Almendares won three of those four games, including a 7–1 victory against Habana on December 13. By the New Year, O'Neil had matched Salazar's hit total in barely half as many at-bats, and O'Neil's spot in Almendares's starting lineup was secure. And although the Scorpions were still looking up at Habana in the standings, O'Neil liked what he saw. "We had the best defense in [Cuban] baseball at that time," O'Neil said. "We could catch the ball. We could really catch the ball. Our manager, Adolfo Luque, uh-huh, a good manager, strict but knew baseball. Fleitas, who was our catcher, was more or less running the ball club. You would call him the manager on the field. Good man, good man. We had some good ballplayers."[24]

Jorge Comellas started for Almendares on January 8, surrendering three first-inning runs to Marianao, and only made it out of the second inning. But the Scorpions rallied for seven runs in the second and won 8–6, cutting Habana's lead to four games. Fortunately for the Lions, the schedule called for a three-day break in Almendares's schedule. And Habana was able to take advantage. On January 9, Fred Martin held Marianao in check to give the Lions a 4–1 victory. Hank Thompson, who went 3-for-4 with a home run and drove in three runs, now led the league's hitters with a .348 average. The next day, Thompson went 2-for-5 to raise his average to .350. Teammate Lou Klein went 3-for-5 and was beginning to creep his way into the batting-title race. With Habana taking advantage of five Cienfuegos errors in the game, the Lions won 11–5. Cocaína García earned his eighth victory of the season and pushed Habana's lead in the standings to five games.

Almendares's brief layoff, however, did little to stall the team's momentum. On January 12, Max Lanier tossed a complete-game, two-hitter to beat Cienfuegos 6–1. Almendares rapped out 14 hits, including three by third baseman Héctor Rodríguez and two each by Fleitas, shortstop Avelino Cañizares, outfielder Lloyd Davenport, and second baseman Jesse Williams. In the other game that day, Habana starting pitcher Terris McDuffie couldn't get out of the second inning as Marianao clubbed 16 hits—four each by Beto Ávila and Roberto "Tarzán" Estalella—to beat the Lions 17–9. Habana's lead once again fell to four games. In going 2-for-4, Thompson raised his league-leading average to .355.

Almendares added another victory, its seventh consecutive win to start January, the following day. Comellas rebounded from his previous bad outing to beat Marianao 4–2. With Havana off, its lead narrowed to 3½ games. Almendares was led by Fleitas, who went 4-for-5 to raise his average to .347, second in the league to Thompson's .355 mark. Scorpions right fielder Roberto Ortiz drove in a pair of runs on a home run. The player who had hit the inaugural home run at El Gran Stadium now had his eighth of the season, to solidify his league lead in that department. "Ortiz," said Max Lanier, "had a lot of power."[25] Lanier would benefit from Ortiz's hitting in his next start against Habana.

Born in Central Senado in Camagüey on June 30, 1917, Roberto Ortiz started playing baseball with Club Senado, the local sugar mill team, in 1935. In 1937 he joined Hershey Sport Club, where he teamed with Fleitas, his future Almendares teammate, to win the 1938 Cuban amateur league championship. Ortiz turned professional in 1939, signing with Washington Senators scout Joe Cambria and with Habana of the Cuban League. The following winter he joined Almendares, the team with which he would play during eleven of his fourteen Cuban League seasons. Because of his uncommon stature among Cubans—Ortiz stood six foot four and weighed more than 200 pounds—he became known as El Gigante del Central Senado, the Giant from Senado Sugar Mill.

Ortiz used his strong frame to drive in a Cuban League–leading thirty-six runs during the 1942–43 season. He led the league in hitting with a .337 average in 1943–44. Cuban baseball historian Roberto González Echevarría called Ortiz "perhaps the most popular baseball player in Cuba in the forties and fifties."[26] Ortiz's popularity was such that he portrayed himself in a 1952 film, *Honor y Gloria*, about his life and baseball career. But his popularity was strained by an ugly incident—possibly the most violent in Cuban League history—on January 7, 1945. Irate over a call, Ortiz attacked Bernardino Rodríguez, knocking the home plate umpire unconscious.[27] Rodríguez had to be hospitalized, and Ortiz, who apologized in a letter published in the Cuban newspapers, was suspended for the remainder of the 1944–45 season.[28]

Another potentially ugly incident involving Ortiz was narrowly averted early in the 1946–47 season. In the first inning of Almendares's November 22 game against Cienfuegos, Ortiz hit what was described as the longest home run of the young campaign. The 380-foot, two-run blast helped stake the Scorpions to a 4–0 lead. When he came to the plate in the third inning, Ortiz was hit by a pitch from Cienfuegos's Ramón Roger, Ortiz's former teammate with Hershey. In Ortiz's next plate appearance, pitcher Homer "Hoot" Gibson plunked him on the elbow. Ortiz had had enough. Ortiz, "holding the bat high in a hostile attitude," and Gibson began to charge at one another. Cienfuegos catcher Myron "Red" Hayworth got between the two would-be combatants. With Ortiz "wielding his bat with the intention of hitting" Hayworth, home plate umpire Amado Maestri and other players intervened before things got out of control. Maestri ejected Ortiz. Almendares manager Adolfo Luque argued that Hayworth should be sent to the showers as well, but Maestri ruled that it had been Ortiz who instigated the incident.[29]

Even without Ortiz, Almendares went on to win the game 11–1 with starting pitcher Agapito Mayor earning the victory. While Mayor would not become a major factor again until the final month of the season, Ortiz continued to deliver home runs and help Almendares to victories. Almendares's next Ortiz-fueled victory came on January 16.

The previous day, Habana had beaten Cienfuegos 6–1 as Cocaína García tossed a complete-game four-hitter to improve his record on the season to 9–1. Lou Klein went 4-for-4, scored three runs, and raised his batting average to .353 to overtake teammate Hank Thompson (.352) and Fleitas (.347) for the league lead. The victory gave Habana a fleeting four-game lead over Almendares, but the Lions soon were dealt a crucial blow. García, the team's most effective starter, contracted pneumonia. So the league's leading pitcher would not start another game until February 2, when he recuperated.

On the night of January 16, Roberto Ortiz went 2-for-5, drove in two runs, and hit his league-leading ninth home run of the season as Almendares defeated Habana 9–1 in front of 45,000 fans at El Gran Stadium. Max Lanier scattered six hits and struck out five to earn the complete-game victory. Almendares's eighth consecutive victory to start the New Year once again cut the Lions' lead in the standings to three games. With Habana's Lou Klein hitless in four at-bats and teammate Hank Thompson going 2-for-4, Thompson regained the league lead in hitting with a .356 average. Fleitas (.343) was back in second, and Klein (.340) had dropped to third. Almendares won its ninth consecutive game on January 17, a 6–4 victory against Marianao. The streak ended January 19 as Cienfuegos rode a seventeen-hit attack to beat Almendares 11–7. With Habana beating Marianao on the strength of Terris McDuffie's complete-game performance the previous day, the Lions went into the Cuban League's "all-star break" holding a 3½-game lead.

The pregame strike orchestrated by members of the recently formed Cuban Professional Baseball Players' Association on December 6 had won several concessions from the league's owners. Aside from salary increases, the players earned the right to stage a game from which all proceeds would go to their union. That Players' Day came on Monday, January 20. Appropriately enough, with Habana holding a 3½-game lead against Almendares in the standings on what otherwise would have been an off day for the league, the all-star contest pitted a team of Habana's Best against a squad of Almendares's Best. Given the status of Habana and Almendares as the league's Eternal Rivals, it didn't matter that both teams included players from Cienfuegos and Marianao. And, of course, Miguel Ángel González and Adolfo Luque managed the two teams.

The roster for Habana's Best included Habana mainstays such as outfielder Pedro Formental, catcher Salvador Hernández, pitcher René Monteagudo, and brothers Carlos and Heberto Blanco. It also featured third baseman Orestes Miñoso, first baseman Lorenzo Cabrera, and pitcher Sandalio Consuegra of Marianao. Almendares regulars Avelino Cañizares, Andrés Fleitas, Roberto Ortiz, Lázaro Salazar, Santos Amaro, Conrado Marrero, and Agapito Mayor were joined on Almendares's Best by outfielder Pedro Pagés and catcher Rafael Noble of Cienfuegos and Roberto Estalella of Marianao. A packed house at El Gran Stadium watched the game, and interest was so great that some fans entered with forged tickets.

For Habana's Best, Miñoso went 3-for-6, drove in a run, and scored three times. Monteagudo went 4-for-5 and Carlos Blanco collected two hits and scored two runs. Hernández had two hits, including a fifth-inning home run, and drove in two runs. Estalella, who went 3-for-4, homered for Almendares's Best. Cañizares went 3-for-5 and Noble delivered two hits. In total, the teams rapped out 32 hits, 19 by Habana, which went on to win the game 13–7. Consuegra, who started the game for Habana's Best, pitched three innings and was credited with the victory. Almendares's Best starter Oliverio Ortiz was charged with the loss after pitching the first three innings. None of that mattered. "What was most satisfying and emotional," *Diario de la Marina* sportswriter René Molina wrote, "was the end of the festivities in which two legitimate stars of our baseball reunited in one instant that will be remembered with gratitude by all who had the good fortune to witness it."[30]

Before the ninth inning, a group of fans persuaded public-address announcer Conde Moré to take to the stadium's public-address system and implore Luque, Almendares's fifty-six-year-old manager, to enter the game. Luque obliged and began warming up on the mound to a rousing ovation. The crowd's anticipation only grew when González came out of the Habana dugout wearing catcher's gear. González approached Noble and asked permission to replace him behind the plate for the inning. "It was a gesture so beautiful, so sincere, so spontaneous," Molina wrote, "that it brought older fans to tears."[31]

In the ninth inning, Luque got Miñoso to fly out to left for the first out. Monteagudo followed by lining a single to right, and Cabrera hit into a force play at second base. A hit by Danni Day put runners at first and second. But González ended the inning by throwing out Cabrera at third base with a perfect throw on an attempted double steal. "On their return to the dugouts," Molina wrote, "a standing ovation accompanied the two old heroes, vestiges of a yesteryear that glimmers from afar but is unforgettable."[32]

Before Luque and González took the field with their respective teams for the Players' Day game, another player from the Cuban League's past breathed his last in the early hours of January 20. At 1:30 in the morning, Negro leagues legend Josh Gibson died of a stroke in a bed in his mother's home in Pittsburgh at the age of thirty-five. By January of 1947 the man purported to have hit more home runs in his career than Babe Ruth was a shell of his once-powerful self, some 20 pounds having melted off his six-foot-one, 200-pound frame. That winter he had declined opportunities to play in Puerto Rico or barnstorm with the Satchel Paige All-Stars. "He was suffering from nervous exhaustion," Gibson biographer Mark Ribowsky wrote. "His immune system disarmed by drink and severe hypertension, he had fallen prey to kidney and liver dysfunction and bronchitis."[33]

Before drink and illness had ravaged Gibson, he was an irrepressible force in the Negro leagues. Playing mostly with the Homestead Grays and Pittsburgh Crawfords between 1929 and 1946, Gibson has been credited with hitting 962 home runs—many against nonleague teams and widely varied competition—according to Negro leagues historian James A. Riley.[34] In his brief forays into Cuba, Gibson displayed the same propensity for the long ball that he had in the Negro leagues. During the 1937–38 Cuban League season, Habana signed Gibson, hoping his bat would lift a team suffering through the worst season in its history. In just 61 at-bats, Gibson batted .344 and drove in 13 runs. His three home runs were the second most behind a three-way tie at four homers for the league lead between Santa Clara's Ray Brown and Almendares's Willie Wells and Roberto Estalella. But Gibson's efforts were not enough to keep Habana from withdrawing from league play on January 25, 1938, and being saddled with an 8–58 record.[35]

With Habana relegated to last place—the Lions went through three managers, José Olivares, Tinti Molina, and Julio Rojo, during the season—Santa Clara won the pennant under Lázaro Salazar, debuting as manager while earning MVP honors. Santa Clara's Sam Bankhead led the league with a .366 average, 47 runs, 89 hits, and 34 RBI.[36] Brown led the league with a 12–5 record for the Leopards. Martín Dihigo managed Marianao and won 11 of the Gray Monks' 35 victories.[37] The season also featured the first night game at La Tropical stadium on December 22. With temporary lights installed, Marianao defeated Almendares 6–5. But the lighting was so poor that additional lights had to be brought in from Miami for other games. Ultimately, efforts to play night games were abandoned until the mid-1940s.[38]

Gibson returned to Cuba the following winter, but this time with a better team, Santa Clara. With Salazar again serving as player-manager, the Leopards won their second consecutive Cuban League pennant and third title in four seasons. Santa Clara teammates Ray Brown and Cocaína García each won eleven games. Santa Clara's Tony Castaño led all hitters with a .371 average, and teammate Santos Amaro batted .346. Gibson's previous team, Habana, fared much better with Miguel Ángel González back at the helm after two winters away, finishing second to Santa Clara. The Habana skipper had signed Martín Dihigo, who went 14–2, including a one-hitter against the league's Cuba team on November 29, to lead all pitchers. But Dihigo lost out on MVP honors to Alejandro Carrasquel of the Cuba team, who won 11 of the team's 25 victories. An ill-conceived rule eliminated any player who had won an individual award from being named most valuable player. Gibson also made a strong case for MVP consideration. He set a Cuban League high mark with 11 home runs in 163 at-bats while batting .356 and driving in 39 runs and leading the league with 50 runs scored.[39]

Shuttling between Almendares's starting rotation and the bullpen, Agapito Mayor had an uneven first two months of the season. Of his first sixteen appearances, nine had come in relief. Mayor did not make his first start until November 6 and did not win a game as a starting pitcher until November 22, an 11–1 victory against Cienfuegos. After picking up his third win of the season, Mayor lost three of his next four decisions. The victory came on December 8, a complete-game 11–6 win against Cienfuegos. And all the while, Mayor often was pitching on short rest, coming out of the bullpen two days after pitching deep into a game he had started or starting a game a couple of days after a relief appearance. "That was nothing back in those days," Mayor said. "I pitched five games in one week once. In those times, you just pitched."[40] But after losing 6–1 to Habana on December 30, Mayor barely pitched during the month of January, making just four relief appearances. Such a stretch of inactivity was uncommon for Mayor.

Born in Sagua la Grande, Las Villas, on August 18, 1915—the same day as Almendares teammate Max Lanier—Mayor began playing baseball for sugar mill teams before joining Fortuna Sport Club in Cuba's national amateur league. He helped lead Fortuna to two consecutive amateur titles in 1936 and 1937. In 1937 Mayor led the league with a 1.13 earned run average.[41] The following year, representing Fortuna, Mayor led Cuba to the gold medal at Central American Games Championship IV, played in Panama City. He went 4–0 as Cuba beat Panama, Nicaragua, Puerto Rico, Mexico, Venezuela, and El Salvador.[42] Later in 1938 Mayor turned professional, joining the Cuban League for the 1938–39 season, and became a vital cog on Almendares's pitching staff.

Years later his wife, Gloria, recalled Mayor beating eventual league champion Santa Clara, 9–0, in his professional debut. "When he started playing for Almendares, it was for a percentage of the gate," Gloria said. "Sometimes he would come home with twenty-five pesos, other times with five pesos, other times with fifty pesos. Later, yes, they started making a salary. But at first it was a percentage of the gate when he started playing with Almendares at La Tropical."[43] Mayor posted a 5–4 record as a rookie. He had his best statistical season in 1941–42 as he went 6–2 with a 1.55 earned run average. And Mayor won seven games in three of the next four winters. But in January of 1947, Mayor had become a nonfactor. And as January turned into February, his Almendares team, which had recently cut Habana's lead to 3½ games, now trailed the league leader by five games. Beginning with his start on February 2—his first starting assignment since December 30—Mayor would firmly reestablish his place in determining the 1946–47 Cuban League champion.

Panama and the Petition

The Dodgers opened their tour of Panama on Monday, March 10, in Panama City. A crowd of 6,500 watched as Brooklyn collected thirteen hits in an 8–1 victory against the Panama Chesterfields. Back in Havana, Yankees president Larry MacPhail railed against the Dodgers. He accused them of skipping out on what he contended was supposed to have been a three-game series and leaving the Yankees to conclude their Cuban trip against a local all-star team. "When we arranged our contract . . . it was with the understanding that the Dodgers were to be our opponents in all three," MacPhail vented. "Instead, they have deliberately walked out on us after playing only two games here and we resent their action very much."[1]

As MacPhail seethed back in Havana, the Dodgers won their next game in Panama, beating the Cervecería team 9–4 on Tuesday as starter Kirby Higbe gave up four runs. The next day, Panamanian champion General Electric topped the Dodgers 7–6 in front of 10,000. Bobby Bragan homered in the game, which was called after seven innings because of darkness. That night, MacPhail fired the first real volley in the ongoing war of words with the Dodgers. The Colonel announced he had orally filed charges with baseball commissioner Happy Chandler against Dodgers manager Leo Durocher, team president Branch Rickey, and traveling secretary Harold Parrott. "There have been from 30 to 35 [newspaper] pieces up to now which are attributed to Durocher or

Rickey or both, which I regard as slanders," MacPhail said. "If Durocher or Rickey or both are guilty, they should be punished."[2]

Chief among MacPhail's complaints were the comments made by Durocher and Rickey implying MacPhail had entertained two known gamblers in his box at El Gran Stadium. "It was the first time in my life that I ever have seen either of them," MacPhail said. "Furthermore, they were not my guests. They were seated in the box next to mine."[3] After MacPhail's announcement, Chandler tried to defuse the situation by asking MacPhail to take some time to reconsider. "Then if he feels the same way," Chandler said, "the matter can be taken up."[4] The day Chandler called for a cooling-off period, the Dodgers defeated the Canal Zone All-Stars 8–4 in Cristóbal, Panama, in a game called after eight innings because of darkness. After the game, reporters asked Durocher about MacPhail's charge that Durocher had engaged in conduct detrimental to baseball. "What does he mean by conduct detrimental to baseball?" Durocher said. "I might have something to say behind the commissioner's closed doors."[5]

The Dodgers players remained unfazed by the acrimony swirling among Durocher, Rickey, and MacPhail. On Friday, March 14, Brooklyn beat a team of Pacific-side Service All-Stars 17–0 in Balboa, Canal Zone. The crowd of 6,000 at Balboa Stadium included General Willis D. Crittenberger, head of the Caribbean Defense Command. On Saturday, 4,000 fans saw the Dodgers beat the Panama All-Stars 6–3 in Panama City. That day, the cooling-off period suggested by Chandler came to an end. MacPhail requested, in writing, that Chandler investigate remarks "allegedly made" by Dodger officials. In his complaint MacPhail wrote that the remarks "if false . . . constitute slander and libel" and "represent . . . conduct detrimental to baseball."[6]

Jackie Robinson began his professional baseball career as a shortstop with the Kansas City Monarchs. But after signing with the Dodgers organization in 1945, he successfully converted to second base for the 1946 International League season with the Royals. Robinson made just ten errors while leading the league with a .349 average and 113 runs scored. As spring training for the 1947 season began, the big question was whether Robinson would make the Dodgers roster. But it wasn't the only one. If Robinson were to reach the majors, what position would he play? Brooklyn already had well-established players at the two positions Robinson had played: Pee Wee Reese at shortstop and Eddie Stanky at second base. *Baltimore Afro-American* sportswriter Sam Lacy noted how difficult it would be to displace Stanky, "a hard-driving, to-hell-with-it performer who matches everything the Rickey-Durocher system plans and dreams. The diminutive fire-brand will be a hard man to dispose of."[7]

Not long after arriving in Havana for spring training, Robinson learned the answer to the question of which position he would play. His most likely path to the majors would be through first base. Even as Robinson continued playing second base in the Royals' games against the Havana Cubans, he started learning the new position from Hall of Fame first baseman George Sisler. The father of Dick Sisler, who had become a Cuban League legend during the 1945–46 season, was in camp as a coach with the Royals. Handed a first baseman's mitt, Robinson was asked how the new glove felt. "I honestly don't know," he responded. "I never had one on before."[8] The Dodgers dismissed Robinson's workouts at first base as "an experiment of no significance,"[9] but before leaving for Panama, Robinson said he was not averse to another position switch. "I'll play where they want me to play," he told *New York Sun* writer Herbert Goren. "I never played first, but I'll try anything."[10]

Privately, however, Robinson wasn't nearly as open to change. "He didn't like it at all, but Rickey convinced him that this was his way of getting up to the majors," Lacy recalled years later. "It was just a case where he had enough problems. He had enough things to be concerned about [than] to give him this additional concern of changing positions and possibly doing poorly."[11] Montreal manager Clay Hopper was no happier about the prospect of Robinson playing first base during the Panama trip. He knew playing Robinson at first base would not help the Royals get ready for the season. If Robinson failed to make the Dodgers, the Royals' second baseman would have spent much of training camp playing out of position. And if Robinson were to be promoted, the Royals' eventual first baseman would have gotten little playing time during spring training. But Hopper's efforts to persuade

Rickey to elevate Robinson to the Dodgers roster during spring training games were rejected.

On March 12, Durocher conceded what had been widely speculated. Robinson would play first base in games against the Dodgers on the Isthmus of Panama. "It's the only infield spot we have for him," Durocher said. "We're all set at second with Ed Stanky. I wouldn't bench that little guy for Rogers Hornsby. [Pee Wee] Reese is a fixture at short and we're going with [Arky] Vaughn at third."[12] First base had been a revolving door for the Dodgers. Ed Stevens and Howie Schultz had shared the position in 1946, and the addition of spring candidates such as Lou Ruchser, Sailor Jack Douglas, and Jack Paepke did little to suggest Brooklyn had found a clear-cut choice. Even though Robinson had never played there, it made sense to try him at first base. "If the colored boy is impressive enough," the *Brooklyn Eagle*'s Harold C. Burr wrote, "he then will receive a trial at the bag with the Dodgers."[13]

If Cuban fans at times had viewed Robinson's presence with indifference, fans in Panama greeted his arrival on March 15 with rabid enthusiasm. Black Panamanian fans saw Robinson as a harbinger of what might be if he were to reach the majors. He and his black teammates were "the toast of Panama City and elsewhere in this nation of dark people," *Pittsburgh Courier* sportswriter Wendell Smith wrote. The players "find themselves 3,000 miles from home and being accorded better treatment here than they have experienced in their own country."[14] Panamanian promoter Carlos Smith, who was black, guaranteed the Dodgers $35,000 to play exhibitions in Panama. That was an enticing sum considering the costly venture of holding camp in Havana. Smith's one caveat: Robinson and the Royals' three other black players—Roy Campanella, Don Newcombe, and Roy Partlow—must be there. They "are heroes here," Smith wrote. "They are looked upon as leaders and pioneers."[15]

More than 6,000 fans packed Mount Hope Park in Cristóbal, Panama, to see the Royals' first game on the Isthmus on Sunday, March 16. Robinson and Campanella treated them to quite a show in the Royals' 9–5 victory against General Electric. The team Wendell Smith described as an "all-Negro native nine" had won the Panama Professional League. And just a few days prior to the game against the Royals, they had beaten the Dodgers 7–6. Robinson went 2-for-4, including a 382-foot home run over the left-field fence. He also beat out a perfect bunt down the third-base line. After early struggles in the exhibition season, Robinson's performance against General Electric improved his spring average to .520. The game also saw Campanella deliver his best performance since camp opened, blasting a 410-foot two-run home run over the center-field fence and scorching a two-run double. "Jackie Robinson and Roy Campanella," Smith wrote, "were as hot as the tropical sun here."[16] Years later, Sam Lacy assessed the importance of the Panama trip. "We were able to see that the Montreal team, with these black players, was drawing larger crowds than the Dodgers themselves when they came into a town," he said. "That gave us sort of a morale boost."[17] While Robinson's hitting thrilled the crowd, his defense was no less significant. In his first game at first base, he handled ten chances cleanly. "Robinson was doing some fancy stepping at first base," Smith wrote, "a new position for him, but one that he will apparently master quickly."[18]

While Robinson was displaying his skills at his new position, Branch Rickey was flying to the Canal Zone from the Dodgers' minor-league camp in Pensacola, Florida. He had hoped the Dodgers players themselves would call for Robinson's promotion to the majors once they had a chance to see him in action. "The players could decide Robinson's fate," Rickey had declared in January. "It's what I prefer—that the Dodgers players make their own decision after seeing him in action."[19] But a groundswell for Robinson's elevation never materialized. Before the Dodgers and Royals left Cuba for Panama, New York Sun writer Herbert Goren described the prevailing sentiment toward Robinson among the Dodgers players as "mainly antagonistic." Robinson, Goren wrote, "will have to undo an undercurrent of resentment. Not all the Dodgers feel that way, but a great many do."[20]

Several players, mostly southerners, had no desire to have a black teammate. Buzzie Bavasi, who became the Dodgers' general manager in 1950, was the GM with the Class-B Nashua Dodgers in 1946. He remembered Rickey "anticipated that we would have a problem, but he thought the problem would come from other clubs."[21] Instead, as Rickey quickly learned upon arriving in Panama, the early enemies came from within. Talk of a petition among the Dodgers players to block Robinson joining the team had bubbled up in Cuba "after workout hours, sometimes at the Hotel Nacional bar, sometimes in more sleazy places in Havana's night scene."[22] Among the mutineers were South Carolina native Kirby Higbe, Georgia-born Hugh Casey, Louisiana native Ed Head, northerner Carl Furillo of Pennsylvania, and Alabama residents Dixie Walker, Eddie Stanky, and Bobby Bragan. "I was born and raised in Birmingham," Bragan said years later of his attitude that spring. "Any time a black came to my house, he went through the back door. If he drank water at a bus station, he drank from a black fountain, and I drank from a white fountain. If he went to the men's room, he went to a black [one]."[23]

Word of the rebellion reached Durocher and Rickey on the night of Sunday, March 16. Kirby Higbe was out drinking when Dodgers traveling secretary Harold Parrott stumbled upon the pitcher at a Canal Zone watering hole. A drunken Higbe, perhaps guilt-ridden over his participation in the mutiny, spilled the beans about the petition. "Ol' Hig just won't do it," Higbe told Parrott. "The ol' man [Rickey] has been fair to Ol' Hig. So Ol' Hig ain't going to join any petition to keep anybody off the club."[24] Armed with knowledge of a possible players' revolt, Parrott immediately informed Rickey and Durocher. Upset and restless, Durocher rousted his coaches from bed and demanded they gather the players.

The midnight meeting convened in a huge empty kitchen behind the mess hall at Fort Gillick, where the Dodgers stayed while in Panama. Dressed in blue silk pajamas and a gold bathrobe, Durocher berated his white players—at one point calling out Dixie Walker by name—over their attitudes toward Robinson:

> You know what you can do with that petition? You can wipe your asses with it. . . . If this fella is good enough to play on this ball club . . . he is going to play on this ball club, and he is going to play for me. I don't care if a guy is yellow or black, or if he has stripes like a fuckin' zebra, I'm the manager of this ball club, and I say he

plays. . . . So, I don't want to see your petition, and I don't want to hear anything more about it. The meeting is over; go back to bed.[25]

Amazingly, the reporters bunking with Durocher at Fort Gillick never caught wind of the petition or the Dodger manager's late-night tirade. It wasn't until something unusual happened—or, more accurately, did not happen—the morning after the meeting that the writers realized anything was going on. It had been Durocher's "hearty practice to rout each and every sluggard [reporter] out of bed at a preposterous hour," wrote the New York World-Telegram's Bill Roeder. "Sometimes even before noon."[26] But on the morning of St. Patrick's Day no such early wake-up came. Durocher had already left for California. The writers awoke, well rested, to find a note on the kitchen table that read: "Good-bye boys. I'm flying to Los Angeles. Personal business, nothing important. See you in Havana, Leo."[27] One reporter, the Brooklyn Eagle's Harold C. Burr, managed to talk to Durocher before he left Panama for California. "Naturally, I want to see him in action at first base," Durocher said. "We've got nine more games with Montreal in Cuba and at Ebbets Field and there's still lots of time left for me to look him over."[28] And with that he was off to California.

Robinson had no idea Durocher had left Panama the morning he was scheduled to play his first spring training game against the Dodgers on Monday, March 17. That morning Robinson and Wendell Smith were "subjected to a raw discrimination" when a waiter at the Hotel Tivoli in Panama City informed them that they could not be served.[29] According to a report in the New York Amsterdam News under the byline Cleto Hernández, the pair had been invited to the hotel by Branch Rickey. But when Robinson and Smith tried to join Rickey and his wife for breakfast, a waiter intervened, saying "superior orders" would not allow them to be served. Robinson and Smith, "indignant" over the slight, left the hotel.[30] Robinson and Smith denied the incident took place in a story in the Pittsburgh Courier. The same story, however, claimed the newspaper had "received information from a reliable source" confirming the episode. Perhaps Smith and Robinson, wanting to avoid controversy as Robinson attempted to break baseball's color barrier, chose to downplay the event. In the *Courier* story, however, Smith described the U.S.-controlled Canal Zone as "every bit as bad as Mississippi."[31]

The remainder of the day went far better for Robinson, despite Durocher being absent for the Montreal star's first game against the Dodgers. With Rickey among the 6,000 fans at Panama City's Olympic Stadium, Robinson displayed his fancy glove work for the first time against the Dodgers. Robinson flawlessly handled thirteen chances at first base. He also went 2-for-4 in a game that ended in a 1–1 tie, called because of darkness in the eighth inning. One of Robinson's hits helped the Royals tie the game in the fourth inning. Overall, it was an impressive performance for Robinson in front of his patron. But Rickey's mind surely was elsewhere. Greeted by Parrott's revelation of a brewing insurrection among the Dodgers players, Rickey feared what word of a revolt against Robinson might do to his grand plans. He moved quickly to quell the rebellion.

His first step was inviting second baseman Eddie Stanky to break-fast at the Hotel Tivoli, where Rickey was staying in Panama. Stanky knew exactly why Rickey had summoned him. "When you gave me that big raise in February," Stanky said, "you told me you were doing it be-cause you might need a favor some day. Well, Mr. Rickey, you've got your favor. Don't worry about a thing."[32] With a key southerner such as Stanky now on board, Rickey went to work on the other rebels. He summoned the players one by one to his hotel room. The most heated exchange came with Bobby Bragan. Years later, Bragan relayed the fol-lowing account of the meeting:

> Rickey: Not you nor anybody else is going to tell me who to play. It doesn't make any difference whether a guy's skin is purple, white, green, black, or blue, he is going to play if he's going to do more than the other guy. Do you understand that?
> Bragan: Yes, sir.
> Rickey: Would you rather be traded, or would you rather play with him?
> Bragan: I'd rather be traded.

Rickey: Are you going to play any differently because he's here?
Bragan: No, I'm not.[33]

Dixie Walker was not among the players summoned to Rickey's hotel room. Walker left Panama on Tuesday, March 18, flying to Miami to meet with his family on "personal business."[34] He would rejoin the Dodgers when the team returned to Havana on March 22.

The same day Rickey watched Robinson for the first time in Panama, his Dodgers also played another game in Balboa. Brooklyn beat the Canal Zone All-Stars 4–3 as Stanky singled to drive in the tying run in the ninth and delivered a game-winning RBI triple in the eleventh inning. The next day, the Dodgers played the All-Stars to a 6-all tie in another contest shortened to eight innings by darkness. It was Brooklyn's second deadlock in three games over two days. Career minor leaguer Roy Kennedy hit a grand slam against future major leaguer Ralph Branca. More significant than the results of any of those games were two developments on March 18. Rickey set the deadline for whether to promote Robinson to the majors at midnight April 16, the night before the Royals were scheduled to open their International League season. In declaring the timeline for his decision, Rickey addressed the issue of Robinson's potential future position. "The problem hasn't reached the stage where anybody has first base sewed up," he said. "It's premature to say that Robinson already has a place on the Dodgers."[35]

The other development took place several countries away, in Tampa, Florida. Baseball commissioner Happy Chandler denied a *Cincinnati Enquirer* story quoting him as warning that "somebody may wind up getting kicked out of baseball."[36] According to *Enquirer* sportswriter Lou Smith, Chandler's remarks referred to the upcoming hearing over Larry MacPhail's charges against Durocher. After the story came out, Chandler denied making those comments, while on a Florida golf course with a group of sportswriters including Smith. "I don't remember saying anything like that," Chandler bristled. "I'll decide what punishment, if any, is necessary after I've heard all the evidence Monday."[37]

The next day, Durocher arrived at Lockheed Air Terminal in Holly-wood, California, to reunite with his wife, Laraine Day. Durocher had met Day in 1945, while she was married to jazz musician Ray Hen-dricks. With Day still in the middle of divorce proceedings against her husband, she and Durocher married on January 21, 1947. Day had been granted a California divorce from Hendricks on January 20 by Superior Court judge George Dockweiler. Under California law, how-ever, Day had to wait a year for the divorce to be finalized. That did not stop Day and Durocher. The day after Dockweiler's decree, the actress flew to Juárez, Mexico, to secure a divorce there. Day then returned to El Paso, Texas, where she married Durocher, "all within the short span of 28 hours."[38]

The judge was not amused. He called Day into court to explain her actions. But Day's attorneys charged Dockweiler with being biased against their client. Their request for a hearing before a different judge was granted. Superior Court judge Edward T. Bishop ruled Dockweiler had shown bias and that "it was probable Miss Day could not obtain a fair and impartial trial before him."[39] Bishop set a March 4 hearing date for Day to show cause why her California divorce should not be set aside. On March 14, Superior Court judge John W. Bull refused to dis-miss proceedings seeking to set aside Day's California divorce and set a new hearing date of April 28.[40] When Durocher landed in Hollywood on March 19, he was in no mood to talk. After getting a hug and kiss from his wife, Durocher told reporters camped out waiting for him, "Whatever you have to say, boys, it's a great big no!"[41] Day was equally empathic, shouting "No, no, no, no, no," as she and Durocher climbed into a waiting limousine and drove away. After just twenty-four hours in town, the couple left for the Dodgers' camp in Havana.

If there was ever any doubt whether Eddie Stanky would allow him-self to be displaced by Jackie Robinson at second base, he showed in Panama why his feistiness would make such a scenario unlikely. As the Dodgers beat Panama General Electric 7–0 in Cristóbal on Wednes-day, March 19, Pee Wee Reese clubbed two home runs and Carl Furillo and Ed Stevens each homered once to back the two-hit pitching of

Vic Lombardi. The next day, the Dodgers played their final exhibition against the Royals on the Isthmus. The Dodgers won 10–3, but Robinson went 3-for-4 despite never hitting a ball out of the infield. On his only out, in his first at-bat, shortstop Pee Wee Reese ranged far to his right for a sensational stop and threw Robinson out by a step.

It was the only time the Dodgers infield would even attempt a play against Robinson. In his second at-bat, Robinson hit a sizzler down the third-base line. Arky Vaughn made a great stop but couldn't make a throw to first. In the fifth inning, Robinson's perfect bunt down the third-base line also drew no throw. Finally, Robinson bunted down the first-base line for his third infield single as "the crowd rose as one and gave Jackie a great ovation."[42] With Robinson on first, Dodgers second baseman Eddie Stanky, angered that the infield had been caught off guard twice by Robinson, asked for a timeout. Once time was called, "the fiery second sacker took the ball Robinson had bunted and threw it over the grandstand and out into the street."[43]

Stanky's display was indicative of the resentment and even downright anger some of the Dodgers players felt toward Robinson. Few were as adamant as Bragan. But despite his preference for being traded, Bragan remained with the Dodgers, and eventually he and other players came to change their views on Robinson. Playing with Robinson "was the greatest thing that ever happened to me," said Bragan, who after his playing career managed a racially mixed Almendares team during the 1952–53 Cuban League season. "Those people, like myself, who might have been a little slow joining Robinson at the breakfast table, we were fighting to see who would eat with him. It was a real transition. He sold everybody."[44] Such a change in attitude, however, did not come as easily for others, especially Dixie Walker, who had failed to muster support for a petition against Robinson.

At different times in his life, Walker has denied and admitted to his role in the petition. Author Roger Kahn wrote that in 1976 Walker had told him the petition was "the stupidest thing he'd ever done." Kahn quoted Walker as saying: "I organized that petition in 1947, not because I had anything against Robinson personally or against Negroes generally. I had a wholesale business in Birmingham and people told me I'd lose my business if I played ball with a black man."[45] But in 1981

Walker told *New York Times* writer Ira Berkow, "I didn't know a thing about any insurrection, as it was later called."[46] Regardless, the stigma of the petition stayed with Walker his entire life, and he was certainly tethered to it in the spring of 1947, as he would come to find out upon his return to Havana.

While the Dodgers were in Panama, their B squad remained in Havana for exhibition games. That roster included a young Gil Hodges, who had returned from two years of military service to play with the Class-B Newport News (Virginia) Dodgers in 1946; future major-league manager Clyde King; Howie Schultz, one of the Dodgers' first-base candidates for 1947; fading major leaguer Cookie Lavagetto; and twenty-year-old Duke Snider, who went on to play eighteen major-league seasons, sixteen of them with the Brooklyn and Los Angeles Dodgers, and be inducted into the Hall of Fame. Even Ol' Kirby Higbe, who had spilled the beans about the petition against Jackie Robinson, took the short flight from Panama early to pitch in a B game in Havana.

The B games came against the Havana Cubans of the Class-C Florida International League. Cuba's first minor-league team was the culmination of efforts to bring organized baseball to Havana that began in 1929. The Class-B Southern League, which at the time included teams in Florida (Jacksonville, Tampa, and Pensacola), Alabama (Montgomery and Selma), and Georgia (Columbus), tried to expand to Miami and Havana. The league even got Pan American Airways to offer a special rate for teams flying from Miami to Havana.[47] Hotelier Charles Green, who had owned the Jacksonville franchise, was vying to own a team in Cuba. But the league's expansion efforts collapsed when plans for a team in Miami and later St. Petersburg, Florida, fell through. Green tried again to expand the Southern League into Cuba in 1931, but the Great Depression helped drive the league out of business by the middle of the 1932 season.[48]

Minor-league baseball finally arrived in Cuba with the founding of the Florida International League for the 1946 season. Aside from the Havana Cubans, the league included the Miami Sun Sox, Miami Beach Flamingos, Lakeland Pilots, Tampa Smokers, and West Palm Beach

Indians. Baldomero "Merito" Acosta, a former major leaguer with the Washington Senators and Philadelphia Athletics from 1913 to 1918 and a Cuban League star from 1913 to 1925, was the Cubans team president. Another founder was Senators scout Joe Cambria, the team's secretary-treasurer.[49] Papa Joe had begun signing Cuban players to professional contracts in the early 1930s—such Cuban League stars as Fermín Guerra, René Monteagudo, Gilberto Torres, and Roberto Ortiz. The Havana Cubans' connection to the Senators also included Senators owner Clark Griffith, who bought 20,000 shares in the team in July of 1946. Acosta and Cambria each controlled 10,000 shares.[50]

Under manager Oscar Rodríguez, the Havana Cubans played their inaugural season at La Tropical stadium in 1946. Rodríguez, who had played in the Cuban League from 1918 to 1929, led the Havana Cubans to the first-half title with a 33–14 record, six games ahead of the second-place Flamingos. The Cubans went 43–27 to finish second by 2½ games to the Smokers in the second half of the season. But Havana lost in the semifinal playoff round. For their second season, the Cubans moved from La Tropical to Bobby Maduro's new El Gran Stadium. The team's ties to the Senators became formalized through a working agreement in which Griffith became the team's vice president.[51]

As the Havana Cubans prepared for their inaugural season at El Gran Stadium, they did so with a revamped roster that included several mainstays of Cuba's amateur ranks, such as Conrado Marrero, Julio "Juquí" Moreno, and Rogelio "Limonar" Martínez. Marrero had been Cuba's most successful and popular amateur baseball player and had completed his first professional season in 1946–47 with Oriente of the National Federation and Almendares of the Cuban League. Moreno began his pro career with the Cuban League's Marianao club in 1945–46 and had played for the National Federation's Havana Reds. Martínez debuted professionally with Almendares in 1945–46 and played with Matanzas of the National Federation in 1946–47.

The Havana Cubans opened their 1947 spring training exhibition season against Brooklyn's Montreal Royals farm team, the defending Class-AAA International League champions. In the six matchups before the Royals left for a series of games in Panama, Montreal won four times and lost twice. Jackie Robinson led the way for the Royals, batting .500 (13-for-26). Once the Royals left Havana to join the Dodgers in the Canal Zone, the Havana Cubans continued their preparations for the upcoming season with games at El Gran Stadium, including some against the Dodgers B squad.

In the first contest on Saturday, March 15, Rafael Rivas, who had gone 27–4 with a 2.03 earned run average during the Cubans' inaugural season, started against Clyde King of the Dodgers. Neither starter fared well, as the Dodgers held a 7–5 lead through three innings and went on to win the game 8–6 in front of 500 fans. In the next matchup on Monday night, the Dodgers B team won 1–0 despite a stellar outing by Conrado Marrero, who struck out eight and limited the Dodgers to four hits. A run surrendered in the first inning was the lone blemish on Marrero's pitching line.

With those games done, the Dodgers B team lost a pair of games against a Cuban all-star team selected by Gilberto Torres. In the second of those games, Torres's squad racked up sixteen hits to beat the Dodgers 8–4 on Wednesday, March 19. Fermín Guerra, the Philadelphia Athletics catcher, went 4-for-4 with two doubles. Orestes Miñoso went 3-for-4 with a single, double, and triple. Kirby Higbe, back from the Dodgers' side trip to Panama, took the brunt of the Cuban selection's attack, surrendering six runs on eight hits. The return of the Dodgers and Royals from Panama to Cuba meant more games between them and the Havana Cubans and Cuban all-star teams. Those games would help decide Robinson's fate for the 1947 season.

Whoever Defeats Almendares Dies

Max Lanier had been announced as Almendares's starting pitcher for its game against league-leading Habana on February 1. But when it came time for the opening pitch, Lanier was not on the mound. Once again the Scorpions' lefty had returned home to St. Petersburg, Florida. Instead manager Adolfo Luque sent veteran Lázaro Salazar to the hill against Habana's predominantly right-handed hitting lineup. The result was as immediate as it was disastrous. Salazar surrendered five hits and allowed a walk in one-third of an inning, and the Lions tallied seven first-inning runs en route to an 8–1 victory. The shelling of Salazar left Habana with a six-game lead in the standings and opened Lanier to some scathing criticism.

"Cuban baseball . . . cannot depend on an athlete who has spent the entire season removing his flannel uniform so he can leave for St. Petersburg by plane," columnist Eladio Secades wrote in the following day's *Diario de la Marina*. "When Max Lanier was with the Gray Monks, immediately after each game, he was in Florida whenever he felt like it. You could not count on him."[1] Throughout the season, Lanier had made several trips to Florida. Once while he was still with Marianao, Lanier—after beating Cienfuegos 7–0 on November 30—flew to St. Petersburg, reportedly to receive treatment on his "ailing left arm."[2] His latest absence with Almendares drew reports of a rift between Lanier and the team. Those reports were denied by team treasurer

Dr. Julio Sanguily, who said Lanier had been given permission to fly to St. Petersburg for three days because his wife had been "gravely ill."[3]

But Cuban baseball historian Roberto González Echevarría wrote that the reasons for Lanier's frequent flights had little to do with personal injury or family illness. According to González, Lanier confessed his trips were nothing more than shopping sprees. The pitcher would return from Florida armed with groceries for himself and teammates such as Fred Martin. "It's hard to get bacon, ham, or anything like that—they let me fly back to St. Pete and I'd bring back enough stuff for four or five families," González quotes Lanier as saying, "and they'd tell me at the airport customs, 'Well, you'd better win today.'"[4]

Given Luque's temper—his intolerance for pitchers unwilling to pitch occasionally involved the threat of gunplay—Almendares's apparently lax attitude toward Lanier's Florida expeditions remains curious. Perhaps it had much to do with the lefty's winning ways since coming to the Scorpions in a trade for catcher Lloyd Basset. Lanier lost his first start for Almendares, a complete-game 1–0 defeat against Cienfuegos. He then rattled off three consecutive complete-game victories, beating Habana 6–1 on January 5, Cienfuegos 6–1 on January 12, and Habana 9–1 on January 19. But Lanier's role in Almendares's resurgence did not spare him from Secades's wrath. His most recent disappearance proved that "nothing about Cuban baseball matters to him," Secades wrote. "Instead of going into battle . . . he again . . . disappears, abandoning the cause of his team, which yesterday needed him with urgent desperation. Because 'the Monster' was in St. Petersburg, Almendares could not start its best pitcher and Habana took another step in its conquest of the pennant."[5]

Having virtually disappeared during the previous month, Agapito Mayor served notice that he was back in his first start in February. After Salazar's clubbing at the hands of Habana on the first day of the month, Mayor took the mound on February 2 and delivered a sterling performance against Cienfuegos. He pitched ten innings and scattered five hits—among them a solo home run to Napoleón Reyes that tied the score at 1–1 in the fourth inning. Almendares secured the 2–1 victory when Roberto Ortiz, who went 2-for-4, slugged a solo home run in the bottom of the tenth inning. On the same day, Marianao defeated Habana 3–1 as Cocaína García, making his first start since his bout of pneumonia, gave up eight hits. The combination of Almendares's victory and Habana's loss cut the Lions' lead to five games.

But Almendares gave back a half game in the standings when Marianao defeated Jorge Comellas 4–3 on February 4. The Scorpions appeared on their way to a victory and again chipping away at Habana's lead. Almendares led the Gray Monks by a score of 3–2, but Comellas loaded the bases on a hit and two walks in the seventh inning. With two strikes against him, Marianao's Tony Castaño lined a single to right field to drive in two runs. Almendares had just fourteen games remaining on its schedule—in a span of three weeks—in which to make up its 5½-game deficit to Habana in the standings. So going into Almendares's February 5 doubleheader against Cienfuegos, any combination of nine Habana victories or Almendares defeats would give Habana the pennant.

With Habana idle that day, Almendares did its part to keep the Lions from getting any closer to clinching. In the first game of the doubleheader, Mayor took the hill on just two day's rest. Before a "discrete gathering that braved the intense cold and five-hour duration" of the game, Almendares's "forgotten man," as *Diario de la Marina*'s René Molina referred to Mayor, outdueled Cienfuegos's Max Manning for a 2–1 complete-game victory.[6] Mayor struck out four and allowed no walks while surrendering eight hits, including two each by Napoleón Reyes, Alejandro Crespo, and Red Hayworth. In his coverage of the game, Molina lamented Mayor's season and extolled his recent reawakening in Almendares's rotation: "In the early days of the season, he was the key pitcher, the perennial choice to pitch against Habana, Luque's trusted man. But one afternoon he exploded opposite the roaring lion and from that moment disappeared from the rotation. . . . Last night, with two days of rest, he was called to arms, as in the first days of the season, and again the southpaw responded, 'Present!'"[7]

With Mayor's second consecutive stellar performance complete, it was Tomás de la Cruz's turn to take on Cienfuegos in the nightcap of the doubleheader. The thirty-two-year-old native of Marianao was in the final year of a distinguished Cuban League career that began with Marianao in the 1934–35 season. He led the league with six victories as a rookie pitcher that season and compiled 65 career wins in his first twelve Cuban League seasons. In the waning years of his career, De la Cruz was still a formidable pitcher. After eight seasons in the minor leagues, De la Cruz finally reached the majors in 1944, going 9–9 with a 3.25 earned run average for the Cincinnati Reds. He led the Cuban League with a 2.30 ERA during the 1944–45 season. And on January 4, 1945, De la Cruz pitched the fourth no-hitter in Cuban League history, a 7–0 victory by his Almendares team against Habana.

In the 1946–47 season, De la Cruz's record stood at three wins and five losses going into his game against Cienfuegos. With the Elephants' Stan Breard and Pedro Pagés each driving in a run, De la Cruz appeared on his way to losing his sixth game of the season. He had given up only three hits in five innings, yet was trailing 2–0. But Almendares got De la Cruz off the hook by scoring seven runs in the bottom of the fifth. Catcher Andrés Fleitas doubled to drive in three runs. Right fielder Roberto Ortiz, who went 2-for-4, hit a two-run homer. Jesse Williams also drove in a run. The seven-run outburst gave De la Cruz the win and Almendares a doubleheader sweep that cut Habana's lead to 4½ games.

▰

After first joining the Cuban League with Marianao for the 1935–36 season, Adrián Zabala had become a mainstay with Cienfuegos beginning in 1941–42. He won nine games during the 1942–43 and 1945–46 seasons—tying teammate Sal Maglie for the team lead during the latter—and 1946–47 was shaping up as another fine season for the native of San Antonio de los Baños. Going into his February 6 start against league-leading Habana, Zabala already had eight victories. And despite also having seven defeats on his ledger, Zabala appeared well on his way toward eclipsing the career high in wins he had set along with Maglie the previous season.

Zabala's career had been closely tied to Maglie's even before the two helped the Elephants to the 1945–46 Cuban League championship. The pair debuted in the major leagues with the New York Giants in

August of 1945. But their time in the majors was short lived. With Zabala holding out in a contract dispute with the Giants before the 1946 major-league season, New York manager Mel Ott informed the lefty in February of 1946 that a return to Class-AAA Jersey City was likely. So Zabala, who had played for Puebla in 1944 and led the Mexican League with a 2.74 earned run average while compiling a 10–2 record, accepted a standing offer from Jorge Pasquel to return to Mexico.[8] By March 31, 1946, Maglie also had jumped his Giants contract to join the Mexican League. And, of course, the two ended up as teammates with Puebla. Maglie went 20–12 with a 3.19 ERA, while Zabala went 11–14 with a 4.92 ERA.[9]

When the 1946 Mexican League season ended, Zabala returned to Cuba for the winter, rejoining Cienfuegos. For much of the season, the left-handed pitcher had been a thorn in the side of the predominantly right-handed-hitting Lions. Habana had beaten Zabala nearly as many times—four—as he had beaten them. But in Zabala's five victories against the Lions, he had held them to six total runs and shut them out once, 9–0 on December 24. So Habana's game against Cienfuegos on February 6 meant the possibility of seeing its lead in the standings narrowed even further. Zabala "always has been a dangerous obstacle and now is in exceptional form," René Molina wrote.[10] But in this game Zabala was not able to limit the Lions' attack. Habana rapped out ten hits, with a three-run sixth inning providing the 4–3 margin of victory. With Habana starter Jim LaMarque's control wavering, manager Miguel Ángel González opted to bring in starting pitcher Cocaína García to preserve the victory, which increased Habana's lead to five games.

Habana saw its lead cut to 4½ games after it lost to Marianao 5–4 on Friday, February 7. Marianao's Roberto Estalella homered in the seventh as the Gray Monks overcame a 4–0 deficit. It almost became the last game played of the 1946–47 Cuban League season. After Almendares's owners had refused to play a scheduled February 12 game against Habana as a benefit for the Cuban Professional Baseball Players' Association pension fund, the league's players threatened to strike. But the Cuban press refused to support them. "When the players' board of directors went to the press box to get the opinion of the writers," René Cañizares wrote in the *Sporting News*, "they were told that they were not dealing fairly with the owners."[11] Eventually the crisis was averted. The parties agreed to have 5 percent of the net receipts from the February 9 game between Almendares and Habana go to the Players' Association. And a game between Cuban and American all-stars would be played on February 10, with proceeds going to the owners.

The day before the newly designated benefit game, Lázaro Salazar won a pitching duel against Canadian Jean Roy as Almendares beat Cienfuegos 3–2. Scorpions outfielder Lloyd Davenport drove in two runs to help Almendares cut Habana's lead to four games. Almendares further whittled away at the Lions' lead in Sunday's benefit game. Max Lanier started for Almendares and Cocaína García for Habana. With Davenport and Roberto Ortiz each driving in a run, Almendares scored three runs in the third inning off García, who was lifted for a pinch hitter in the fourth. It was not the best of outings for Lanier, who walked nine batters, but he was bailed out by his defense. In the seventh inning, Habana loaded the bases with one out against Lanier before Davenport made a spectacular catch in deep left field on a line drive by Habana's Lou Klein. Almendares second baseman George Hausmann made a great play on a sharply hit grounder to end the game and give the Scorpions a 3–1 victory, their fourth in a row. Habana's lead was now just three games as the league paused for another all-star break.[12]

In fact, two all-star games were played on Monday, February 10. But they lacked the fan interest of the all-star game that had been played on January 20 and were declared an "economic failure" by *Diario de la Marina* writer René Molina. "The memory of the previous all-star game that had a theatrical ending," he wrote, "and the intense cold convinced ticket buyers that they preferred to wait for the bitter duels that lie ahead between the Eternal Rivals."[13] In the first game of the doubleheader, Cienfuegos manager Martín Dihigo and new Marianao skipper Pipo de la Noval directed the squads. The Pipo All-Stars included Havana second baseman Carlos Blanco, Almendares outfielder

Santos Amaro, and Marianao outfielder Roberto Estalella. The Dihigo All-Stars included Cienfuegos pitcher Luis Tiant Sr., along with first baseman Buck O'Neil and pitcher Conrado Marrero of Almendares. Despite Blanco going 2-for-4 and driving in three runs, the Dihigo All-Stars won 5–4.

The nightcap of the doubleheader featured more of the Cuban League's best players. The American All-Stars, managed by Miguel Ángel González, included Habana teammates Henry Kimbro, Lou Klein, Hank Thompson, and Lennie Pearson; Almendares's Lloyd Davenport, George Hausmann, and Gentry Jessup; and outfielder Danny Gardella and pitcher Max Manning of Cienfuegos. The Cuban All-Stars, managed by Adolfo Luque, included Almendares teammates Avelino Cañizares, Roberto Ortiz, Andrés Fleitas, and Tomás de la Cruz; Habana's Pedro Formental, Heberto Blanco, and Salvador Hernández; Napoleón Reyes, Adrián Zabala, and Pedro Pagés of Cienfuegos; and Marianao's Orestes Miñoso and Tony Castaño. Despite the packed lineups, a mere 5,000 fans were in attendance at El Gran Stadium as Jessup and Kimbro each drove in a run to give the American All-Stars a 2–0 victory. "The ideal would have been to provide one simple match," Molina wrote, "a unique and true all-star game."[14]

Habana came out of the second "all-star break" looking to stop its slide in the standings. And the Lions barely had to do anything against Marianao to make that happen on Tuesday, February 11. Pitchers for the Gray Monks issued fourteen walks, including six in the first inning. Those allowed the Lions to score three runs while barely swinging at a single pitch. Aristónico Correoso walked the first three batters of the game—Henry Kimbro, Pedro Formental, and Lou Klein—to load the bases before being pulled. Reliever Lino Donoso fared no better, walking the only two batters he faced to force home Kimbro and Formental and give Habana a 2–0 lead. Sandalio Consuegra came on in relief and finally recorded the first out, inducing Lennie Pearson to pop up to Marianao third baseman Orestes Miñoso in foul territory. But Consuegra walked Heberto Blanco to bring home Klein with Habana's third run of the inning. Mercifully, Habana catcher Salvador Hernández grounded into a double play to end the inning. But the Lions had all the runs they would need for a rain-shortened, eight-inning 5–0 victory that increased their lead over Almendares to 3½ games.

The next day, Almendares again cut into Habana's lead. As he had eight times already during the season, Habana manager Miguel Ángel González sent Fred Martin to the mound against Almendares. Martin had won five of those previous matchups, twice beating Agapito Mayor, whom he would face on Wednesday. But this matchup belonged to Mayor. He held Habana to three hits while not allowing a single batter to reach second base. With Mayor dominating the Lions' lineup, Almendares got all the runs it needed in the third inning when Buck O'Neil, Avelino Cañizares, and Andrés Fleitas each scored on base hits. Roberto Ortiz hit his league-leading eleventh home run in the sixth inning, and Almendares came away with a 5–0 victory that cut Habana's lead to 2½ games. "When everyone had logically thought that the battle for first place had ceased with the Lions' [previous] victory," René Molina wrote, "the miracle of resurrection was observed last night in an indubitable way."[15]

Almendares's seemingly inexorable climb up the standings continued on Thursday as the Scorpions defeated Cienfuegos 6–2 behind the complete-game pitching of Lázaro Salazar. With Habana idle, Almendares had crept to within two games of the league leaders. González needed to stop the bleeding. The Habana manager filed a protest with the Cuban League charging that Almendares had used an ineligible player, third baseman Héctor Rodríguez, in Wednesday's 5–0 victory by the Scorpions. Back on January 22, Rodríguez, while using a kitchen knife, had severed a tendon in his hand. Believing the injury would force him to miss the remainder of the season, Almendares placed Rodríguez, who had been batting .305 at the time of the injury, on the inactive list.

But the injury had healed sufficiently for manager Adolfo Luque to insert Rodríguez back into the lineup against Habana. The problem? Two years earlier, the league had adopted a rule change stating that any player inactive because of injury or illness had to wait at least 30 days before returning to action. Rodríguez had only been out 22 days. Given that Rodríguez had already played in two Almendares victories—one against Habana and one against Cienfuegos—a ruling in González's favor could lead to the forfeiture of those victories and prove devastating to Almendares's chances of overtaking the league leaders. Instead of trailing Habana by 2½ games, the Scorpions could be facing a five-game deficit with only twelve days remaining in the season.

League president Dr. Rafael Inclán, secretary Carlos Robreño, and treasurer Paul J. Miller gathered on February 14 to rule on González's protest only to make a surprising discovery. No one could find a record of the previously agreed-upon change having ever been written into the official rules. And a four-hour search failed to turn up any documentation. At eleven that night, the league officials adjourned until the following day. *Diario de la Marina* columnist Eladio Secades beseeched league officials not to take the "radical" step of voiding Almendares's victories should documentation of the rule change be unearthed. He pointed out the rule did not require a specific punishment for the violation. "Almendares can be fined for using an ineligible player," Secades wrote, "but to take away from Almendares and its fans the legitimate joy of a victory that brings them closer to the glories of the pennant is unfair and is also very dangerous."[16]

Habana's real problem during its slide in the standings wasn't Héctor Rodríguez's sudden presence in the Almendares lineup. It was the Lions' suddenly weak hitting. "Habana cannot hit," Secades wrote. "The organization famous for its red beatings is showing clear symptoms of pernicious anemia. Not Klein, not Thompson, not Pearson is hitting the ball as they did during those joyful days" earlier in the season.[17] Since beating Almendares 8–1 on February 1, Habana had won only two of six games. During that stretch, the heart of the Lions' batting order—Lou Klein, Hank Thompson, and Lennie Pearson—had combined to bat 10-for-64 for a .156 average. In those six games they had driven in just four runs, as the Lions were held to one run or none three times. Despite their struggles, Thompson was still tied with Almendares's Andrés Fleitas for the league lead with a .323 batting average, and Klein was fourth in hitting with a .305 mark.

But February 15 brought more bad news for the Lions. The day began with Habana learning its protest of Wednesday's game lacked legal grounds. The league ruled in favor of Almendares because the rule change cited by Miguel Ángel González had never been entered into the official record. Then, Habana's struggles at the plate continued that afternoon against Almenedares as the Lions fell "like toy soldiers against the homicidal rifle of lefty Max Lanier," according to René Molina's coverage of the Scorpions' 6–2 victory.[18] That was especially true of the heart of Habana's order. Klein, Thompson, and Pearson combined for zero hits in twelve at-bats. Lanier struck out five and did not walk a batter as he allowed only two hits in his complete-game performance.

Lanier might have shut out Habana had it not been for an error by shortstop Avelino Cañizares that allowed two runs to score in the eighth inning. Meanwhile, Almendares roughed up Habana starter Terris McDuffie, who had dominated the Scorpions in his previous start against them on January 24. But this time the Scorpions scored two in the first inning and chased Habana's "clown pitcher" in the second. McDuffie faced nine batters, surrendered six hits, and allowed four runs. Almendares's seventh consecutive victory cut Habana's lead to just one game. With both teams able to spend the next week trying to beat up on the two lesser teams in the league, Cienfuegos and Marianao, a three-game series between Habana and Almendares in the final week of the season loomed large.

Almendares's seven-game winning streak finally ended on February 16. Marianao starting pitcher Sandalio Consuegra limited the Scorpions to six hits as the Gray Monks won 6–0. Ángel Castro, whose batting average had been hovering around .200, drove in three runs, and Beto Ávila went 4-for-4 and scored twice. On the same day, Habana beat Cienfuegos 7–2 as Cocaína García tossed a complete-game two-hitter to end the Lions' two-game losing streak. It was García's tenth win of the season, but only Habana's second victory in six games. Klein, Thompson, and Pearson, who had struggled badly during Habana's slump, came alive at the plate. Klein and Thompson each went 2-for-4 and Pearson went 3-for-5. Each drove in a run.

As members of the Brooklyn Dodgers began arriving in Havana for spring training, the Lions were beating Marianao 3–0 on February 19 and Cienfuegos 10–5 on February 20. Habana's Fred Martin held Marianao to three hits in a complete-game victory, his ninth of the season. Against Ciefuegos, Habana rapped out 14 hits, including a 4-for-4 performance by Lou Klein, who doubled twice and scored four runs. He had batted .115 (3-for-26) during the seven-game stretch before Habana's three-game winning streak. But during the streak, Klein batted .667 (8-for-12). His resurgence at the plate gave Klein a .322 batting average, elevating him into first place for the league's batting title over Marianao's Ávila (.321), teammate Thompson (.319), and Almendares's Fleitas (.317).

While Habana was rattling off three straight victories to halt its slide, Almendares rebounded from its loss to Marianao with a three-game winning streak of its own. Agapito Mayor, one of the driving forces in Almendares's stunning climb up the standings in February, won his fourth consecutive complete-game start on February 18. Two of those first three victories had come against Cienfuegos, and the Elephants once again were the victims—this time by a 2–0 score after twice losing 2–1 to Mayor in the first week of the month. George Hausmann drove in all the runs the Scorpions would need with a two-run single in the second inning. Then on just two days' rest, Mayor entered a game against Cienfuegos on Friday, February 21, pitched 4⅓ innings in relief, and picked up the victory as Almendares won 9–4.

Earlier on that Friday, the Dodgers had held their first workout at El Gran Stadium. On Saturday, Jackie Robinson arrived in Havana to join his Montreal Royals teammates for spring training. At El Gran Stadium, it was Almendares's hitting that carried the afternoon against Marianao. Among the Scorpions' seventeen hits were a home run by Santos Amaro, triples by Roberto Ortiz and Hausmann, and a double by starting pitcher Tomás de la Cruz. Héctor Rodríguez had three hits. Avelino Cañizares, Buck O'Neil, Hausmann, Ortiz, Amaro, and De la Cruz had two hits apiece. De la Cruz, in his complete-game 12–2 victory, allowed eight hits while striking out four and walking just one batter. It was the Scorpions' tenth victory in its past eleven games. "We just thought we could win," Lanier said of the streak. "Everybody went out there and played great ball."[19] The next day, Almendares and Habana would begin their scheduled three-game, three-day series against each other to determine the 1946–47 Cuban League championship. Habana topped the standings with a record of 40 wins and 22 losses. Almendares, in second place at 39–24, had a 1½-game deficit to make up on the league leaders. "We had to win thirteen games to be able to win the championship," Agapito Mayor remembered years later. "And Habana only had to win one [of the final three], so it was a very, very difficult series. . . . If we lost one game, it was over."[20]

Havana awoke on Sunday, February 23, to the words of *Diario de la Marina* columnist Eladio Secades proclaiming the sentiment that filled the city. "Since yesterday the shouts from the streets, the emotion from the grandstand, the public enthusiasm is for Almendares," he wrote. "The phrase of faith in the blue can be heard everywhere."[21] It was true. Almendares had mounted a remarkable comeback. At the start of the month, the Scorpions were looking up in the standings at Habana, six games behind the league leaders. Eleven victories in fourteen games had lifted Almendares to within a game and a half of the lead. But a difficult task still lay ahead if the Scorpions were to win the pennant. Three games in three days against Habana. Lose once, and Almendares would need Cienfuegos to beat Habana in the season finale. That would leave the Eternal Rivals tied and force a playoff. But sweep the Lions, and the Scorpions would be champions.

For the first game of the series, Almendares manager Adolfo Luque sent left-hander Max Lanier to the mound against the Lions. Habana manager Miguel Ángel González countered with Pedro "Natilla" Jiménez, choosing the righty to start against Almendares's heavily right-handed-hitting lineup. With ten wins and three losses, Cocaína García was Habana's top pitcher, but the lefty was potentially vulnerable to Almendares's righty hitters. Right-handed pitcher Fred Martin, who was second on the Lions with nine victories, was an option for González. But starting Jiménez, whose record was 6–2, allowed

González to keep Martin as his ace in the hole for the second game, should Habana lose the first to Lanier. El Monstruo had won four of his five starts against the Lions since coming to Almendares in a mid-season trade. "He didn't pitch well" with his former team, Marianao, Almendares catcher Andrés Fleitas said. "Once he was with Almendares, he started pitching well. I think playing with a better team inspired him. He pushed himself."[22]

After Marianao beat Cienfuegos 3–0 in the meaningless first game of Sunday's doubleheader, what Lester Bromberg of the *New York World-Telegram* described as "37,000 banner-waving, shrieking fans" filled El Gran Stadium for the day's marquee matchup.[23] The crowd also included "twenty-five sobersides Dodgers," who were passing time before their exhibition games by taking in the action that had Havana in a frenzy.[24]

It appeared as though Lanier might not fare as well in this outing as he had in his previous starts against Habana. The Lions tagged Lanier for three first-inning hits, including a run-scoring double by Lou Klein. Lennie Pearson drove in the other run as Habana took a 2–0 lead. But Almendares bounced back in the top of the second inning, scoring three times themselves as Buck O'Neil, Lanier, and Avelino Cañizares each drove in a run. The Scorpions added another run in the sixth.

Five errors proved to be Habana's downfall. Habana shortstop Hank Thompson booted a potential double-play grounder that led to one Almendares run. Another run scored on Lions catcher Salvador Hernández's errant throw trying to catch a runner going to third base. While Habana's defense was coming apart, Lanier settled down after his first-inning jitters. He struck out only two batters and surrendered nine hits, but he gave up only one walk and never allowed Habana to string together enough hits to mount a comeback. The result was a 4–2 Almendares victory that cut Habana's league lead to just a half game. "I didn't have much trouble the first game," Lanier remembered years later.[25]

Before baseball games were being organized in the 1890s to fund Cuba's fight for independence from Spanish rule, José Martí took an interest in the sport while in exile in the United States. The father of Cuban independence noted, "In every neighborhood there is a baseball game. Children . . . in New York like baseball and pistols more than they like books. . . . They go into the streets and hide from the police to play baseball in the courtyards."[26] Martí launched the War of Independence, Cuba's third and final revolt against Spain, on February 24, 1895. His orchestrated uprising began simultaneously against Spanish troops in four Cuban cities—Bayate, Ibarra, Guantánamo, and Baire.[27] But the insurrection came to be known for just one of those cities, as El Grito de Baire, the Cry of Baire.

It was on the national holiday commemorating the start of that war that the second of three games between Almendares and Habana to decide the 1946–47 Cuban League championship was set to be played: Monday, February 24. The damp and rainy day began with Andrés Fleitas nursing a cold and fever when he arrived at the ballpark for the three o'clock contest. With a .308 average coming into the game, the Almendares catcher had fallen behind Habana's Lou Klein (.328), Marianao's Beto Ávila (.324), and Habana's Hank Thompson (.313) in the race for the league's batting title. But Fleitas's presence in the Scorpions' lineup was vital, so the trainer administered a simple remedy: a shot of brandy.[28]

With Fleitas's playing time secured, Agapito Mayor took the mound to start the game for Almendares. Mayor's wife was too nervous to attend the crucial game. "I didn't go to the game he pitched. I said, 'No, I'm not going to go,' and I stayed home," Gloria Mayor recounted years later. "I heard it on the radio."[29] Agapito Mayor's Habana counterpart in that game was Fred Martin. "Miguel Ángel wanted to give the game to his favorite pitcher," Agapito recalled. "His star was Fred Martin. He always put him pitching against me."[30]

The game remained scoreless through 3½ innings before Almendares drew first blood in the bottom of the fourth. After Lloyd Davenport led off the inning with a walk, Roberto Ortiz tried, unsuccessfully, to lay down a sacrifice bunt. Swinging away, the Scorpions slugger drove a pitch to deep center field, where Habana's Pedro Formental tracked it down for the first out. But after Davenport stole second base, Santos Amaro singled over third baseman Lou Klein's head to drive in

Davenport with Almendares's first run of the game. The narrow advantage continued until the seventh inning, when a tactical decision by Miguel Ángel González allowed another Almendares run and opened the Habana manager to vocal criticism.

Lennie Pearson led off the top of the seventh with a single to center field and advanced to second base on Hank Thompson's sacrifice bunt. González, wanting a right-handed hitter to bat against the lefty Mayor, sent infielder Carlos Blanco to pinch-hit for left-handed-hitting right fielder Woody Bell. The strategy didn't work. Blanco lifted a blooper into shallow left field. Almendares shortstop Avelino Cañizares caught the ball despite colliding with left fielder Santos Amaro, who was already camped under the Texas leaguer. With two outs, Mayor intentionally walked Habana catcher Salvador Hernández. Martin grounded into an unassisted force play at second to end the Lions' threat. But González's real strategic mistake came in the bottom half of the inning.

Despite having experienced outfielders—Henry Kimbro, René Monteagudo, Pablo García, and Cocoliso Torres—on the bench, González opted to keep the right-handed-hitting Blanco, an infielder by trade, in the game in right field, a position he had never played. With one out, Almendares's George Hausmann reached on an infield hit. Habana shortstop Hank Thompson stopped the ball but was unable to make a throw to get Hausmann, who was known in Cuba as Ardilla, or Squirrel, because of his speed. Up to the plate stepped the Scorpions' right-handed-hitting catcher. "Fleitas, who normally hit to the other side, hit a line drive to right field that totally confused Carlos Blanco," according to broadcaster Felo Ramírez, who called the game for radio station COCO.[31] Blanco froze for a moment before realizing he needed to back up on what writer René Molina called a "savage drive."[32] It was too late. The ball landed over Blanco's head in right-center field and rolled to the fence for a triple that drove home Hausmann to give Almendares a 2–0 lead. Blanco "misjudged the fly ball," Lanier said. "That put us in good position."[33]

It did more than that, producing a run that proved crucial, as Habana rallied in the top of the eighth inning. Blanco's brother, Heberto, tripled to left-center field with one out in the frame. Pablo García, pinch-hitting for Pedro Formental, hit a long sacrifice fly to bring home

Heberto Blanco and cut Almendares's lead to 2–1. But that was the only run the Lions could muster, as Lou Klein and Alberto "Sagüita" Hernández failed to connect for the final two outs of the inning. Habana mounted another threat in the top of the ninth. Pearson led off with a single to center, but when Thompson tried to bunt him over, Mayor pounced on the ball and threw out Pearson at second base. Kimbro, who had entered the game in place of Carlos Blanco, grounded out to Buck O'Neil at first base for the second out. After Salvador Hernández walked, Torres pinch-hit for Martin. Mayor induced Torres to pop up. "Behind home plate," Fleitas said, "I had to catch the last out in the crowd."[34]

The misty rain that had fallen since early morning did not cease until after Fleitas made the final out. When he squeezed the foul ball that vaulted Almendares into first place by a half game, Agapito Mayor embraced his catcher "in an uncontrollable overflow of joy," Diario de la Marina's René Molina wrote.[35] Years later Mayor would say, "If I don't win that game, we never would have been champions. If I had lost, it would have been over."[36] In the stands, the crowd erupted in an ovation "without precedent," according to Molina.[37] The loudest shout at the end of the day, however, came from Habana manager Miguel Ángel González, whose cry "according to those who heard it in the clubhouse reached the skies."[38] Molina was cutting in his assessment of González's managerial machinations: "Mike, who has seen the seemingly indestructible advantage enjoyed by his cast crumble, seems to have lost equanimity and the mental capacity that characterize him as a mentor."[39]

The crucial final contest of the three-game series remained to be played the next day. A victory by Almendares would give the Scorpions the championship. But a victory by Habana would mean Almendares would have to hope Cienfuegos could defeat the Lions in the season finale on Tuesday just to force a playoff for the title. Despite much yet to be decided, the sportswriters at Sunday's game had released their vote for the season's most valuable player. Fleitas received 20 of the possible 25 votes to earn the honor. Habana's Klein received the other 5. Was the writers' choice of Almendares's catcher a harbinger of what would take place on Monday? The more important question was this: Who would pitch?

⚑

Speculation in the February 25 editions of *Diario de la Marina* focused again on who would pitch that Tuesday's potentially decisive game, which was scheduled to start at three o'clock. For Habana, both Cocaína García and Terris McDuffie were well rested, neither having pitched in more than a week. McDuffie was still nursing a sore arm, so "everything suggests that González will need to appeal to 'Coca,'" the newspaper predicted.[40] For Almendares, a theory that had gained momentum was that Max Lanier, on just one day's rest, would take the mound. But Scorpions manager Adolfo Luque hadn't given any indication. "If it's not Lanier," a story previewing the game concluded, "then the choice would be between Tomás de la Cruz and Jorge Comellas."[41]

Fans began lining up outside El Gran Stadium an hour before the gates opened at ten in the morning. By eleven the stands were filled. Two hours before the opening pitch, the overflow had spilled onto the field and ropes had to be used to cordon off spectators along the first- and third-base lines. "It was incredible," Fleitas said. "I calculated that there were close to forty thousand fans, with the thirty-thousand-plus that fit in the stadium and the two to three thousand that were on the field."[42] Among the spectators were Jackie Robinson and other players from the Montreal Royals and Brooklyn Dodgers. Outside the gates of the packed stadium, thousands were turned away. Hoping for a glimpse of the historic game, a group of young men risked electrocution by climbing the light towers just beyond the left-field fence. The stadium's chief electrician was dispatched to urge them to abandon their perch. They refused. "It was bedlam," Felo Ramírez said. "Cuba was paralyzed. The country shut down. For the last game, the parliament didn't hold a session. All the representatives of the government were at the game. No one worked that day. It was something contagious, the fanaticism."[43]

In the Almendares clubhouse, a deal was being brokered to determine the Scorpions' starter. Luque approached Lanier about pitching in the decisive game. "We'll give you five hundred dollars if you pitch the third game and win it," Luque offered. Lanier countered with his own proposal. "I won't pitch it that way," he said. "I'll pitch it for five hundred dollars, win or lose, because I only have one day's rest."[44] It was a bold stance by Lanier, given Luque's penchant for erupting against a player unwilling to bow to his will. "He didn't let anybody step on his toes," Lanier said. "I liked him. He treated me like his own son."[45] Perhaps it was Luque's warm feelings for Lanier; the manager, after all, had given his pitcher leeway to fly back to Florida several times during the season. Perhaps it was that Lanier had been a stalwart in the rotation since coming to Almendares from Marianao in the trade in December. Perhaps Luque simply understood the importance of the game. Whatever his motivation, he acquiesced.

Luque was not always so accommodating with reluctant pitchers. While managing Almendares during the 1939–40 Cuban League season, Luque removed Negro leagues star Ted "Double Duty" Radcliffe from a game at La Tropical stadium. Afterward a loud bang rang out in the clubhouse. Fellow Almendares pitcher Rodolfo Fernández had to knock Luque's arm to hinder the manager's aim. Luque had tried to shoot Radcliffe, who "the enraged manager claimed was not giving his all," Cuban baseball historian Roberto González Echevarría wrote. "It was stated in court that Luque had slammed a door hard in anger, and the episode came to be known as *el portazo de Luque* (Luque's door slam)."[46]

Later in Luque's career, with Marianao, it was Terris McDuffie who experienced the manager's gun-wielding ways. Hall of Fame major-league manager Tommy Lasorda, who pitched for Marianao and Almendares during the 1950s and called Luque "the worst human being I have ever known,"[47] described the encounter in his 1985 book *The Artful Dodger*. While pitching for Marianao in 1952–53, McDuffie one day balked at Luque's order to pitch on two days' rest. McDuffie's refusal prompted Luque to retrieve a pistol from his office and point it at McDuffie's head. That was enough to persuade the pitcher to head for the mound, and he proceeded to throw a two-hitter. But Luque didn't resort to such tactics with Lanier. And when it was announced over the stadium's public-address system that the lefty would take the mound for Almendares on less than forty-eight hours' rest, "a deafening ovation ignited from one end of the stands to the other."[48] Among the fans was the wife of Lanier's teammate Agapito Mayor. Gloria Mayor could not bear the stress of watching her husband pitch the previous day, but "after he won, the next day I went, when Lanier pitched," she recalled. "I was very fond of Lanier, but it was not the same as watching Mayor pitch. I said, 'OK, now I'll go, and whatever God wants will happen.'"[49]

For Habana, it would not be Cocaína García or McDuffie countering Lanier. Instead, rookie right-hander Lázaro Medina was announced as the Lions' starter. What followed in the stands was "a long murmur that was mixed with uncertainty, mistrust, and resignation," René Molina wrote.[50] During a pregame ceremony at home plate, Andrés Fleitas was presented with a check, the proceeds of a collection taken up by brothers Luis and Raúl Pazo Fernández for Fleitas's having been named the league's most valuable player the previous day. Even before Medina took the mound, the Almendares catcher sensed what might be coming. "Miguel Ángel González, I don't know if he made a mistake or not, but he put his faith in rookie Lázaro Medina for the last game," Fleitas recalled. "He didn't last long."[51]

A sign of how the game would play out came in the first inning when Almendares right fielder Roberto Ortiz made a superb catch on a drive by Habana's Lou Klein. "The magnificent trap," René Molina wrote, "exposed the spirit of the fight, the confidence, the enthusiasm of those who had come from so far down to produce the surprise of the year."[52] Almendares took the early lead, scoring a run in the second inning. After Héctor Rodríguez walked, the Scorpions executed a hit-and-run with Buck O'Neil grounding to Lou Klein. The Habana third baseman charged the ball and threw out O'Neil at first. On the play, Rodríguez rounded second and kept running for third. Klein returned to the bag in time to make the out, but first baseman Lennie Pearson's errant throw landed in the cordoned-off crowd along the left-field line, allowing Rodríguez to race home.

Medina got into more trouble in the third inning. To open the frame, he walked Avelino Cañizares and surrendered a scorching single to left by George Hausmann. Fleitas's sacrifice bunt put runners on second and third. Cañizares and Hausmann scored when Lloyd Davenport lined a Medina pitch inside the right-field foul line that bounced into the crowd for a ground-rule double. Ortiz's single to left field drove home Davenport, giving Almendares a 4–0 lead. Medina got out of the inning without further damage, but he was out of the game after the fourth inning. The Scorpions put the game away with a five-run outburst off reliever Pedro "Natilla" Jiménez in the seventh inning. Santos Amaro drove in a run with a single, Lanier and Cañizares each walked with the bases loaded to force in a run, and O'Neil and Lanier scored when second baseman Heberto Blanco couldn't handle a sharply hit grounder by Hausmann that caromed into center field.

While his teammates were hitting their way through four Habana pitchers, Lanier was overpowering Habana's batters. He held the Lions scoreless until the eighth inning, when Klein drove in Habana's only two runs on a bad-hop single that bounced over Cañizares's head at shortstop. "I don't think anyone could have beaten him that game," Fleitas said. "He threw many different pitches, fastballs, curves, off-speed pitches, but on that day, he said his fastball felt good. He threw nothing except fastballs. I calculate he was throwing ninety, ninety-plus [miles per hour] the entire game."[53] From the stands, then-seventeen-year-old fan Leonardo Agüero watched the culmination of Almendares's miraculous comeback. "Of those three [final] games, I saw two," he recalled years later. "I saw the first game and the third game. . . . Max Lanier's games, I saw both. I'll remember that my whole life. They were games for the ages."[54] When the final out was recorded, fans ran onto the field, mobbing the players. "Max Lanier was practically suffocating," Fleitas said, "because the fans rushed the field."[55]

After the players clawed their way off the field, they celebrated their unlikely championship in the Almendares clubhouse, where Lanier continued receiving the spoils of war. "The fans really went crazy over there," Lanier recalled. "One of them come to the door and wanted to speak to me. When I did, he handed me a hundred dollar bill. They kept knocking and I had seventeen hundred dollar bills."[56] Once the clubhouse celebration concluded, Lanier left intending to return to his apartment so he could pack up and catch a flight to his home in St. Petersburg, Florida. But when he appeared outside the stadium, the lingering crowd mobbed the Almendares pitcher. "I couldn't get out of the ball park," Lanier recalled. "All of them wanted my clothes and everything. I run back in and called a taxi that picked me up underneath the stands."[57] As the cab drove off with Lanier, three truckloads of fans followed the taxi to Lanier's apartment and then on to the airport to wish him bon voyage. "I guess they were just excited," Lanier said, "and wanted to see me as long as they could."[58]

In the press box, Eladio Secades was writing the column that would appear in the next day's *Diario de la Marina*. In it Secades would muse about how differently things appeared less than two months earlier when Habana had held a commanding six-game lead. "What, you don't remember? Cuba was a display of red rags," Secades wrote. Then, referring to Almendares owner Dr. Julio Sanguily, "July Sanguily's phrase diagnosing the death of any who would dare to beat Almendares was the object of ridicule and bloody satires. The boast was laughable. Whoever defeats Almendares, dies. . . . No one believed in the return of the dead."[59] But rise from the dead is what Almendares had done, and the Scorpions' revival ignited a wild celebration that spread through the streets of Havana and across Cuba. "It was something incredible," Mayor recalled. "The entire city flooded the streets. It was the biggest victory in [Cuban] baseball. Incredible."[60] Gloria Mayor remembered how screaming fans stormed the streets after the game. "We had to lock the doors to the house," she said, "because we thought fans would knock the house down."[61]

Outside El Gran Stadium, jubilant Almendares fans carried a red-painted toy lion in a small, makeshift white casket for a "funeral procession" through the streets of Havana. El Velorio del León, the Lion's Wake, had begun at a nearby funeral home and meandered past the stadium, where Fleitas joined some 150 or 200 fans. "That was wonderful," he recalled. "That was the fanaticism that existed. They grabbed me and made me join them walking from the stadium through the streets. . . . I walked, but I had to stop. I lived near the Hotel San Luis. I told them, 'I can't walk anymore.' I was tired from the game."[62] The procession continued without Fleitas toward the Colón Cemetery and concluded when the fans cast the departed lion's casket adrift on the nearby Almendares River. Elsewhere, Cuba's capital took on a carnival atmosphere as thousands took to the streets. Fans packed trolley cars, filled bars, danced in improvised congas, set off fireworks, and released blue balloons. "Whew, they turned it out," O'Neil remembered. "Everybody was excited. They had people riding all over the streets in cars, hanging onto streetcars, blowing horns, with ribbons and banners and everything. Oh, Havana was outstanding, really."[63] And the revelry spread beyond the capital. "It wasn't just Havana. It was general," Fleitas recalled. "All the Cuban territories, Santiago de Cuba, Matanzas, Santa Clara, Pinar del Río, and Havana. . . . It was the championship with the most enthusiasm."[64] Fan Leonardo Agüero described the celebration, which lasted two or three days, as "a national festival."[65]

René Molina put the celebration into a larger context. "I confess that on only two occasions have I felt that same impression of collective bustle in Havana," he wrote, "when the peace treaty was signed after the recent world war and when Dr. Grau San Martín climbed to power" by winning Cuba's presidential election in 1944.[66] Once dawn broke on Wednesday, February 26, once all the festivities of the previous night had ceased and the collective hangover was beginning to set in, there was also the realization that the 1946–47 Cuban League season was not, in fact, over. Two meaningless games remained to be played. Habana, having choked away a six-game lead to lose the championship, barely put up a fight on Wednesday in an 8–3 loss to hapless Cienfuegos. On Thursday the season officially concluded with Cienfuegos beating Marianao 2–1 in a battle of the league's two cellar-dwelling teams.

Cienfuegos's back-to-back victories kept the Elephants from finishing in last place—by themselves. They tied Marianao with a record of 25 wins and 41 losses. Managing and playing in his final Cuban League season, Cienfuegos's Martín Dihigo, a Cuban baseball icon, finished his managerial career with a record of 142 wins and 129 losses. He batted .091 in just eleven at-bats and had a 1–3 record as a pitcher. Cienfuegos teammate Adrián Zabala tied Marianao's Sandalio Consuegra for the league lead with 11 victories. Habana's Manuel "Cocaína" García had the best winning percentage with a 10–3 record (.769). The hitting categories were dominated by players from Almendares and Habana. The Lions' Lennie Pearson drove in a league-leading 45 runs, and Almendares's Roberto Ortiz led with 11 home runs. Habana's Lou Klein finished with a .330 average to win the batting title, topping Marianao's Beto Ávila (.323), teammate Hank Thompson (.320), and Almendares's Andrés Fleitas (.316). Fleitas, who also led the league with 83 hits and drove in 43 runs, earned MVP honors. "As far as I'm concerned," Fleitas said, "it was one of the greatest series, one of the greatest championships Cuba has ever seen."[67]

Opening Day, Brooklyn

The Dodgers played their final exhibition game in Panama on Friday, March 21, defeating Panama General Electric 5–0. The next day, the Dodgers and Royals flew back to Havana to continue spring training. Outfielder Dixie Walker was not on the flight. The Georgia native and longtime Alabama resident had been in Panama for Leo Durocher's late-night tirade denouncing the petition against Jackie Robinson. But Walker left Panama a day later to be with family in Miami. He returned to Havana by boat to rejoin the Dodgers. Upon his arrival in Cuba, Walker was summoned to Dodgers president Branch Rickey's room at the Hotel Nacional. As he had with Bobby Bragan and other petition conspirators in Panama, Rickey wanted to confront Walker face-to-face about the petition and the possibility of Robinson being promoted to the Dodgers.

Walker did not react well to Rickey's confrontation. "He really reamed me out," he told *New York Times* writer Ira Berkow in 1981. "I was so mad at him accusing me of being a ringleader that a few days later I wrote him this letter requesting to be traded."[1] Handwritten on a yellow piece of paper and dated March 26, 1947, Walker's letter read:

Dear Mr. Rickey,

Recently, the thought has occurred to me that a change of ball clubs would benefit both the Brooklyn Dodgers and myself. Therefore, I would like to be traded as soon as a deal could be arranged. My association with you, the people of Brooklyn, the press and radio has been very pleasant, and one I can truthfully say I am sorry has to end. For reasons I don't care to go into, I feel my decision is best for all concerned.[2]

Walker was the only Dodger to request a trade in writing. Rickey eventually granted his wish, sending "the People's Cherce" from Brooklyn to the Pittsburgh Pirates after the 1947 season. But Walker wasn't the only Dodger to resent Robinson's presence. "The white players did not want us there," Don Newcombe said. "They knew we were there to take a white boy's job."[3]

At least one white player on the Dodgers did not allow his southern upbringing to dictate how he treated Robinson. Kentuckian Pee Wee Reese refused to entertain talk of petition. "The one that really stopped that was Pee Wee Reese," said Buzzie Bavasi, Class-B Nashua's general manager in 1947. "Reese, who was from Louisville, took over and told all the other young men on the team that Robinson was a hell of a player. It was very clear he was in Robinson's corner."[4] Despite Walker's being one of his best friends on the team, when Walker tried to get Reese to sign the petition against Robinson's potential promotion to the majors, he declined. Reese "looked at it and I just flatly refused," he said. "I just said, 'Hey look, man, I just got out of the service after three years. I don't care if this man is black, blue, or what the hell color he is. I have to play baseball.'"[5]

Jorge Pasquel's failed attempts to sign Dodgers for the Mexican League earlier in spring training seemed an odd strategy. Despite his millions, the Mexican League was in financial trouble—a fact Pasquel all but admitted before he flew to Cuba to deal with his league's impending crisis over player contract holdouts. "The fact that I have much money has been mistakenly interpreted," he said in a press release. "That's no reason for giving it away."[6] Pasquel was trying to cut many league salaries in half. And almost all of the 120 Mexican League players on Cuban League rosters—approximately 80 percent of the players in Mexico—had joined groups intent on holding out for more money from the Mexican League. Tomás de la Cruz led the group of Cuban players, Roland Gladu and Jean Roy led the white North American players, Lloyd Davenport the Negro leaguers, and Beto Ávila the Mexican players.[7]

During his recent trip to Havana, Pasquel did not speak to holdouts Max Lanier or Lou Klein. "They know they must reach an understanding with me regarding their salaries for 1947. Lanier was paid $25,000 in 1946. He won only five games for my Veracruz team. That's $5,000 per victory, and that's too much," Pasquel said. "Klein also wasn't the player in Mexico that he was in Cuba this winter."[8] Pasquel's penchant for hyperbole was on full display. In fact, Lanier had gone 8–3 with a stellar 1.93 earned run average in his first Mexican League season. The *Sporting News* listed Lanier's 1946 salary at $14,000.[9] And Pasquel's slap at Klein also was unfounded, given Klein's .335 batting average in his first season in Mexico.

More likely, Pasquel's exaggerations were an attempt to rationalize the Mexican League's sudden need for austerity. Such financial constraints led Pasquel to abandon—at least temporarily—his attempts to lure more stars south of the border. Would stopping his raids of expensive major leaguers quell the rebellion among his league's players and its teams over the exorbitant contracts he had already given out? It wasn't enough to save two teams from financial trouble. During a March 11 meeting in Mexico City, it was announced that the Nuevo Laredo and Torreón teams had withdrawn from the league. The league had lost approximately 1.25 million pesos, or $250,000 in U.S. money, during the 1946 season.[10] And two league mainstays, Monterrey and Puebla, were on the verge of dropping out as well. But Pasquel assured his fellow owners that "there will always be a Mexican League."[11] The desertions left a six-team league with clubs in Veracruz, Monterrey, San Luis Potosí, Tampico, Mexico City, and Puebla. The circuit would open on Thursday, March 27, instead of March 13 or 20 so players from

Nuevo Laredo and Torreón could be dispersed among the remaining teams.

A week before the delayed start of the 1947 Mexican League season, some nineteen players, including twelve banned by organized baseball, were not listed on any Mexican League rosters.[12] Among those not agreeing to renewed contracts were former New York Giants George Hausmann, Danny Gardella, and Roy Zimmerman and ex–St. Louis Cardinals Klein, Lanier, and Fred Martin. "The only reason I went [to Mexico] was because I just wasn't making enough money [in the majors]," Lanier said years later. "They offered me a good salary, but they just didn't keep their promise. That was the problem down there. They cut our salaries in half."[13] It had been reported that many of these players had signed big, multiyear contracts to play in Mexico. But the Associated Press quoted unnamed league officials refuting those claims, saying the players had "signed one year contracts with option clauses, but they have to bargain for the salaries each year."[14]

Leo Durocher briefly returned to the Dodgers' base camp in Cuba on Friday, March 21. The next day, he served as first base coach as the Dodgers beat a Cuban all-star squad 5–2. Durocher's wife, Laraine Day, watched the proceedings from a box seat behind the Dodgers dugout.[15] The couple were back in Havana ahead of Durocher's March 24 hearing in Sarasota, Florida, before baseball commissioner Happy Chandler over the complaint filed by Larry MacPhail. The Yankees president accused Durocher and Rickey of libel, slander, and conduct detrimental to baseball for insinuating he had hosted known gamblers in his private box at El Gran Stadium.

The list of witnesses to be interrogated by Chandler was lengthy: on the Yankees side, MacPhail, part owner Dan Topping, coach Charlie Dressen, and traveling secretary John "Red" Corriden; on the Dodgers side, Durocher, traveling secretary Harold Parrott, who had ghost-written Durocher's Brooklyn Eagle columns, former Dodgers outfielder Augie Galan, and former Brooklyn scout Ted McGrew. Missing from the hearing was Branch Rickey. The day before the hearing, MacPhail referred to Rickey as "the one we're gunning for."[16] The Dodgers president had to fly from Havana to Lucasville, Ohio, for the funeral of his brother-in-law John Moulton. Rickey had unsuccessfully requested a postponement of the hearing. With Rickey absent, the Dodgers were represented at the hearing by part owner Walter O'Malley, Branch Rickey Jr., writer Arthur Mann, and former Missouri senator George H. Williams. MacPhail, Topping, and American League president Will Harridge represented the Yankees.

The hearing convened in the glass-enclosed penthouse of the Sarasota Terrace Hotel. Durocher, the first scheduled witness, entered the hearing at 3:45 p.m., 45 minutes late after setting up his wife in another hotel, away from the press's prying eyes. After spending 45 minutes in the hearing, Durocher "retired to the bar, where he sipped a coke, showered the press with 'no comments,' and took bows."[17] The hearing lasted four and a half hours. Like Durocher, none of the witnesses discussed what took place behind those closed doors. They had been sworn to secrecy by Chandler. Years later, Durocher recounted the events of the hearing in his 1975 autobiography. After Chandler instructed MacPhail to read the offending "Durocher Says" articles from the *Brooklyn Eagle*, Durocher insisted, "I didn't mean anything derogatory about you. . . . Maybe I have needled you a little bit in there, but to me it was nothing personal."[18] When the Brooklyn manager offered to apologize publicly, MacPhail tore up the articles and hugged Durocher.

But if MacPhail was satisfied, it quickly became apparent Chandler was not. The commissioner asked Durocher about crap shooting and high-stakes card games in the Dodgers clubhouse before turning his inquiries to Durocher's quotes about Engelberg and Immerman. Durocher told Chandler that "although I had never seen the quotes in the paper and couldn't remember exactly what I said, word for word, I sure had spoken my mind."[19] Chandler finally dismissed Durocher from the hearing with an admonition: "You cannot discuss one word of this with anyone. When you walk out this door you are forever silenced."[20]

With Durocher out of the room, the hearing continued with testimony from the remainder of the witness list. Although he did not testify, *New York Sun* sportswriter Herbert Goren submitted an affidavit in which he reportedly shot down MacPhail's defense that Engelberg and Immerman had not been his guests at El Gran Stadium. According to Goren's affidavit, Engelberg said that while he and Immerman did sit in the box adjoining MacPhail's, they were in fact MacPhail's guests.[21] But according to Dan Daniel of the *Sporting News*, Chandler never learned of Engelberg's assertion he had received his tickets from MacPhail. Rickey, perhaps trying to extricate himself from the feud with MacPhail, did not allow Dodgers part owner Walter O'Malley to present Goren's affidavit to the commissioner during the hearing.[22]

In the hotel bar, the one person with whom Durocher discussed the hearing was Chandler's wife, Mildred. She reassured the Dodgers manager there was nothing to worry about. The other members of the Dodgers contingent at the hearing apparently agreed. After the hearing, Harold Parrott sent a telegram to Rickey saying, "BROOKLYN WINS ANOTHER."[23] Once the hearing concluded, Chandler said he would reserve judgment until after he had reviewed all the evidence. He also announced he would meet privately with Rickey and MacPhail on Friday, March 28.[24]

Back in Havana from their side trip to Panama, the Dodgers beat Gilberto Torres's Cuban all-stars 5–2 on Saturday, March 22. Ralph Branca held the Cuban team to one hit over six innings, while the Dodgers tagged Conrado Marrero for all five of their runs. The next day, the Dodgers shelled Torres's all-star selection 12–4. Orestes Miñoso, Lorenzo "Chiquitín" Cabrera, and Pedro Pagés each had a pair of hits for the Cuban squad, but pitchers Sandalio Consuegra, Lino Dinoso, Antonio Nápoles, and Ray Gavilán combined to give up nineteen hits. Dodgers catcher Bruce Edwards and pitcher Vic Lombardi had three hits each, while Eddie Stanky, Gene Hermanski, Pee Wee Reese, and Dick Whitman each collected two. If Dixie Walker's mind weighed heavy from his meeting with Rickey, he showed no sign, going 2-for-4 and scoring a pair of runs.

On Wednesday, March 26, the Dodgers and the Montreal Royals opened a seven-game series, with the Dodgers winning 6–0. Jackie Robinson was out of the Royals lineup because of a stomach ailment, the result of the local cuisine, which was heavy on fried food. "That plus the fact that he was under constant pressure emotionally," *Baltimore Afro-American* sportswriter Sam Lacy said, "gave him problems he would normally never have."[25] Roy Campanella went 1-for-1 for the Royals. Teammate Kevin Connors went 1-for-4. The six-foot-five first baseman, who also played for the Boston Celtics from 1946 to 1948, later became more famous as Hollywood actor Chuck Connors than he ever did as a Dodgers farmhand. Catcher Mike Sandlock was a teammate of Connors on the Royals and later on a Cuban League championship Almendares team. "He wanted to be an actor so bad," Sandlock said. In 1951, when Sandlock was going to play with the Triple-A Hollywood Stars, Connors "got in my ear, and he says, 'When you get there, do some talking for me. I want to be up there.' Suddenly he got hooked up in L.A. The next thing you know, he got his foot in the door with acting."[26]

Durocher finally got to see Robinson in action as the Dodgers won the next meeting on Friday, March 28. Robinson, back in the lineup despite his ongoing stomach problems, went 1-for-3, but "he was far off his usual brilliant form, being guilty of two errors,"[27] Roscoe McGowen wrote in the *New York Times*. The two plays Robinson booted at first base led to four of the Dodgers' runs as Brooklyn beat the Royals 5–2.

That day, the hearings addressing MacPhail's charges against Durocher and Rickey shifted to the Pennsylvania Hotel in St. Petersburg, Florida. Instead of testimony from multiple witnesses, this second meeting with Chandler included only Rickey and MacPhail. The Associated Press's story previewing the meeting declared that "no one now expects the Commissioner to do anything drastic to any of the leading figures in the quarrel, including manager Leo Durocher."[28]

Like the hearing in Sarasota, this meeting lasted four and a half hours and ended without resolution. MLB's secretary-treasurer, Walter Mulbry, informed the press that Chandler would probably call another hearing after he investigated "a number of things which have developed."[29] Again Chandler instructed the participants not to speak about the proceedings. During the meeting, Rickey reportedly denied accusing MacPhail of entertaining gamblers in his private box at El

Gran Stadium on the nights of March 8 and 9.[30] In his autobiography, however, Durocher wrote that Rickey had not repudiated the quotes attributed to the Dodgers president by the *New York Sun*'s Herbert Goren. Instead, Durocher contended, Rickey told Chandler that even if the quote hadn't been his exact words, "they had expressed his feelings exactly and [Rickey] would stand behind Goren's quote in its entirety."[31]

One indication, however, that the feud between Rickey and MacPhail had somehow been tamped down came during a break in the hearing. MacPhail told reporters, "I would like to talk privately to Mr. Rickey when he comes out if you fellows would give us a chance."[32] The lengthy discussion between the team owners "appeared amiable enough."[33] According to the *Sporting News*'s Dan Daniel, MacPhail demanded during the hearing that Chandler issue a statement about Rickey's denial so as to vindicate MacPhail and repair the Yankees president's reputation. "Chandler said that he could not give out his decision piecemeal," Daniel wrote. "He also said that he had not yet ended his investigation."[34] The consensus among reporters who had covered the meeting was that it would at least result in "an order to Durocher to stop writing columns in the *Brooklyn Eagle*, and a general order forbidding any major league manager from writing for a newspaper."[35]

Nine former major-league players were still unsigned on the eve of the opening of the 1947 Mexican League campaign. Former Cardinals teammates Max Lanier and Fred Martin had yet to reach an agreement with Jorge Pasquel following their 1946–47 Cuban League seasons with Almendares and Habana, respectively. Another ex-Cardinal, Lou Klein, who had played for Veracruz the previous season and Habana during the winter, was not on a roster. Former New York Giants second baseman George Hausmann had returned to San Antonio, Texas, following the conclusion of his Cuban winter-league season with Almendares. Harry Feldman, Ace Adams, Roy Zimmerman, Danny Gardella (who had played with Cienfuegos in the winter), and Habana catcher Salvador Hernández also were no-shows in Mexico.[36]

An estimated crowd of 30,000 jammed into Mexico City's Delta Park—where capacity was 22,000—for the opener between the Mexico City Reds and the Veracruz Blues. Mexico's president Miguel Alemán threw out the ceremonial first pitch. But the absence of key players and the contraction of the league from eight to six clubs meant "the inaugurals were in marked contrast to the fanfare that accompanied them last year,"[37] according to the *Sporting News*. Cuban-born Ramón Bragaña tossed a three-hitter to lead Veracruz to a 6–2 victory against Mexico City. El Profesor, as Bragaña was known in Cuba, surrendered a hit to Ed Stone in the first inning and then retired seventeen consecutive batters before Stone recorded another hit in the eighth.[38]

Bragaña, who was born in Havana on May 11, 1909, was far from the only Cuban connection in the Mexican League that season. Ray Dandridge, who had played with the Cuban League's Marianao team and with Oriente of the rival National Federation during the winter of 1946–47, made his debut as Mexico City's manager. He held that post following the surprise retirement of Ernesto Carmona, one of the founders of the Mexican League and Mexico City's longtime president and manager. Former New York Giants pitcher Adrián Zabala, who had led Cienfuegos with eleven wins in 1946–47, lost his opening-day assignment as Puebla fell 4–1 to San Luis Potosí. On March 30, Zabala led Puebla, managed by Cuban League legend Adolfo Luque, to an 8–5 victory against the same team. Another Cuban baseball legend, Martín Dihigo, who had managed Cienfuegos to a third-place finish in 1946–47, managed San Luis Potosí, the team that replaced the defunct Torreón franchise. And Lázaro Salazar, a longtime pitcher with Almendares, was the player-manager for Monterrey.

Mexico's Beto Ávila, the subject of a brief tryout with the Dodgers earlier in spring training in Havana, decided to join the Mexican League's Puebla team rather than accept an assignment with the International League's Montreal Royals. "I'd rather get one more year's experience in Mexico than in the minors,"[39] said Ávila, who later played with the Cleveland Indians starting in 1949 and won an American League batting title (.341) in 1954. By March 22, Max Lanier and Fred Martin were en route to Mexico to meet with Pasquel in an effort to iron out their respective contracts.[40] With both players banned from organized baseball, reaching an accord with Pasquel appeared to be their only option for playing professional baseball during the summer.

■

Barely more than a week remained before the Dodgers were to break camp in Cuba, and Leo Durocher had watched Jackie Robinson play only once. Durocher's itinerary—traveling from Panama to California to Havana to Florida and back to Cuba—and Robinson's stomach issues had prevented the pair from crossing paths any more than that. Durocher's second impression of Robinson came on Saturday, March 29. It was only slightly better than his first, as Kirby Higbe blanked the Royals for a 7–0 victory. Robinson played for seven innings at first base and went 0-for-2, but he drew a walk in the fourth inning and stole second base on a pickoff play. Despite his stomach problems, Robinson wanted to play "because people might think I was quitting if I didn't."[41]

In that morning's edition of the weekly *Pittsburgh Courier*, Wendell Smith, citing "an unimpeachable source," reported that Robinson would be promoted to the Dodgers on April 10 and would play first base when the team opened the season against the Boston Braves on April 15 in Brooklyn. "The only obstacle in his way currently is the possibility of a wholesale rebellion on the part of the present members of the Brooklyn Club," wrote Smith,[42] perhaps a veiled reference to the Dixie Walker–led petition that had come to the attention of Durocher and Rickey in Panama. Smith's story also declared that Robinson had been informed about his promotion as early as March 5, before the Royals had left Havana on the Panama trip. It was actually Smith who had informed Robinson, making it reasonable to conclude that Smith's unimpeachable source could have been Branch Rickey. Apparently Robinson was not impressed, because he laughed in Smith's face.[43]

But if Robinson's future with the Dodgers was indeed a fait accompli, the final week of spring training in Havana gave no such indication. Robinson's stomach problems limited his effectiveness and playing time, leaving his chances for promotion unclear. When the Royals recorded their first victory in six games against the parent club—a 6–5 win in front of only 800 fans at El Gran Stadium on Sunday, March

30—Robinson did not play, because he was receiving medical attention. Instead he sat in a box seat at the conclusion of the game. Curiously, Durocher was also absent, showing up only at the end of the thirteen-inning marathon.[44]

Branch Rickey certainly gave no public indication of Robinson's future with the club. After insisting that the Dodgers players themselves would decide Robinson's fate, Rickey struck a different tone as the Dodgers beat the Royals 1–0 in a practice game on Monday, March 31. "No player on this club will have anything to say about who plays or who does not play on it," Rickey said as he sat in his box seat at El Gran Stadium. "I will decide who is on it and Durocher will decide who of those who are on it does the playing."[45] In that game, Robinson was suddenly playing second base instead of first, because Royals manager Clay Hopper wanted to see more of Kevin Connors at the corner position. *New York Times* sportswriter Roscoe McGowen wrote that the move raised the question "as to whether his [Robinson's] trial at first base—for a possible promotion to the Brooks at that post—has ended."[46] Adding to the puzzlement was the fact Durocher only watched pregame workouts and batting practice from a seat behind the dugout and was gone by game time.

Although the petition against Robinson had not become general knowledge, perhaps the first public indication of how much it had raised the ire of Branch Rickey and Leo Durocher came on Tuesday, April 1. Durocher, putting in a full appearance for the Dodgers' 6–1 victory against the Royals, was asked about the team's lineup while holding court with the writers before the game. The Dodgers manager named only three players—second baseman Eddie Stanky, shortstop Pee Wee Reese, and catcher Bruce Edwards—as undoubted starters. What about "the People's Cherce," fan favorite Dixie Walker? "No comment" was Durocher's only response.[47] Walker had not been having a particularly good spring, but it was an odd response to a question about one of the team's most popular and productive players.

Four days later, the April 5 editions of the *Baltimore Afro-American*—citing "unimpeachable sources"—reported that Rickey had quashed a player petition seeking to block Robinson's promotion to Brooklyn. The story accurately reported that the petition had been prepared while the Dodgers and Royals were playing in Panama. No Dodgers players involved in the petition were named in the story, but the *Afro-American* reported that Rickey had "learned about the move before all signatures had been obtained. He called in the ring leaders and informed them in no uncertain terms that he would take care of picking the Brooklyn players. . . . Nothing further was heard of the petition."[48]

During the April 1 game between the Dodgers and Royals, Robinson once again found himself playing second base. But Lou Ruchser instead of Connors was at first base. Robinson returned to first base the following day as the Dodgers beat the Royals 12–2. He went hitless in three at-bats and drew a walk. Robinson also had an assist and made ten putouts at first without an error. Rickey had agreed to Robinson's temporary return to second base—at Clay Hopper's request—to "show some fellows who never had seen him there just how good a second baseman he is."[49] The Dodgers president also reiterated his earlier position that if Robinson did not earn a spot on the Dodgers by April 17, he would not be called up during the 1947 season. "There has been no decision," Rickey said, "nor will there be until several minds have met on the subject."[50]

Despite Rickey's stated plan of playing Robinson at first base in the remaining exhibition games, the Royals infielder once again played second base on April 3, a game won by the Dodgers 3–2. Rickey discounted the switch because it came in an unscheduled practice game. What could not be easily discounted happened when the Dodgers beat the Royals 6–3 on Saturday, April 5. Robinson's chances for promotion to the Dodgers were dealt a blow when Bruce Edwards, sliding back to first base, bowled over Robinson, who hurt his right arm and back. After lying on the ground for several minutes while he was being attended to, Robinson slowly left the field and the game. Still sore from his collision with Edwards, Robinson sat in the stands the next day as the Dodgers beat the Royals 6–0 on Easter Sunday in the final exhibition game at Havana's El Gran Stadium.

The Dodgers and Royals broke camp after the game and left Havana by boat. Up to that point, it had been the most expensive spring-training camp in history, at a cost of $50,000. With Havana behind them, the Dodgers headed north for a series of exhibition games in the United States leading up to the team's season opener. Robinson, whose average stood at .437 (21-for-48) in fourteen exhibition games, was still nursing his back injury as the Dodgers played exhibition games against the St. Louis Cardinals in Miami and the minor-league Charleston Rebels in South Carolina. By then the immediate fate of Robinson's black teammates had been decided. Roy Campanella was promoted to Montreal and Don Newcombe returned for another season with Nashua of the Class-B New England League to work on his curve ball. Roy Partlow had been released on March 25. But Robinson's future remained unclear. "We had our doubts," Newcombe said. "We knew it was eventually going to happen. After the year he had in Montreal, they could not stop it. The only problem was determining when it would happen."[51]

▰

With Rickey abandoning his original hope of having the Dodgers players lobby for Robinson's promotion, it fell to Durocher to publicly ask the Dodgers president to elevate Robinson to Brooklyn. But a telephone call assured that Durocher never got the chance. It came during an April 9 meeting of the Dodgers brain trust in Rickey's Montague Street office. "You can't do that," Rickey pleaded with the person on the other end of the line.[52] When the called ended, Rickey explained it was commissioner Happy Chandler handing down the verdict from the two hearings in Florida. Harold Parrott, the Dodgers' traveling secretary who had ghostwritten Durocher's *Brooklyn Eagle* columns, was fined $500, and the Dodgers had been hit with a $2,000 fine. "What happened to me?" Durocher asked. "You have been suspended for one year," Rickey informed him. "For what?" Durocher protested. Chandler had suspended Durocher for conduct detrimental to baseball.[53]

Despite the setback, Rickey acted swiftly the next day when Robinson returned to the field for the first time since hurting his back five days earlier in Havana. As Robinson, playing his final exhibition game against the Dodgers at Ebbets Field on Thursday, April 10, popped up into a double play in the fifth inning, Rickey's assistant Arthur Mann posted a terse release in the press box: "The Brooklyn Dodgers today purchased the contract of Jackie Roosevelt Robinson from the Montreal Royals. He will report immediately."[54] Arthur Daley of the *New York Times* postulated that Rickey had used Durocher's suspension as cover for announcing Robinson's promotion. "He practically smuggled him in," Daley wrote. "Just as the excitement of the Durocher episode reached its apex, Rickey quietly announced that Jackie was being signed to a Dodger contract."[55]

New York's mainstream press recorded baseball's seismic change in relatively muted tones in the following day's editions. The *New York Times*, for example, stretched an eight-column headline, "Dodgers Purchase Robinson, First Negro in Modern Major League Baseball," across the lead of its Sports section—on page 20. While the *Daily News* and *New York Post* each featured Robinson in back-page headlines, the *Journal American* buried a brief Robinson item below a banner headline about Durocher.[56] The black press, however, trumpeted the news. A banner headline across the front page of the *Baltimore Afro-American* blared: "DODGERS SIGN UP JACKIE." In the article, Robinson's reaction to the history-making announcement was subdued. "I'm extremely grateful for the confidence which Mr. Rickey and the Brooklyn officials have placed in me," he said, "and they can be sure that I will give them the very best I have at all times."[57] Robinson's wife, Rachel, was more ebullient. "It is the most thrilling news I've had since Jackie Jr. was born," she said. "Tomorrow morning I start apartment hunting in Brooklyn."[58] While Rachel began her search for a New York home on Friday, April 11, Robinson headed to Ebbets Field, where he would don Dodgers flannel for the first time in that day's exhibition game against the New York Yankees.

He arrived at the stadium to find no locker available and had to hang his clothes and newly issued number 42 uniform from three hooks on the wall of the Brooklyn clubhouse.[59] New teammates, such as outfielder Gene Hermanski and pitchers Ralph Branca and Johnny Van Cuyk, greeted Robinson warmly. Others were not as welcoming. After all, Dixie Walker had said earlier he wasn't concerned about Robinson as long as Robinson remained with Montreal. Apparently in response to those quotes, Walker had received an unprecedented reception in his own ballpark the previous day. The Dodgers' most popular player had been "vociferously booed" by "certain members of the Harlem delegation among the 14,282 fans" attending Robinson's Ebbets Field debut with the Royals.[60] Before the first exhibition game against the Yankees, Walker denied having been opposed to Robinson's promotion from Montreal. The Dodgers right fielder insisted he had been misquoted when Robinson was first signed in 1945. "What I said was that it was Montreal's business when they signed him, not mine," Walker said. "The only thing that matters now is whether he can help the team. It's up to him to prove he is the best man for the position."[61]

Editorials in the New York newspapers weighed in with various opinions on Robinson's elevation to the majors: The *New York Times*, in a page 16 editorial, concluded, "If Robinson had been a white man [his] name would have been there [on the roster] long before this."[62] Bill Corum of the *New York Journal American* called it "the most important forward step the national pastime has made in years, and it would have had to blush to call itself the national pastime if this hadn't been done when the opportunity arose."[63] The *Daily Mirror*'s Dan Parker noticed "no resumption of the War Between the States as the major league color line was finally torn down."[64] And Leonard Cohen of the *New York Post* argued that Robinson's "color doesn't matter to us, and shouldn't matter to others. He should rise or fall on his skill and sportsmanship, as anyone else."[65]

But Robinson's three games in a Dodgers uniform against the Yankees were mere exhibitions. The games—and therefore his presence in the majors—would not officially count until Opening Day. The Robinsons awoke in room 1169 at the McAlpin Hotel in midtown Manhattan on the morning of Tuesday, April 15. It was a bright, cool day with temperatures in the sixties. Hours before the first game of the 1947 season, Jackie Robinson rode the subway to Ebbets Field for his official major-league debut against the Boston Braves. Clyde Sukeforth, who had scouted Robinson in the Negro leagues and now was serving as interim manager for the suspended Durocher, asked Robinson how he felt and informed the newest Dodger he would start at first base. Despite his playing the position in spring training, it was not a foregone conclusion Robinson would play there—let alone start—in the first game of the season. "You could have knocked me over with a handkerchief," he said after the game. "I didn't have any idea I'd be in there right away."[66]

Once he made his way to the field for pregame warm-ups, Robinson became "the most-photographed man on the field," according to *Baltimore Afro-American* writer Sam Lacy.[67] Perhaps the most famous image from the photo session shows the Dodgers' starting infield—Spider Jorgensen, Pee Wee Reese, Eddie Stanky, and Robinson—standing together on the top step of the dugout, Stanky with his arm resting on Robinson's shoulder. In the stands, Rachel Robinson sat with five-month-old Jack Jr. She arrived at Ebbets Field after having a difficult time securing a taxi willing to take her to Brooklyn. Once in her seat, it was clear she and Jack Jr. were not wearing clothes warm enough for the day's chilly conditions. So the woman next to her, a member of Roy Campanella's family, held Jack Jr. inside her fur coat to protect him from the cold.[68]

Rachel Robinson was one of an estimated 14,000 black fans who packed into Ebbets Field to witness history. If those estimates were correct, more than half of the 26,623 fans in attendance—5,000 fewer than the stadium's capacity—were black.[69] It's no wonder "the huge opening day throng . . . expressed wholehearted approval of Jackie's presence in the lineup," as Sam Lacy wrote.[70] Once the game was under way, Red Barber, the Dodgers radio broadcaster for WHN, described Robinson in this way: "Jackie is very definitely brunette."[71] Robinson recorded eleven putouts at first base and went hitless in three at-bats. He grounded out in his first major-league at-bat in the first inning, flied out to left field in the third, and hit into a double play in the fifth inning, robbed of a hit by Braves shortstop Dick Culler's diving stop. In the seventh, Robinson reached on a bunt attempt when an errant throw caromed off his shoulder. He eventually came around to score the decisive run as the Dodgers won 5–3.

The black press hailed Robinson's debut. The *Pittsburgh Courier* devoted no fewer than seven headlines to Robinson's debut. Among them: "JACKIE SCORES WINNING RUN," "Robbie's Bunt Turns Tide," "Jackie Now 'Darling of The Brooks,'" "Robinson Mobbed by Cameramen and

Fans at Historic Opener," and "Jackie Romps Home From Second Base as 26,000 Cheer." Lester Rodney of the communist *Daily Worker* wrote, "It's hard this Opening Day to write straight baseball and not stop to mention the wonderful fact of Jackie Robinson."[72] But despite being the most socially significant moment in baseball history, Robinson's debut received shockingly subdued coverage in the mainstream press. The *New York Times* relegated its coverage to page 32, and neither headlines nor copy referred to Robinson's race or the breaking of baseball's color barrier. Roscoe McGowen's lead story didn't mention Robinson until the sixth paragraph. Although Arthur Daley's column the previous day had noted, "There is no way of disguising the fact that he is not an ordinary rookie,"[73] Daley waited eleven paragraphs in his coverage of Robinson's debut before mentioning him, and described the occasion as "quite uneventful."[74]

Robinson would go on to bat .297 with 12 home runs, 48 runs batted in, and a National League–leading 29 stolen bases during the 1947 season. But his rookie year was filled with tension and turbulence. He endured a slew of brushbacks from opposing pitchers and racial taunts from the stands and opposing dugouts. Perhaps none of the invectives were as vile as those hurled by Philadelphia Phillies manager Ben Chapman during a three-game series that began in Brooklyn on April 22:

> "Hey, nigger, why don't you go back to the cotton fields where you belong."
> "They're waiting for you in the jungles, black boy."
> "Hey, snowflake, which one of those white boys' wives are you dating tonight?"
> "We don't want you here, nigger."
> "Go back to the bushes."[75]

Incensed by the constant abuse from Chapman and the Phillies players, Eddie Stanky finally lashed out during the third game of the series: "Listen, you yellow-bellied cowards. Why don't you yell at somebody who can answer back."[76] Chapman's insults also drew the ire of fans, who wrote commissioner Happy Chandler to complain; mainstream and black press columnists, who criticized Chapman; and influential newsman Walter Winchell, who blasted the Phillies manager on his national radio show. National League president Ford Frick interceded with the Phillies management, and Chapman was "advised to keep his bench comments above the belt."[77]

Frick also played a role in averting another potentially disastrous incident as the St. Louis Cardinals were set to begin a three-game series in Brooklyn on May 6. Players on the Cardinals were prepared to stage a strike if Robinson was in the lineup for the series. According to Stanley Woodward of the *New York Herald Tribune*, the strike was instigated by a member of the Dodgers, who then backed out. "Subsequently, the St. Louis players conceived the idea of a general strike within the National League on a certain date," Woodward wrote.[78] Frick met with Cardinals owner Sam Breadon at the Hotel New Yorker to head off the strike. "I didn't have to talk to the players myself. Mr. Breadon did the talking to them," Frick said. "From what Breadon told me afterward the trouble was smoothed over."[79] Frick also insisted that the National League firmly supported Robinson and that any player attempting anything like a strike would be indefinitely suspended from baseball.

Amid the swirl of taunts, Robinson also received threatening letters, including a pair of anonymous missives that came to light while the Dodgers were in Philadelphia on May 9. Police disclosed that one letter warned Robinson to "get out of baseball."[80] Despite the turmoil, Robinson earned rookie of the year honors in 1947, and the shockwaves of his debut would be felt in the sport for decades to come. With Robinson performing well, more black players joined him in the majors. They represented an untapped source of talent, and other major-league teams weren't about to let the Dodgers corner the market on that talent. During his midnight tirade in Panama, Leo Durocher had warned his white players that Robinson was "only the first. . . . There's many more coming right behind him."[81] And even though the suspended Durocher wasn't there to see it, he was proven correct during the 1947 season. Larry Doby, formerly of the Newark Eagles of the Negro National League, became the second African American player in the majors and first in the American League when he made his debut on July 5. Later that month, a pair of former Kansas City Monarchs followed, with Hank Thompson, who had played for Habana during the winter, and outfielder Willard Brown each joining the St. Louis Browns, on July 17 and 19, respectively. On August 26, former Memphis Red Sox and Birmingham Black Barons pitcher Dan Bankhead debuted with the Dodgers.

The impact of black players on that era is undeniable, and the ripple effects of their inclusion in the major leagues were felt beyond those fields. Well before Robinson made his major-league debut, the race had been on for major-league teams to sign as many African American players as possible. The Negro leagues were the most concentrated pool for that talent. As major-league teams began persuading Negro league players to jump their contracts—often without compensating the players' previous teams—the Negro leagues began a slow but inexorable decline toward eventual extinction. Newark Eagles owner Effa Manley foresaw the end after Branch Rickey went around her and her husband, Abe, to sign away Don Newcombe in April of 1946. "What will become of colored baseball leagues," Effa Manley asked *Baltimore Afro-American* writer Sam Lacy, "if players are picked out by major league owners without consulting the team management?"[82]

A House United

Rumors began swirling not long after Habana manager Miguel Ángel González had watched his team's seemingly insurmountable six-game lead in the standings evaporate. Almendares had rallied to claim the Cuban League championship on February 25, and already there was a report that González might sell his team to Jorge Pasquel for $200,000, more than six times what he had paid to become the sole owner of the franchise in December of 1946.[1]

The other rumor was that Dodgers manager Leo Durocher wanted to hire González as a coach. The thought was that if González would divest himself of a team filled with ineligible players, the veteran manager could be welcomed back into organized baseball. González had asked the St. Louis Cardinals to release him from his contract as their third-base coach after the 1946 major-league season. He wanted to continue as owner and manager of the Habana club in the Cuban League. But Happy Chandler had made it clear that such a move would not absolve González of the commissioner's five-year ban for consorting with ineligible players.

As speculation over his future grew in February of 1947, González did little to quell the rumors. Although he would not say whether he had been approached about selling his team, he admitted his willingness to sell "if the price is right," according to *New York Times* writer Roscoe McGowen. McGowen also reported that González talked about the possibility of suing "'if necessary' to establish his right to work again in organized baseball—in case he decides that is what he wants to do." Although Branch Rickey denied he was considering hiring González, Durocher added grist to the rumor mill by pointing out that González had become a free agent once Cardinals owner Sam Breadon released him in 1946. And a source McGowen described as being "connected with the Dodgers" speculated that Chandler "wouldn't have a leg to stand on" if González sold the Habana club and attempted to revive his coaching career in the majors.[2]

González's future was not the only unresolved question after the 1946–47 Cuban League season ended. The future of the Cuban League itself was in doubt because of Chandler's ban on ineligible players. Even as the Cuban League remained outside the auspices of organized baseball, the *Sporting News*'s Dan Daniel gave voice to the possibility of Havana as a potential major-league city. "Havana could be in the major leagues," he wrote on March 5. "However . . . it is going to find itself very much confined and very much restricted in its baseball outlook and material, as regards the Cuban League, unless it complies with Commissioner A. B. Chandler's demand that it clean out the ineligibles."[3]

By April of 1947, Cuban League officials had been meeting in secret, trying to secure organized baseball's blessing for the league. Miguel Ángel González, Almendares part owner Dr. Julio Sanguily, and Bobby Maduro, owner of El Gran Stadium, were dispatched to meet with Chandler and George M. Trautman, president of the National Association of Professional Baseball Leagues, the governing body of the minor leagues. Their efforts paid off later that month when Chandler and Sanguily reached an accord. The Cuban League no longer would be off limits to players within organized baseball. In return, the Cuban League would release, and refrain from signing in the future, any players deemed ineligible by organized baseball. Among those banned by Chandler, only González would be permitted to remain in the Cuban League. González had been given a "special dispensation" by Chandler to continue as Habana's owner and manager, although he would not be allowed to return to the majors as a coach. In assessing the pact, Dan Daniel deemed it a "death blow" to the Mexican League, "which is hanging on the ropes anyway. The agreement also is the forerunner of a wider and more vital pact in which all Latin-American baseball will come under the jurisdiction of the commissioner."[4]

At a meeting in Columbus, Ohio, on May 12, the executive committee of the major leagues "favorably" considered the Cuban League's application.[5] The league's entry into organized baseball as an unclassified minor-league circuit became official after a July 11 meeting in Columbus between Cuban League officials, Trautman, and the executive committee of the National Association.[6] "The National Association is happy to co-operate with the Cuban Winter League in their expressed desire to accept the National Association rules and standards of play," Trautman said. "The new agreement affords us the opportunity to work in greater harmony with our good neighbors from the south."[7]

Since it began in 1878, the Cuban League had operated independently, handling its own affairs and signing players as it saw fit. That was about to change. Under the agreement, a maximum of 32 National Association players—8 for each of the Cuban League teams—would be allowed to play in any Cuban League season. Players with four years or fewer of professional experience would be allowed to participate in the Cuban League until March 1.[8] Cuban League president Rafael Inclán would submit a list of 60 players from which the 32 would be chosen by Trautman. The new operating rules also meant Mexican League jumpers such as Max Lanier and Fred Martin would be banned from playing in the Cuban League. The same would be true of Cuban players ruled ineligible by organized baseball. Trautman, however, reinstated a dozen Cuban players—Andrés Fleitas, Tony Castaño, Agapito Mayor, Salvador Hernández, Gilberto Valdivia, Mosquito Ordeñana, Oliverio Ortiz, Antonio "Pollo" Rodríguez, Armando Roche, Ramón Roger, Jorge "Cocoliso" Torres, and Daniel Doy—provided they applied for reinstatement before October 20. Trautman had concluded they had not jumped their contracts to play in the Mexican League. They had been ruled ineligible "for various, lesser violations of National Association rules,"[9] no doubt referring to their having played with and against ineligible players. But what would become of those Cuban players who had not been granted amnesty?

▰

Even with several former major leaguers holding out, the 1947 Mexican League rosters read like a who's who of the 1946–47 Cuban League season. Almendares manager Adolfo Luque, unlike Habana manager Miguel Ángel González, had not been given a dispensation by organized baseball. Banned from working in Cuban baseball, Luque was managing Puebla, and during the season he married Mexican actress Ivonne Recek Saade. After quitting as Marianao's manager in Cuba, Armando Marsans had signed to take the helm of the Tampico team. And although Martín Dihigo's Cuban League career had ended with the winter of 1946–47, the former Cienfuegos manager continued to manage with the Mexican League's San Luis Potosí team. Veteran Almendares pitcher Lázaro Salazar was serving as player-manager for Monterrey.

The on-field rosters were equally stocked with Cuban League talent. Mexico City had Alex Carrasquel, Ray Dandridge, Fred Martin, and Roberto Ortiz. Monterrey included Carlos Blanco and Andrés Fleitas. Puebla featured Beto Ávila, Sandalio Consuegra, Sal Maglie, Agapito Mayor, Napoleón Reyes, and Adrián Zabala. Avelino Cañizares, Roberto Estalella, and Roland Gladu dotted San Luis Potosí's roster. Héctor Rodríguez, Murray Franklin, and Gilberto Valdivia were with Tampico. And Tony Castaño, Lloyd Davenport, Booker McDaniels, and Terris McDuffie joined Ramón Bragaña with Veracruz. With few if any other options available to them, the major leaguers who had been holding out started trickling back to the Mexican League. Former St. Louis Browns catcher Myron "Red" Hayworth, who had played for Cienfuegos in the winter, reported to San Luis Potosí by the end of April. Former St. Louis Cardinals infielder Lou Klein returned to the fold on May 17, joining Monterrey, where he teamed with Almendares second baseman George Hausmann.

But Max Lanier wasn't ready to join his former teammates—Klein with the Cardinals and Hausmann with Almendares—back in Mexico. Unable to reach an agreement with Jorge Pasquel to return to the

Mexican League, Lanier began entertaining the idea of playing semi-pro ball in April of 1947. "I won't take a cut in salary to play in the Mexican League," Lanier said at the time, "and I've contacted Jorge Pasquel my last." On April 19 he confirmed he had been in contact with a semipro team in Cleveland. "I've got a lot of ball games left in this ole wing," Lanier said. "I'm perfectly willing to get rid of some of them for some semipro outfit."[10] In fact, Lanier sent a telegram to the semipro team essentially begging for a job: "Heard that you had a baseball club. I would like to pitch for you this summer. If you would be interested, wire me collect."[11] With no offer forthcoming, Lanier finally gave in, returning to Veracruz on June 17.

As Cleveland Indians ace Bob Feller was compiling the fifth twenty-win season of his major-league career, he announced on August 11 a postseason barnstorming tour that would include him pitching five games in the recently organized-baseball-sanctioned Cuban League. After the conclusion of the American portion of the schedule, Feller would pitch five games from October 21 to November 8 for Almendares. The Scorpions would be managed by Fermín Guerra, who had protected his good standing with organized baseball by not playing for the Cuban League the previous winter.

"Commissioner A. B. Chandler ruled that ball players could engage in thirty days of post-season competition beginning Oct. 8," said Indians business manager Rudy Schaffer, "so there is no question on that score." Bill Veeck, however, wasn't quite so sure. The Indians owner was recuperating from a second operation on his right leg, which had been partially amputated the previous year, when he was asked about Feller. The pitcher had not sought Veeck's permission before accepting an offer to play in Cuba. "Until I talk with Feller I have no idea what stand I will take," Veeck said. For his part, Feller didn't see any reason he could not play in Havana. "What's all the fuss about?" he asked.[12]

It quickly became apparent Feller's intentions were irrelevant. On August 12 baseball's secretary-treasurer, Walter Mulbry, told a reporter he believed commissioner Happy Chandler would not allow the barnstorming trip "even though there is nothing in the rules to prevent Feller or any other major league player from playing in the Cuban League during the thirty-day barnstorming period."[13] By August 14 Chandler put the kibosh on Feller's trip. His directive to all sixteen major-league teams prohibited major-league players from playing as members of the Cuban League during the 1947–48 season: "Players may play during the barnstorming period outside of the continental United States if their schedules are approved by the commissioner and they do not play with or against ineligible players."[14] Aside from not having pre-clearance from the commissioner, Feller's trip seemed to fit under the rules. The trip would occur during the approved barnstorming period. The Cuban League had been welcomed back into organized baseball's good graces, so playing with or against ineligibles would not be an issue. But Chandler nixed the visit because "It's a league, isn't it? Major League players cannot participate in games of other leagues anywhere."[15]

Chandler's edict also nixed plans for the other three teams in the Cuban League to feature big-league players. Larry Doby of the Indians and Hank Thompson of the St. Louis Browns reportedly were among those being considered. Only minor leaguers would be permitted to play in the Cuban League. "My plans to play in Cuba have been made in good faith, with the stipulation I would not play with or against ineligible players," Feller said. "I intend to ask him [Chandler] to clarify his ruling."[16] Feller even offered to donate $15,000 to $20,000 to the American League players' pension fund if Chandler would approve Feller's barnstorming schedule to include games in Cuba. "I want to prove," he said, "that I'm not going to Cuba for any selfish interest."[17] Feller would never set foot in Havana while wearing a Cuban uniform.

⚑

With the Cuban League welcomed into organized baseball, ineligible Cuban players faced the prospect of not being allowed to play in their homeland in the winter. But the Cuban Professional Baseball Players' Association made sure that would not happen. The Players' Association, under the direction of Almendares pitcher Tomás de la Cruz and emboldened by the economic boom of the previous two years, decided in June to form a rival league for the winter of 1947–48. The Liga

Nacional would play at La Tropical with four teams: Alacranes, Leones, Cuba, and Santiago, with Dr. Jesus Portocarrero serving as the league's president. Hoping to capitalize on the familiarity of the Eternal Rivals, the Liga Nacional's Alacranes and Leones teams' names were blatant rip-offs of the long-standing Almendares and Habana teams of the Cuban League.

Alacranes would be owned by Dr. Julio Marrero and managed by Adolfo Luque; Leones would be owned by Dr. Miguel de León and managed by Salvador Hernández; Cuba would be owned by Colonel Gonzalo García Pedroso and managed by Silvio García; and Santiago would be owned by Dr. Eduardo Sabás Alomá and managed by Napoleón Reyes. Each owner agreed to guarantee $30,000 for players' salaries and donate 20 percent of net profits to the Players' Association. The twenty-five-man roster for each team had to include at least three rookies and no more than eight American players. Contracts were to be negotiated collectively by the Players' Association.[18] The irony was that the previous winter the Cuban League had operated as an outlaw league, while the National Federation played with organized baseball's blessing at La Tropical. Now with the Cuban League a part of organized baseball, La Tropical stadium would host an outlaw league.

Postponed one day by the lingering inclement weather of a hurricane that had passed west of Havana, the Cuban League opened on Friday, October 10. Despite the rainy conditions, some 12,000 fans gathered at El Gran Stadium to watch Habana and Marianao play to a 3–3 tie before a downpour forced the game to be called after eight innings. Habana, managed by Miguel Ángel González, returned with many of the players from the heartbreaking previous season, and Tomas "Pipo" de la Noval returned as Marianao's manager. But Cienfuegos and Almendares were under new management this season. Former New York Yankees pitcher and future Hall of Famer Vernon "Lefty" Gómez replaced Martín Dihigo as Cienfuegos's manager. With Luque set to manage in the outlaw Liga Nacional, Fermín Guerra piloted Almendares.

Compared to González's team, Guerra's would feel a much greater impact from the latest schism in Cuban baseball. Because of their affiliation with the Mexican League, Fred Martin, Sagüita Hernández,

Lázaro Medina, and Carlos Blanco, who had played for Habana during the 1946–47 season, would be playing for the Liga Nacional's Leones club. But Almendares lost many more players, ineligible because they had played in Mexico, including key pitchers Max Lanier, Agapito Mayor, and Tomás de la Cruz, shortstop Avelino Cañizares, third baseman Héctor Rodríguez, leading home run hitter Roberto Ortiz, and catcher and league MVP Andrés Fleitas. Mayor and Fleitas had been granted amnesty by Trautman, but out of loyalty to the Players' Association, which founded the Liga Nacional, they had chosen to play in the outlaw league and aid Alacranes' championship bid.

Even before the Liga Nacional opened its inaugural season, there were issues. Once again Julio Blanco Herrera had invested a substantial amount of money to upgrade La Tropical. But after spending $50,000 on renovations, he balked at putting up any money to guarantee player salaries. Tomás de la Cruz's efforts to secure a larger guarantee from the league's four owners—$60,000 apiece instead of just $30,000— were unsuccessful. Max Lanier and Fred Martin were lobbying to have a two-month advance on their salaries deposited in an American bank before they would sign their contracts. And a legal battle was being waged over the radio rights to broadcast the league's games. Station COCO's contract had been voided because Station CMW wanted exclusive rights—convenient, perhaps, given that league president Jesús Portocarrero also happened to be secretary and chief counsel for the RHC Network, which owned CMW.[19]

Adding to the Liga Nacional's issues was the acrimony between the players who had joined the outlaw league and those who had remained in the Cuban League. On October 26, police detained Tomás de la Cruz after Habana manager Miguel Ángel González and the owners of El Gran Stadium, Bobby Maduro and Miguel Suárez, accused the president of the Players' Association of threatening Habana players unless they joined the league at La Tropical. De la Cruz apparently took particular issue with Habana players such as Woody Bell, Henry Kimbro, Hank Thompson, and Lennie Pearson. "I personally went to see Lennox Pearson and Thompson, because they had signed contracts with us to play at Tropical and received $2,000 each," Cruz said. "As they jumped the least they could do was to return the money."[20]

The Players' Association had 108 members, only 27 of whom had been ruled ineligible by organized baseball. But on the day before the Liga Nacional season opened, the union decided to shed 13 members. The association's directors agreed unanimously to "dishonorably expel" those who "betrayed the cause of the Association."[21] Those excommunicated for the transgression of participating in the Cuban League instead of the Liga Nacional were: Pedro Pagés, Cocaina García, Orestes Miñoso, Chiquitín Cabrera, Rafael Noble, Mosquito Ordeñana, Mario Arenciba, Catayo González, Conrado Marrero, José María Fernández, Pipo de la Noval, Daniel Doy, and Lino Dinoso.

On the night of Thursday, October 30, between 32,000 and 40,000 fans packed into La Tropical stadium for the inaugural Liga Nacional game between Leones and Alacranes. It pitted Alacranes lefty Agapito Mayor against Leones right-hander Fred Martin in a rematch of the penultimate game of the 1946–47 Cuban League season. *Información* sportswriter Fausto Lavilla described the scene:

> A human chain snaked around the playing field, minimizing it and forcing special rules to be established. There were spectators on the beams that supported the roof, and the daring sat calmly on the slopes of the roof. Thousands sought refuge in the grove that blooms in deep left field. Others climbed the fences that separate the stadium from the brewery, and there were also those who witnessed the game from the top of the players' clubhouse. Two hours before hostilities began, the grandstands already were filled and the chief umpire, Amado Maestri, was consulted about whether the doors should be closed to prevent overflow. The arbitrator responded: "I am willing to hold the game on a handkerchief."[22]

With the throng of fans situated, Salvador Hernández's Leones club defeated Adolfo Luque's Alacranes team by a score of 3–0. In many ways the scene was reminiscent of the Cuban League's inaugural game at El Gran Stadium to open the 1946–47 season. Adding to the success of opening night was the fact that a mere 3,000 fans had attended the corresponding game competing for Cuban baseball fans' attention at El Gran Stadium that night.[23]

![flag ornament]

Aside from the early attendance disparity, there were other signs all was not well in the organized-baseball-sanctioned Cuban League. In the first month of the season, Almendares owner Dr. Julio Sanguily complained about the quality of the minor-league players who had been made available to the Cuban League. "We were promised the best minor league players from AAA down and also major league players during the barnstorming period," Sanguily was quoted as saying in the *Sporting News*. "But Commissioner Chandler's ukase against major leaguers participating in our games was a solar-plexus blow administered to the Cuban Professional League."[24] According to the article, Sanguily complained that Roy Campanella, of the Brooklyn Dodgers' Montreal Royals farm team, had not been permitted to play in Cuba, and he also speculated that the Cuban League might lose between $100,000 and $200,000 if it did not have better players to compete with against the Liga Nacional.

But after the story was published, Sanguily quickly denied criticizing organized baseball. He was described as being "satisfied" with organized baseball efforts. Sanguily also expected "more minor league stars next season" for the Cuban League and was "confident the pro league will win the fight against the 'outlaw' organization."[25] Sanguily's complete attitude turnaround appeared to be bolstered during a December 1947 convention in Miami when the National Association declared that any minor-league player, not just those with less than five years' experience, would be eligible to play in the Cuban League, starting the following winter. In another development, Major League Baseball decided it would henceforth allow players with no more than forty-five days of major-league experience to play in Cuba as well.[26]

While the Cuban League was receiving encouraging news, the Liga Nacional began to unravel. Some players jumped back to organized baseball and the Cuban League, the most notable of whom was Fleitas. The reigning MVP from the 1946–47 Cuban League season had opted to join the Liga Nacional's Alacranes team, but his tenure there lasted all of thirteen at-bats before he returned to the Cuban League, signing a three-year $10,000 contract with Almendares and incurring the wrath of his fellow Liga Nacional players and the Cuban press.[27] The Santiago team, struggling financially because of a lack of fan interest, withdrew from the league on December 15, and its players were dispersed among the remaining three teams. Luis Rodríguez Olmo and Sandalio Consuegra moved to Leones, Luis Tiant Sr. and Danny Gardella joined Cuba, and Booker McDaniels and Lázaro Salazar switched to Alacranes.

Although Santiago was the only Liga Nacional team to fold, it was not the only one dealing with attendance problems. La Tropical had the early attendance advantage, but fans began to flock in greater numbers to games at El Gran Stadium as the Cuban League season advanced. Then an ugly incident further damaged the Liga Nacional's image on December 22 when a melee broke out during a game between the Cuba and Leones teams. A close call at second base ended Cuba's rally and sparked a brawl, in which a Cuba player struck an umpire and was ejected. Three players involved in the skirmish were arrested. When the Cuba team refused to continue, umpire Amado Maestri declared the game a forfeit, awarding victory to the Leones club. Between players jumping their contracts, dwindling attendance, and on-field incidents, rumors of a premature conclusion to the season were rampant. In response, the Liga Nacional's board of directors issued a statement saying, "We are going to continue our schedule to the end."[28]

The New Year didn't bring any better news for the Liga Nacional. In early January the Players' Association confirmed that two club owners had left the league, forcing the union to take over the operation of those teams.[29] Later in the month another prominent player, former Indians pitcher Paul Calvert, became the latest to jump the league. Calvert, who had played for Marianao during the 1946–47 season, left the Leones club and returned to Marianao after learning he had been reinstated in organized baseball by George M. Trautman of the National Association. Calvert "literally leaped from his chair when he read the wire restoring him to good standing, and personally telephoned [Marianao] Owner Eloy García to agree to a winter contract."[30]

As doubts about the Liga Nacional's viability continued to mount, hope of ending hostilities between organized baseball and the Mexican League began to emerge. The first indication came in the form of an announcement from the Mexican League on January 20. Walter Mulbry, baseball commissioner Happy Chandler's assistant, would be in Mexico on January 21 and would meet with Mexican baseball commissioner Alejandro Aguilar Reyes. According to the announcement, the meeting had been requested in a telegram signed by Chandler. It would be the first official encounter between organized baseball and the Mexican League since the latter began raiding major-league teams of their players in early 1946. Although the agenda was not specified, the reason seemed obvious. Jorge Pasquel still held the title of Mexican League president, but he was now subordinate to Aguilar, who upon taking office in October of 1947 had said the league "is ready for friendship with organized baseball."[31]

Following the audience with Mulbry, Aguilar declared that "all differences between the Mexican League and organized baseball in the United States have ended" and predicted his league would be formally recognized by organized baseball "in the near future."[32] Aguilar's statement also said any future agreement between the leagues would include the full restoration of any ineligible player's status in organized baseball. Asked about a future reconciliation, Chandler would not speculate on whether he would be willing to reinstate banned players. But he said, "I'd like to see baseball in both countries get together. But until I hear from Mulbry there's nothing to be said or done."[33]

In Cuba, news of a possible path back to the majors was greeted with joy by the players who had jumped to Mexico. Max Lanier, who was pitching with Alacranes of the Liga Nacional, said that although Cubans had been "wonderful" and were "some of the most enthusiastic fans," he and other onetime big leaguers were ready to get back to playing in America again. "If this thing is really true and goes through, it would make me very happy," said Lanier, who acknowledged making a "mistake in going to Mexico" and believed "two years of banishment is enough." Sal Maglie, Lanier's teammate in Cuba, also longed to return to the United States, saying, "I'm tired of foreign food."[34]

Within a week, their hopes of a rapid resolution were dashed. On January 26, Jorge Pasquel bombastically declared himself to be the true power behind the Mexican League. "If Chandler wants to do anything," Pasquel said while in New York, "he must talk to me personally." The Mexican League president boasted he would continue signing players from the United States and insisted his league would expand from six to eight teams. "In 1945 they said we'd last two months," Pasquel snarled. "Well, we're still going, and we expect to continue."[35] The next day, Aguilar resigned as Mexican League commissioner. And with him went the progress he had achieved with Mulbry. "If Aguilar has resigned," Mulbry said, "I have no comment to make about any further negotiations." And Mulbry did not strike an optimistic note over chances of continuing discussions with Pasquel: "We have no plans in that direction."[36]

Pasquel's grand plans for expansion hit the skids when members of the Cuban Players' Association refused to accept slashed contract offers for the 1948 season. With the Mexican League establishing a top monthly payroll of $10,000 for each team, Pasquel sent players in Cuba contract offers for roughly half of what they had made during the 1947 season. So after Tomás de la Cruz called a meeting of the union in February, he announced the players had decided they would not re-sign with the Mexican League and would instead play a summer league in Cuba with the same teams from the Liga Nacional. "Sooner, or later, he [Pasquel] was bound to have trouble with the other club owners," De la Cruz said. "So I advised him to build up his Mexican teams with Mexican players. That is best. We can perform in Cuba in the summertime."[37]

That would be easier said than done. Although players who had jumped to Mexico such as Max Lanier, Fred Martin, George Hausmann, and Sal Maglie had said they were on board for De la Cruz's plan, significant hurdles remained. Other players from the Liga Nacional had plans to spend their summers playing in Venezuela or the Negro leagues. Holding a summer league in Cuba would compete for fans with the Havana Cubans of the Florida International League. And it wasn't long before Pasquel was boasting he had commitments for the 1948 season, scheduled to begin on March 25, from players such as Lanier, Silvio García, Claro Duany, Pedro Pagés, and Monte Irvin.

After the previous season's heartbreaking loss, Habana gained a measure of revenge as the Cuban League season concluded on February 24. Habana lost to Cienfuegos in the first game of the day's doubleheader, but Marianao beat Almendares 8–7 in the nightcap, giving the Lions the pennant by a one-game margin. Habana's Henry Kimbro led the league with a .346 batting average, and Hank Thompson topped all hitters with 51 runs batted in. Despite Almendares's second-place finish, pitcher Conrado Marrero earned MVP honors. He led the league with a 12–2 record and a 1.12 earned run average.

With the Cuban League season over, the Liga Nacional set its sights on a greener field. The outlaw league was now scheduled to finish its season on March 21, and its plan was to play the final month at El Gran Stadium. Playing at Havana's new stadium would give Liga Nacional teams better facilities than those to which they had been accustomed. More important, however, was the potential to draw more fans than they had at La Tropical. El Gran Stadium had been a boon to the Cuban League in its first two seasons of existence. For the 1946–47 season, the Cuban League had a gross gate of $850,000, the highest in league history. The second year at the new stadium hadn't matched that level, but that season's $650,000 gate was the second-best mark ever.[38] La Tropical had generated no such windfall for the Liga Nacional, and even one month at the new stadium could help some of the outlaw league's clubs get in the black.

But El Gran Stadium's owners rejected those plans, denying the Liga Nacional the use of the new stadium. The *Sporting News*'s Pedro Galiana quoted an unnamed member of Compañía Operadora, the company that ran El Gran Stadium, on the stance. "We are now backing Organized Ball in all angles and cannot give our park to the 'outlaws,'" the stadium member said. "We had the Liga Cubana in the winter time and we are going to have the Havana Cubans of the Florida International

League in the summer. That is good enough for us."[39] El Gran Stadium's rejection of hosting outlaw games and its embrace of the minor-league Havana Cubans meant Tomás de la Cruz's idea of a summer Cuban league was dead before it even had a chance to be formed. On April 8 the Havana Cubans opened their Florida International League season at El Gran Stadium. Under the direction of manager Oscar Rodríguez, the Class-C farm team of the Washington Senators won its third consecutive league championship as Antonio Lorenzo went 23–8 with a 2.23 earned run average to earn MVP honors. Conrado Marrero went 20–11 with a league-leading 1.67 ERA, and Luis Alomá was 19–6 with a 1.77 ERA.

Unable to secure El Gran Stadium for the final month of the season, the Liga Nacional concluded its season on March 21 at La Tropical. Leones, buoyed by the additions of Puerto Rican outfielder Luis Rodríguez Olmo and pitcher Sandalio Consuegra after the Santiago club folded and its players were dispersed, led second-place Cuba by four games on the final day of the season. Alacranes finished six games behind. After going 2–4 with Santiago, Consuegra became Leones' best pitcher, going 11–4 with his new team. Olmo batted .318 with 8 home runs and 47 runs batted in to become most valuable player. He received 15 of the 16 votes from the sportswriters.[40]

Former Cuban League players figured prominently in the less successful efforts of the Cuba and Alacranes teams. Ex-Cienfuegos outfielder Roland Gladu led the league with a .330 batting average for Cuba. Former Cienfuegos pitcher Adrián Zabala had the league's best winning percentage at .650 (13 wins and 7 losses). Danny Gardella, who was among the first players to jump a major-league contract for the Mexican League, and who joined Cuba after Santiago disbanded, led the Liga Nacional with 10 home runs. Former Almendares shortstop Avelino Cañizares scored a league-leading 53 runs and collected 114 hits for Alacranes. Roberto Ortiz, formerly with Almendares, clubbed a league-high 21 doubles and drove in a league-best 55 runs for Alacranes. Third baseman Héctor Rodríguez displayed the same speed he had with Almendares, leading the Liga Nacional with 19 stolen bases. Alacranes tried to bolster its ranks by trading Ramón Bragaña, Santos

Amaro, and Pollo Rodríguez to Cuba for Sal Maglie. The former Giants pitcher was 11–9 with Cuba and went 3–0 with Alacranes. Maglie's fourteen victories led the league, but they were not enough to pull his new team out of last place.

The Liga Nacional was dealt perhaps its final blow as the season was winding down. In December, Leones owner Miguel de León, who was a member of the Cuban House of Representatives, had announced his team would go by the name Habana, usurping the established name of Miguel Ángel González's Cuban League team.[41] But a Cuban court, in the closing days of March, prohibited the Alacranes and Leones teams from using "Almendares" and "Habana" in referring to themselves. The Eternal Rivals' names had been established as trademarks in the Cuban League since 1938 and 1939, respectively.[42] "Some doubt now exists as to whether the Liga Nacional will attempt to operate next season," Pedro Galiana wrote in the *Sporting News*, "because of the many financial problems and the inability to use the New Stadium and two of the traditional club names."[43]

Representatives from Cuba, Puerto Rico, and Panama met in Havana on April 12 to establish the Caribbean Professional Baseball Confederation. Among the dignitaries from Cuba were Cuban League chairman Rafael Inclán, Almendares part owner Dr. Julio Sanguily, Marianao part owner Eloy García, and Habana's Miguel Ángel González. They gathered along with baseball officials from the other two countries, as well as officials from the National Association, to create a Caribbean "world series." The Confederation reconvened on April 21 to admit Venezuela and establish the framework for the proposed series. A two-day gathering on August 21–22 in Havana finalized the rules.

The series would begin play in Havana on February 20, 1949, with the champions from Panama and Puerto Rico playing against each other and the Cuban and Venezuelan champs facing off. The scheduled opening of the series would require Cuba, Puerto Rico, and Venezuela to conclude their respective winter leagues earlier than usual, by February 18. Each team would play twice against the others in a round-robin tournament scheduled to end on February 26. Only players who appeared on the rosters of their respective teams before January 31 would be eligible, and the National Association would allow one hundred minor-league players to participate in the four winter leagues. "The players who come to the Caribbean Conference will do so on their own volition," said Robert L. Finch, public relations director for the National Association. "We are serving as a clearing house."[44] The Confederation also set which cities would host the next three Caribbean Series: San Juan, Puerto Rico, in 1950; Caracas, Venezuela, in 1951; and Panama City, Panama, in 1952.

With the Liga Nacional blocked from using any of the traditional Cuban team names and its native players applying for reinstatement into organized baseball, Tomás de la Cruz's outlaw league never played another season. In June 1948, De la Cruz floated the idea of forming a league with teams from Cuba, Mexico, and the United States that would be stocked with ineligible players from the three countries.[45] It never materialized. By August 1948, Salvador Hernández had been granted his reprieve by organized baseball, and before long many other higher-profile Cuban players—Agapito Mayor, Jorge Comellas, Héctor Rodríguez, Avelino Cañizares, Santos Amaro, Heberto Blanco, Carlos Blanco, and Tony Castaño among them—were allowed to return to the Cuban League for the 1948–49 season. "Permitting favorites of Cuban fans to return is giving the 'outlaws' a knockout punch," Pedro Galiana wrote in the *Sporting News*. "With no Cuban players to organize another league, the ineligibles haven't a chance to start another venture at La Tropical Park."[46]

But not all players were immediately welcomed back into the Cuban League's and organized baseball's good graces. Former major leaguers such as Max Lanier, Sal Maglie, George Hausmann, Fred Martin, and Danny Gardella remained on the outside looking in. And big-name Cuban players such as Roberto Ortiz, Napoleón Reyes, Roberto Estalella, Adrián Zabala, Sandalio Consuegra, and René Monteagudo had to sit out the 1948–49 Cuban League season. They were still barred by organized baseball for having played in Mexico. "I'd gladly swim the Gulf of Mexico back to the States," the *Sporting News* quoted one unnamed player as saying, "if I ever know there is a chance to be reinstated."[47]

Perhaps the biggest injustice was Adolfo Luque's continued banishment. An icon of Cuban baseball, Luque had not been given dispensation to manage in the Cuban League because he had committed the sin of managing in the Mexican League. Luque's managerial counterpart, Miguel Ángel González, had been spared that indignity. But González, himself an iconic baseball figure in Cuba, still was blocked from returning to the major leagues. In July, González met with members of the Cardinals and commissioner Happy Chandler during the All-Star Game in St. Louis, hoping to return to the third-base coaching box in which he had spent so many seasons. "Some day I will be back in Organized Baseball," González said. "I feel that I did no wrong and should be eligible to return to a big league job."[48] But Walter Mulbry, speaking for Chandler's office, said that González's status "remains unchanged."[49]

Had anyone ever taken Jorge Pasquel up on his bold bet regarding the Mexican League's viability, the marker would have come due in September of 1948. Back at the start of the 1946 Mexican League season, Pasquel responded to naysayers by offering to "place $5,000,000 in an American bank to offset $5,000,000 that they will put up to back their claims that our league will fold."[50] Turned out neither he nor the league would have the funds to back that bet. On September 20, 1948, the Mexican League shut down for the season because its teams had lost too much money. The league was to have concluded on October 24, but on the night of September 19 the managers of the remaining four teams—who included Cubans Lázaro Salazar for Monterrey and Napoleón Reyes for Puebla—were summoned by commissioner Octavio Rueda Margo, who informed them "the season is over. Tell your players that I am not paying a single cent more."[51]

The league lost an estimated 2.5 million pesos, about $362,000, over the course of the three seasons of Pasquel's unbridled spending.

At a meeting of the Mexican League's team owners on October 28, Pasquel resigned as president, although he and his brothers maintained ownership of the Veracruz club. "There will be no more raids by the Mexican League," the new president of the league, Dr. Eduardo Quijano Pitman, declared. "We will offer only the greatest of friendship toward Organized Baseball and hope . . . the Mexican League will become a part of Organized Baseball."[52]

The 1948–49 Cuban League season opened on October 8 as a crowd of 21,000 at El Gran Stadium saw Habana cruise past Marianao 17–5. The season concluded on February 17 with Almendares, once again managed by Fermín Guerra, holding an eight-game advantage over Habana for the league title. Former Negro leagues star Monte Irvin, who would make his major-league debut with the New York Giants in 1949, led the league with 10 home runs and drove in 53 runs. He helped give Guerra his first championship as a manager. Among Irvin's teammates was future actor Chuck Connors. But Irvin's team did not include longtime and popular Almendares players such as Roberto Ortiz, who remained banned. After the season, Havana's weekly sports newspaper *América Deportiva* declared, "Latin American baseball has suffered a deep humiliation this winter" when Chandler "refused to reinstate its best ball players even to play only in their country's winter leagues."[53]

With the Cuban League season concluded, Almendares represented Cuba in the inaugural Caribbean Series at El Gran Stadium. Irvin once again provided a key bat, hitting two home runs and driving in 11 runs while batting .389. Almendares swept six games en route to winning the title on February 25. Al Gionfriddo, a former Pirate and Dodger outfielder whose famous catch had robbed Joe DiMaggio of a game-tying home run in the 1947 World Series, batted .533, Héctor Rodríguez hit .458, and Connors weighed in with a .391 average. Agapito Mayor recorded three of Almendares's six victories. Only 55,000 fans attended the six-day tournament, but National Association president George M. Trautman declared it a success. He called the first Caribbean Series "the realization of the dream of baseball leaders of Cuba,

Panama, Puerto Rico, and Venezuela" that "has proven the possibility of using the game as the best good neighbor policy to tighten friend-ship ties."[54]

The remaining players banned by organized baseball generally fell into two categories: those who had not signed contracts with their major-league teams but were still tied to them by baseball's reserve clause when they went to play in Mexico, and those who had jumped their major-league contracts. Players such as Danny Gardella, Mickey Owen, Roland Gladu, Luis Rodríguez Olmo, René Monteagudo, Napoleón Reyes, Adrián Zabala, and Roberto Estalella were in the former group. Players such as Max Lanier, Fred Martin, Murray Franklin, George Hausmann, Sal Maglie, Roy Zimmerman, Ace Adams, Harry Feldman, Alejandro Carrasquel, and Lou Klein were in the latter. Gardella had sued organized baseball for $300,000 over his five-year ban, charging that Major League Baseball was a monopoly and challenging its reserve clause. In March of 1949, Gardella had company in the courtroom.

On March 8, attorney John L. Flynn filed a lawsuit in New York federal court on behalf of Max Lanier and Fred Martin. The lawsuit accused organized baseball of operating a monopoly in violation of an-titrust law and sought $2.5 million in damages, $1.5 million for Lanier and $1 million for Martin. The pair also sought to be reinstated in or-ganized baseball. In his affidavit, Lanier argued that various baseball rules violated United States antitrust laws and "that the reserve clause is also a violation of such laws and the standard uniform form of play-ers' contract . . . is so unjust, harsh, and one-sided that it constitutes no contract whatsoever."[55]

On April 1, U.S. District Court judge Edward A. Conger refused to grant an injunction ordering organized baseball to reinstate Lanier and Martin, pending the result of their lawsuit. He ruled such an in-junction would be premature. "To grant the Plantiffs' application," Conger ruled, "would disturb the status quo, would restore them to po-sitions they resigned voluntarily, and would accord them preliminarily on papers alone the relief to which they might ultimately, after trial, be entitled."[56] On April 19, Conger denied Gardella's request for immediate reinstatement, citing the same reasons, saying that granting an injunction "would necessitate a premature disposition on disputed issues of law and fact."[57] And on June 2, the U.S. District Court of Appeals agreed and refused to order the reinstatement of Lanier, Martin, and Gardella. The three-judge panel ruled it was "not prepared to say that . . . the reserve clause violates the anti-trust acts."[58]

With that ruling, any hope of seeing an early end to their five-year banishment appeared dashed for Lanier, Martin, Gardella, and the rest of the banned players. Three days later, however, that changed. No longer facing the threat of a court order, baseball commissioner Happy Chandler on June 5 reinstated every player who had been suspended for jumping to the Mexican League. All that was required was for them to formally apply for their reinstatement. In his letter to the players, Chandler called it "a fair thing to do," and acknowledged the effect of the recent favorable appeals court ruling. "The threat of compulsion by a court order having been ended," Chandler wrote, "I feel justified in tempering justice with mercy in dealing with all of these players."[59]

And so a conflict that began three years earlier and embroiled dozens of players and three baseball leagues in three countries ended on relatively peaceful terms. News of Chandler's reversal was cheered in Cuba. "Many congratulations on your generous gesture," Almendares owner Mario Mendoza cabled the baseball commissioner. "Receive the blessing of five million Cuban fans."[60] But by the time Adolfo Luque was reinstated by Chandler, no managerial posts were available for the 1949–50 Cuban League season. So Miguel Ángel González hired his former longtime rival as an assistant coach on his Habana team. A final gesture from Chandler came when he allowed Cuban-born major leaguers, regardless of service time, to play in the Cuban League.

The move, which allowed Cuban players such as Roberto Ortiz (Washington Senators), Napoleón Reyes (New York Giants), René Monteagudo (Philadelphia Phillies), and Orestes Miñoso (Cleveland Indians) to again play in the Cuban League, was widely hailed on the island: *Diario de la Marina* columnist Eladio Secades declared that Chandler's decision "will forever kill any ill feelings against Organized Ball in all Latin American countries"; *El Mundo* sports editor Sergio Varona wrote, "The Commissioner's gesture will never be forgotten"; *Alerta* sports editor Fausto Miranda opined that Chandler "will never know how much good his decision has done"; and an editorial in *El Cristo* proclaimed, "Now everybody loves Organized Baseball and will fight to keep our league in a long-time understanding with both the National Association and the big leagues."[61]

Epilogue

Inclusion in organized baseball and the cessation of hostilities against those who had played in the Mexican League ushered in a golden age for the Cuban League in the 1950s. Whatever the Cuban League may have lost in autonomy by being under the umbrella of the National Association, it more than gained in stability. Before the 1943–44 season, Eternal Rivals Almendares and Habana were the only consistently stable franchises in the league. During the first half of the twentieth century teams such as Fe, Santa Clara, Matanzas, and others were founded and rose to prominence, only to fade, withdraw, and disappear forever. With the economic boom that followed World War II and the construction of El Gran Stadium in the heart of Havana, the league settled down with the four teams—Almendares, Habana, Cienfuegos, and Marianao—that would comprise its membership for the remainder of its existence.

Organized baseball's war against the Mexican League threatened the stability not only of individual Cuban teams but of the entire Cuban League. The peace treaty between organized baseball and the Cuban League ended that threat. Gone were baseball commissioner Happy Chandler's sanctions. Gone were insurgencies in the form of homegrown rival circuits to challenge the Cuban League. Throughout the 1950s, the Cuban League would have ready access to players willingly made available by organized baseball. The Caribbean Series, launched in 1949, became an annual event that continues into the twenty-first century. Bobby Maduro, who had built El Gran Stadium, bought the then Class-B Havana Cubans of the Florida International League. Under the name Havana Sugar Kings, the franchise joined the Triple-A International League. The team's motto—"Un paso más . . . y llegamos!" (One more step . . . and we're there!)—referred to its players being one step away from the majors. But it also declared Maduro's aspiration of one day owning a major-league team in Havana.

Buoyed by an influx of new talent after the breaking of its color barrier, Major League Baseball also experienced a boom time during the 1950s. Jackie Robinson's promotion to the Brooklyn Dodgers in 1947 triggered a flood of black players, and of black and white Latino players, into the majors. Their impact, particularly in the National League, was undeniable. Beginning with Robinson in 1949, black players were voted as the league's most valuable players in sixteen of twenty-one seasons. Robinson and Dodgers teammates Roy Campanella and Don Newcombe won the award in five of six seasons from 1949 to 1956, with Campanella winning it three times.

Teams that embraced the torrent of talent were rewarded. The Brooklyn Dodgers, initially the most aggressive organization in signing Negro league players, saw their success soar. During the thirteen seasons between 1947 and 1959, the Dodgers won seven National League pennants. The New York Giants, the first major-league team to field an all-black outfield in Willie Mays, Monte Irvin, and Hank Thompson in 1951, won two National League pennants in the 1950s. With former New York Cubans owner Alex Pompez scouting and funneling Latino and black players to the Giants, the team enjoyed years of success.

Teams that dragged their feet when it came to signing black players, however, paid a price. The New York Yankees, who won fifteen American League pennants during the seventeen seasons between 1947 and 1964, resisted integration in baseball. The team passed on more than one opportunity to acquire Willie Mays before he signed with the Giants in 1950. The Yankees finally bought Elston Howard from the Kansas City Monarchs in 1950. The team became one of the last major-league clubs to integrate when Howard debuted in 1955, and he was the only black player on the Yankees roster until 1957. By not pursuing Latino and African American talent as aggressively as other teams, the Yankees slipped into mediocrity for a decade beginning in 1965.

The flood of black players into the majors also rang the death knell for the Negro leagues. For decades, black baseball had been an institution and a successful enterprise in the African American community. For some, like Ray Dandridge, the breaking of baseball's color barrier came too late. He joined the New York Giants' Triple-A Minneapolis Millers at age thirty-five but never reached the majors. For younger players such as Robinson, Mays, and Hank Aaron, who got their starts in the Negro leagues, access to the majors allowed them to compete on a level playing field with their white counterparts. Their predecessors in black baseball could only dream of such an opportunity. But as major-league teams began signing more black players, often without compensating the Negro league teams to which they had been under contract, the quality of play diminished and teams folded. The Negro National League disbanded in 1948. A shell of the Negro American League limped along for some time, but by the mid-to-late 1950s, the Negro leagues faded into history.

In Mexico, Jorge Pasquel may have been ousted as the ruling force behind the Mexican League in 1948, but he never lost his penchant for flamboyance. Whether it was shooting a charging leopard in Africa or getting caught up in a fan riot during a Mexican League game, Pasquel managed to find his way into the headlines even while reduced to the role of mere owner of the Veracruz Blues. But he no longer made headlines by challenging organized baseball. With him no longer running the Mexican League, the circuit ended its attempts to raid major-league players. After years of overtures, the Mexican League joined organized baseball as a Double-A circuit on January 21, 1955. Less than two months later, Pasquel, whose money brought the league to the height of avarice and the brink of ruin, died in a plane crash in San Luis Potosí on March 7. The plane went down in a mountainous area 225 miles northwest of Mexico City. He was only forty-eight years old.

Throughout the 1950s, the Cuban League prospered until the communist revolution. Fidel Castro and his band of rebels rode victoriously into the city of Havana on January 8, 1959. Castro's rise to power forever altered the future of the country, the lives of its people, and the course of a sport that had been ingrained in the island's culture for almost a century. The last hurrah for the Havana Sugar Kings came during the 1959 Junior World Series. The Sugar Kings defeated the Minneapolis Millers, whose roster included a twenty-year-old Carl Yastrzemski, in a thrilling seven-game series that concluded in Havana with Castro and nearly 3,000 armed soldiers among the 25,000 fans in attendance at El Gran Stadium. My father's cousin Leonardo Agüero was among the fans at El Gran Stadium who stormed the field after the Sugar Kings' game-7 victory. "I was behind third base, right there above the dugout in the first row," he recalled years later. "When they got the last out, I jumped on the field and I was trampled by fans. I went to look for something, a base, a glove, a player's cap, but I couldn't get anything."

As Castro began nationalizing the country's various industries in 1960 and 1961, relations between Cuba and the United States rapidly deteriorated. Bobby Maduro's dream of an expansion major-league team in Havana ended when the Sugar Kings were forced to relocate to Jersey City, New Jersey, on July 13, 1960. International League president Frank Shaughnessy revoked the franchise and gave Maduro forty-eight hours to find a city to which to transfer the team. The transfer was so abrupt that a strip of flannel with the words "Jersey City" had to be stitched on the uniforms for the team's debut in the United States. "If Cuba had remained free, Cuba would have a major league team," longtime Almendares catcher Andrés Fleitas once told me. "The franchise in Montreal would have been Cuba's. They were trying to determine if Cuba could support a major-league team. And indeed they showed it could, because thirty to thirty-five thousand fans would go see Habana and Almendares and Cienfuegos and Marianao."

Citing a lack of security, baseball commissioner Ford Frick barred Americans from participating in the upcoming 1960–61 Cuban League season. The season proceeded without U.S. players, as Cienfuegos beat

Almendares by a one-game margin to win the final professional winter-league season played on the island. Among the players was Luis Tiant Jr., whose father had played in Cuba from 1926 to 1948. For the younger Tiant, 1960–61 was his lone season in the Cuban League, as he left to play in Mexico the following summer and did not return until the filming of his 2009 documentary, *The Lost Son of Havana*.

Tiant's only season in the Cuban League was more than Hall of Famer Tony Pérez could experience. He was an eighteen-year-old minor-league player for the Class-D New York–Pennsylvania League when the Cuban League was disbanded. Years later, he lamented never having had the "good fortune" to play professional baseball in his homeland. "I was raised watching Cuban baseball," Pérez said on August 20, 2011, during the Cuban Cultural Center of New York's tenth annual congress, which focused on Cuban baseball history. "I didn't dream of playing in the majors. I didn't dream of playing in the United States. What I thought about was playing for one of the four teams that played at El Stadium del Cerro in that era. . . . It's still one of the things that I carry with me. I couldn't play in front of my family."

By the end of 1961, Castro abolished professionalism in baseball in Cuba and nationalized the sport. At the time, Cubans represented the largest contingent of Latin American–born players in the majors. And many of those players remained in exile, playing the rest of their careers in the United States. But with access to Cuban talent cut off, their numbers in the majors dwindled over the following decades, overtaken by players from the Dominican Republic, Puerto Rico, and Venezuela until defections began to increase the Cuban presence beginning in the late 1990s. "That man," Fleitas said of Castro, "showed up and destroyed baseball in Cuba."

With travel between Cuba and the United States severely restricted, only Cuban players who had not returned home after Castro's revolution—players such as Pérez, Tiant, Orestes "Minnie" Miñoso, Tony Oliva, Camilo Pascual, Mike Cuellar, and Pedro Ramos—were able to continue playing in the United States for several decades. Many of Cuba's greatest postrevolution players, such as Omar Linares, Orestes Kindelán, and Víctor Mesa, never had to chance to play in the majors.

"I'm sure," Cuban baseball historian Peter Bjarkman said, "Linares and Kindelán could have both played in the majors." It wasn't until 1980 that Bárbaro Garbey—among the mass exodus of Cubans to reach the United States during the Mariel Boatlift—became the first member of the Cuban national baseball team to defect since Castro closed Cuba's borders. His major-league career lasted just 226 games spread across three seasons. But the idea of defection was suddenly a possibility.

In the 1990s, what began slowly with the defections of pitchers René Arocha in 1991 and Ariel Prieto in 1995 soon led to a spate of escapes from the island. More often than not, the most successful defectors in terms of reaching the majors and succeeding there were pitchers, among them Liván Hernández (1995), who went on to record 178 career wins; Liván's half brother Orlando "El Duque" Hernández (1997), who won 90 major-league games; and José Contreras (2002), who won 78. That trend continued into the new century, with Marlins right-hander José Fernández, 2013 National League Rookie of the Year, and fireballing Cincinnati Reds closer Aroldis Chapman, who has saved 30 or more games in three consecutive seasons from 2012 to 2014, the most notable examples.

But in recent years, some of Cuba's best hitters also have defected and arrived in the majors with stunning results. In each his first three seasons in the majors, 2012–14, outfielder Yoenis Céspedes has hit at least 21 home runs and driven in 80 or more runs for the Oakland A's and Boston Red Sox. Los Angeles Dodgers outfielder Yasiel Puig burst onto the majors with a .319 batting average in 2013. And José Abreu hit .319 with 35 home runs and 103 RBIs for the Chicago White Sox in 2014, unanimously winning the American League Rookie of the Year award. Before the start of the 2014 major-league season, Bjarkman described Abreu as "easily the best hitter that's come out of Cuba to the majors, certainly after the revolution, and there probably weren't many before the revolution that had the natural skills as a hitter that he has." On December 17, 2014, U.S. president Barack Obama announced his decision to restore diplomatic relations with Cuba for the first time in more than fifty years. Following the announcement, Major League Baseball issued a statement saying it was "closely monitoring the White House's announcement regarding Cuban-American relations. . . . we will keep our Clubs informed if this different direction may impact the manner in which they conduct business on issues related to Cuba." With this historic shift in U.S.-Cuba relations, perhaps someday Cuban players will again be able, like their predecessors before Castro's revolution, to freely play in the major leagues without having to defect.

Appendix

Table 1. Almendares 1946–47 Cuban League Results

Date	Opponent	W/L	Score	Winning Pitcher	Losing Pitcher	Record
Oct. 26	Cienfuegos	W	9–1	Jorge Comellas	Alex Carrasquel	1–0
Oct. 28	Habana	W	1–0	Bill Tanner	Jim LaMarque	2–0
Oct. 30	Marianao	W	7–4	Jorge Comellas	Sandalio Consuegra	3–0
Nov. 1	Cienfuegos	W	4–3	Tomás de la Cruz	Homer Gibson	4–0
Nov. 2	Habana	W	8–3	Agapito Mayor	Jim LaMarque	5–0
Nov. 3	Marianao	L	9–3	Jesús Valenzuela	Bill Tanner	5–1
Nov. 6	Habana	L	3–2	Fred Martin	Lázaro Salazar	5–2
Nov. 7	Cienfuegos	W	3–0	Jorge Comellas	Alex Carrasquel	6–2
Nov. 9	Cienfuegos	L	8–7	Martín Dihigo	Bill Tanner	6–3
Nov. 13	Cienfuegos	W	9–4	Gentry Jessup	Homer Gibson	7–3

continued

Table 1—*Continued*

Date	Opponent	W/L	Score	Winning Pitcher	Losing Pitcher	Record
Nov. 17	Marianao	W	7–5	Gentry Jessup	Sandalio Consuegra	8–3
Nov. 18	Habana	L	4–0	Fred Martin	Agapito Mayor	8–4
Nov. 19	Marianao	W	8–2	Tomás de la Cruz	Oliverio Ortiz	9–4
Nov. 21	Habana	W	4–2	Gentry Jessup	Pedro Jiménez	10–4
Nov. 22	Cienfuegos	W	11–1	Agapito Mayor	Adrián Zabala	11–4
Nov. 24	Marianao	L	16–0	Paul Calvert	Tomás de la Cruz	11–5
Nov. 25	Marianao	W	2–1	Agapito Mayor	Jesús Valenzuela	12–5
Nov. 28	Habana	L	3–2	Pedro Jiménez	Gentry Jessup	12–6
Nov. 29	Cienfuegos	L	6–1	Alex Carrasquel	Agapito Mayor	12–7
Dec. 5	Habana	L	7–6	Fred Martin	Jorge Comellas	12–8
Dec. 8	Cienfuegos	W	11–6	Agapito Mayor	Jean Roy	13–8
Dec. 9	Cienfuegos	L	4–1	Max Manning	Tomás de la Cruz	13–9
Dec. 11	Marianao	L	1–0	Paul Calvert	Alberto Leal	13–10
Dec. 13	Habana	W	7–1	Gentry Jessup	Fred Martin	14–10
Dec. 15	Habana	L	4–3	Lázaro Medina	Tomás de la Cruz	14–11
Dec. 17	Marianao	W	5–0	Jorge Comellas	Paul Calvert	15–11
Dec. 19	Marianao	W	3–1	Tomás de la Cruz	Sandalio Consuegra	16–11
Dec. 22	Cienfuegos	L	1–0	Max Manning	Max Lanier	16–12
Dec. 25	Habana	L	5–2	Fred Martin	Agapito Mayor	16–13
Dec. 26	Marianao	L	3–0	Paul Calvert	Tomás de la Cruz	16–14

Date	Opponent	W/L	Score	Winning Pitcher	Losing Pitcher	Record
Dec. 26	Marianao	L	6–4	Oliverio Ortiz	Gentry Jessup	16–15
Dec. 27	Cienfuegos	L	5–1	Jean Roy	Jonas Gaines	16–16
Dec. 29	Marianao	W	5–3	Jonas Gaines	Paul Calvert	17–16
Dec. 30	Habana	L	6–1	Cocaína García	Agapito Mayor	17–17
Dec. 31	Habana	L	5–3	Pedro Jiménez	Tomás de la Cruz	17–18
Jan. 1	Cienfuegos	W	5–2	Lázaro Salazar	Max Manning	18–18
Jan. 3	Marianao	W	5–0	Jorge Comellas	Paul Calvert	19–18
Jan. 5	Habana	W	6–1	Max Lanier	Fred Martin	20–18
Jan. 7	Cienfuegos	W	2–1	Lázaro Salazar	Jean Roy	21–18
Jan. 8	Marianao	W	8–6	Tomás de la Cruz	Sandalio Consuegra	22–18
Jan. 12	Cienfuegos	W	6–1	Max Lanier	Max Manning	23–18
Jan. 13	Marianao	W	4–2	Jorge Comellas	Jim Lindsay	24–18
Jan. 16	Habana	W	9–1	Max Lanier	Fred Martin	25–18
Jan. 17	Marianao	W	6–4	Alberto Leal	Sandalio Consuegra	26–18
Jan. 19	Cienfuegos	L	11–7	Jean Roy	Lázaro Salazar	26–19
Jan. 22	Marianao	W	2–0	Gentry Jessup	Paul Calvert	27–19
Jan. 24	Habana	L	4–2	Terris McDuffie	Max Lanier	27–20
Jan. 30	Marianao	L	4–1	Aristónico Correoso	Gentry Jessup	27–21
Jan. 30	Marianao	W	4–1	Conrado Marrero	Sandalio Consuegra	28–21
Feb. 1	Habana	L	8–1	Fred Martin	Lázaro Salazar	28–22

continued

Table 1—*Continued*

Date	Opponent	W/L	Score	Winning Pitcher	Losing Pitcher	Record
Feb. 2	Cienfuegos	W	2–1	Agapito Mayor	Alex Carrasquel	29–22
Feb. 4	Marianao	L	4–3	Sandalio Consuegra	Jorge Comellas	29–23
Feb. 5	Cienfuegos	W	2–1	Agapito Mayor	Max Manning	30–23
Feb. 5	Cienfuegos	W	7–2	Tomás de la Cruz	Walter Nothe	31–23
Feb. 8	Cienfuegos	W	3–2	Lázaro Salazar	Jean Roy	32–23
Feb. 9	Habana	W	3–1	Max Lanier	Cocaína García	33–23
Feb. 12	Habana	W	5–0	Agapito Mayor	Fred Martin	34–23
Feb. 13	Cienfuegos	W	6–2	Lázaro Salazar	Max Manning	35–23
Feb. 15	Habana	W	6–2	Max Lanier	Terris McDuffie	36–23
Feb. 16	Marianao	L	6–0	Sandalio Consuegra	Jorge Comellas	36–24
Feb. 18	Cienfuegos	W	2–0	Agapito Mayor	Max Manning	37–24
Feb. 21	Cienfuegos	W	9–4	Agapito Mayor	Jean Roy	38–24
Feb. 22	Marianao	W	12–2	Tomás de la Cruz	Aristónico Correoso	39–24
Feb. 23	Habana	W	4–2	Max Lanier	Pedro Jiménez	40–24
Feb. 24	Habana	W	2–1	Agapito Mayor	Fred Martin	41–24
Feb. 25	Habana	W	9–2	Max Lanier	Lázaro Medina	42–24

Table 2. Habana 1946–47 Cuban League Results

Date	Opponent	W/L	Score	Winning Pitcher	Losing Pitcher	Record
Oct. 28	Almendares	L	1–0	Bill Tanner	Jim LaMarque	0–1
Oct. 29	Cienfuegos	W	4–3	Lázaro Medina	Adrián Zabala	1–1
Oct. 31	Marianao	W	1–0	Cocaína García	Oliverio Ortiz	2–1
Nov. 2	Almendares	L	8–3	Agapito Mayor	Jim LaMarque	2–2
Nov. 3	Cienfuegos	W	10–2	Pedro Jiménez	Martín Dihigo	3–2
Nov. 6	Almendares	W	3–2	Fred Martin	Lázaro Salazar	4–2
Nov. 11	Marianao	W	6–1	Pedro Jiménez	Paul Calvert	5–2
Nov. 14	Cienfuegos	W	10–2	Jim LaMarque	Martín Dihigo	6–2
Nov. 16	Marianao	W	11–1	Cocaína García	Max Lanier	7–2
Nov. 17	Cienfuegos	W	5–0	Lázaro Medina	John Williams	8–2
Nov. 18	Almendares	W	4–0	Fred Martin	Agapito Mayor	9–2
Nov. 21	Almendares	L	4–2	Gentry Jessup	Pedro Jiménez	9–3
Nov. 23	Marianao	L	3–2	Oliverio Ortiz	Lázaro Medina	9–4
Nov. 24	Cienfuegos	L	8–1	Adrián Zabala	Fred Martin	9–5
Nov. 26	Cienfuegos	W	4–3	Jim LaMarque	Adrián Zabala	10–5
Nov. 27	Marianao	L	4–3	Sandalio Consuegra	Lázaro Medina	10–6
Nov. 28	Almendares	W	3–2	Pedro Jiménez	Gentry Jessup	11–6
Dec. 4	Cienfuegos	W	11–7	Cocaína García	Walter Nothe	12–6

continued

Table 2—*Continued*

Date	Opponent	W/L	Score	Winning Pitcher	Losing Pitcher	Record
Dec. 5	Almendares	W	7–6	Fred Martin	Jorge Comellas	13–6
Dec. 6	Marianao	W	4–0	Lázaro Medina	Max Lanier	14–6
Dec. 8	Marianao	W	3–0	Pedro Jiménez	Sandalio Consuegra	15–6
Dec. 10	Cienfuegos	W	9–1	Cocaína García	Adrián Zabala	16–6
Dec. 13	Almendares	L	7–1	Gentry Jessup	Fred Martin	16–7
Dec. 15	Almendares	W	4–3	Lázaro Medina	Tomás de la Cruz	17–7
Dec. 16	Cienfuegos	W	3–0	Cocaína García	Max Manning	18–7
Dec. 18	Cienfuegos	W	6–4	Jim LaMarque	Walter Nothe	19–7
Dec. 20	Marianao	L	12–2	Oliverio Ortiz	Pedro Jiménez	19–8
Dec. 22	Marianao	W	10–0	Cocaína García	Sandalio Consuegra	20–8
Dec. 24	Cienfuegos	L	9–0	Adrián Zabala	Jim LaMarque	20–9
Dec. 25	Almendares	W	5–2	Fred Martin	Agapito Mayor	21–9
Dec. 28	Marianao	L	7–6	Jim Lindsay	Terris McDuffie	21–10
Dec. 29	Cienfuegos	L	4–2	Adrián Zabala	Fred Martin	21–11
Dec. 30	Almendares	W	6–1	Cocaína García	Agapito Mayor	22–11
Dec. 31	Almendares	W	5–3	Pedro Jiménez	Tomás de la Cruz	23–11
Jan. 1	Marianao	W	6–2	Terris McDuffie	Oliverio Ortiz	24–11
Jan. 4	Cienfuegos	W	12–9	Jim LaMarque	Adrián Zabala	25–11
Jan. 5	Almendares	L	6–1	Max Lanier	Fred Martin	25–12

Date	Opponent	W/L	Score	Winning Pitcher	Losing Pitcher	Record
Jan. 6	Marianao	L	5–3	Oliverio Ortiz	Cocaína García	25–13
Jan. 9	Marianao	W	4–1	Fred Martin	Paul Calvert	26–13
Jan. 10	Cienfuegos	W	11–5	Cocaína García	Max Manning	27–13
Jan. 12	Marianao	L	17–9	Aristónico Correoso	Terris McDuffie	27–14
Jan. 15	Cienfuegos	W	6–1	Cocaína García	Adrián Zabala	28–14
Jan. 16	Almendares	L	9–1	Max Lanier	Fred Martin	28–15
Jan. 18	Marianao	W	11–0	Terris McDuffie	Catayo González	29–15
Jan. 21	Cienfuegos	L	5–2	Adrián Zabala	Jim LaMarque	29–16
Jan. 24	Almendares	W	4–2	Terris McDuffie	Max Lanier	30–16
Jan. 25	Marianao	W	7–2	Fred Martin	Sandalio Consuegra	31–16
Jan. 26	Cienfuegos	W	6–0	Jim LaMarque	Jean Roy	32–16
Jan. 28	Marianao	W	5–3	Fred Martin	Paul Calvert	33–16
Jan. 28	Marianao	W	3–2	Pedro Jiménez	Oliverio Ortiz	34–16
Jan. 31	Cienfuegos	L	2–1	Adrián Zabala	Jim LaMarque	34–17
Feb. 1	Almendares	W	8–1	Fred Martin	Lázaro Salazar	35–17
Feb. 2	Marianao	L	3–1	Paul Calvert	Cocaína García	35–18
Feb. 6	Cienfuegos	W	4–3	Jim LaMarque	Adrián Zabala	36–18
Feb. 7	Marianao	L	5–4	Sandalio Consuegra	Fred Martin	36–19
Feb. 9	Almendares	L	3–1	Max Lanier	Cocaína García	36–20

continued

Table 2—*Continued*

Date	Opponent	W/L	Score	Winning Pitcher	Losing Pitcher	Record
Feb. 11	Marianao	W	3–1	Lázaro Medina	Aristónico Correoso	37–20
Feb. 12	Almendares	L	5–0	Agapito Mayor	Fred Martin	37–21
Feb. 15	Almendares	L	6–2	Max Lanier	Terris McDuffie	37–22
Feb. 16	Cienfuegos	W	7–2	Cocaína García	Jean Roy	38–22
Feb. 19	Marianao	W	3–0	Fred Martin	Paul Calvert	39–22
Feb. 20	Cienfuegos	W	10–5	Jim LaMarque	Alex Carrasquel	40–22
Feb. 23	Almendares	L	4–2	Max Lanier	Pedro Jiménez	40–23
Feb. 24	Almendares	L	2–1	Agapito Mayor	Fred Martin	40–24
Feb. 25	Almendares	L	9–2	Max Lanier	Lázaro Medina	40–25
Feb. 26	Cienfuegos	L	8–3	Ramón Roger	Jim LaMarque	40–26

Table 3. Brooklyn Dodgers 1947 Spring Training Results

Date	Site	Opponent	W/L	Score
Feb. 28	Havana	Boston Braves	W	8–0
Mar. 1	Havana	Boston Braves	L	5–2
Mar. 4	Caracas	New York Yankees	L	17–6
Mar. 5	Caracas	New York Yankees	W	8–7
Mar. 6	Caracas	New York Yankees	L	4–0
Mar. 8	Havana	New York Yankees	W	1–0 (10)
Mar. 9	Havana	New York Yankees	L	4–1
Mar. 9*	Havana	Havana Cubans	W	8–6
Mar. 10	Panama City	Panama Chesterfields	W	8–1
Mar. 11	Panama City	Cervecería	W	9–4
Mar. 12	Panama City	General Electric	L	7–6 (7)
Mar. 13	Cristobal, Canal Zone	Canal Zone All-Stars	W	8–4 (8)
Mar. 14	Balboa, Canal Zone	Pacific Service All-Stars	W	17–0
Mar. 14	Panama City	General Electric	W	4–3
Mar. 15	Panama City	Panama All-Stars	W	6–3
Mar. 15*	Havana	Havana Cubans	W	8–6
Mar. 17	Panama City	Montreal Royals	T	1–1 (8)
Mar. 17	Balboa, Canal Zone	Canal Zone All-Stars	W	4–3 (11)
Mar. 17*	Havana	Havana Cubans	W	1–0
Mar. 18	Cristobal, Canal Zone	Canal Zone All-Stars	T	6–6 (8)
Mar. 19	Cristobal, Canal Zone	General Electric	W	7–0
Mar. 19*	Havana	Cuban Selection	L	8–4
Mar. 20	Panama City	Montreal Royals	W	10–3
Mar. 21	Panama City	General Electric	W	5–0
Mar. 22	Havana	Cuban All-Stars	W	5–2
Mar. 23	Havana	Cuban All-Stars	W	12–4
Mar. 26	Havana	Montreal Royals	W	6–0
Mar. 28	Havana	Montreal Royals	W	5–2

continued

Table 3—*Continued*

Date	Site	Opponent	W/L	Score
Mar. 29	Havana	Montreal Royals	W	7–0
Mar. 30	Havana	Montreal Royals	L	6–5
Mar. 31	Havana	Montreal Royals	W	1–0
Apr. 1	Havana	Montreal Royals	W	6–1
Apr. 2	Havana	Montreal Royals	W	12–2
Apr. 5	Havana	Montreal Royals	W	6–3
Apr. 6	Havana	Montreal Royals	W	6–0
Apr. 7	Miami	St. Louis Browns	W	12–4
Apr. 8	Charleston, S.C.	Charleston Rebels	W	9–2
Apr. 10	Brooklyn	Montreal Royals	L	4–3
Apr. 11	Brooklyn	New York Yankees	W	14–6
Apr. 12	Brooklyn	New York Yankees	L	8–1

*Dodgers B squad game

Table 4. Montreal Royals 1947 Spring Training Results

Date	Site	Opponent	W/L	Score
Mar. 4	Havana	Havana Cubans	L	6–5
Mar. 5	Havana	Havana Cubans	T	5–5 (12)
Mar. 6	Havana	Havana Cubans	W	7–0
Mar. 7	Havana	Cuban Selection	W	7–4
Mar. 11	Havana	Havana Cubans	L	4–1
Mar. 12	Havana	Havana Cubans	W	13–2
Mar. 13	Havana	Havana Cubans	W	11–1
Mar. 14	Havana	Havana Cubans	W	7–3
Mar. 16	Cristobal, Canal Zone	General Electric	W	9–5
Mar. 17	Panama City	Brooklyn Dodgers	T	1–1 (8)
Mar. 20	Panama City	Brooklyn Dodgers	L	10–3
Mar. 26	Havana	Brooklyn Dodgers	L	6–0
Mar. 28	Havana	Brooklyn Dodgers	L	5–2
Mar. 29	Havana	Brooklyn Dodgers	L	7–0
Mar. 30	Havana	Brooklyn Dodgers	W	6–5
Mar. 31	Havana	Brooklyn Dodgers	L	1–0
Apr. 1	Havana	Brooklyn Dodgers	L	6–1
Apr. 2	Havana	Brooklyn Dodgers	L	12–2
Apr. 5	Havana	Brooklyn Dodgers	L	6–3
Apr. 6	Havana	Brooklyn Dodgers	L	6–0
Apr. 10	Brooklyn	Brooklyn Dodgers	W	4–3

Table 5. Players Who Jumped from Organized Baseball to the Mexican League, and Their Cuban League Connection

Player	MLB team[a]	Mexican League team[b]	Cuban League team[c]
Ace Adams	New York Giants	Veracruz	None
Alejandro Carrasquel	Chicago White Sox	Veracruz	Cienfuegos
Roberto Estalella	Philadelphia Athletics	Veracruz	Marianao
Harry Feldman	New York Giants	Veracruz	None
Murray Franklin	Detroit Tigers	Tampico	Marianao
Danny Gardella	New York Giants	Veracruz	Cienfuegos
Roland Gladu	Brooklyn Dodgers	Nuevo Laredo	Cienfuegos
George Hausmann	New York Giants	Torreón	Almendares
Red Hayworth	St. Louis Browns	Torreón	Cienfuegos
Lou Klein	St. Louis Cardinals	Veracruz	Habana
Max Lanier	St. Louis Cardinals	Veracruz	Marianao/ Almendares
Sal Maglie	New York Giants	Puebla	Cienfuegos
Fred Martin	St. Louis Cardinals	Mexico City	Habana
Charlie Mead	New York Giants	Veracruz	None
René Monteagudo	Philadelphia Phillies	Torreón	Habana
Luis Olmo	Brooklyn Dodgers	Mexico City	Santiago/ Leones
Roberto Ortiz	Washington Senators	Mexico City	Almendares
Mickey Owen	Brooklyn Dodgers	Veracruz	None
Napoleón Reyes	New York Giants	Puebla	Cienfuegos
James Steiner	Boston Red Sox	Nuevo Laredo	Santiago/ Alacranes
Vern Stephens	St. Louis Browns	Veracruz	None
Adrián Zabala	New York Giants	Puebla	Cienfuegos
Roy Zimmerman	New York Giants	Nuevo Laredo	Cienfuegos

[a]Major-league organization that owned player's rights
[b]Mexican League team with which player signed with initially
[c]Team during the 1946–47 Cuban League or National Federation seasons

Notes

Chapter 1. The Year of Dick Sisler

1. Williams, *Cuba*, 32.
2. Pérez, "Between Baseball and Bullfighting," 505.
3. Casas, Alfonso, and Pestana, *Viva y en juego*, 18.
4. Ibid.
5. Miñoso, *Just Call Me Minnie*, 17.
6. Ibid., 7, 8, 11–12.
7. Ibid., 10.
8. Ibid., 17.
9. Interview with Orestes "Minnie" Miñoso, June 2000.
10. Miñoso, *Just Call Me Minnie*, 14.
11. Testa, *Sal Maglie*, 19–20.
12. Ibid., 20, 24, 31.
13. Ibid., 32.
14. Ibid., 35, 38.
15. Ibid., 27, 43.
16. Roberts and Rogers, *Whiz Kids*, 114–15.
17. Figueredo, *Cuban Baseball: A Statistical History*, 187.
18. González Echevarría, *The Pride of Havana*, 217, 186.
19. Figueredo, *Cuban Baseball: A Statistical History*, 187.
20. Nowlin and Krieger, "La Tropical Park," 4.
21. Figueredo, *Cuban Baseball: A Statistical History*, 189, 192–93.
22. Santana Alonso, *El Inmortal del béisbol* 42–43.
23. Ibid., 200.
24. González Echevarría, *The Pride of Havana*, 17, 23.
25. Ibid., 17.

26. Ibid., 145.

27. Wilson, *Early Latino Ballplayers*, 77.

28. Testa, *Sal Maglie*, 46.

29. Ibid., 47–48.

30. Miñoso, *Just Call Me Minnie*, 18, 20.

31. Ibid., 20–21.

32. Ibid., 10.

33. Interview with Orestes "Minnie" Miñoso, June 2000.

34. Miñoso, *Just Call Me Minnie*, 23.

35. Ibid., 24.

36. McKelvey, *Mexican Raiders in the Major Leagues*, 44.

37. Ibid., 57.

38. Virtue, *South of the Color Barrier*, 127.

39. Interview with Luis Tiant Jr., 2001.

40. Riley, *Encyclopedia of the Negro Baseball Leagues*, 784.

41. René Molina, "Dick Sisler debutó conectando dos homers que dieron el éxito al Habana," *Diario de la Marina* (Havana), December 12, 1945, 14.

42. René Molina, "Dick Sisler pasó la bola sobre la cerca grande, pero el Habana perdió," *Diario de la Marina*, January 24, 1946, 14.

43. Miñoso, *Just Call Me Minnie*, 25.

44. Roberts and Rogers, *Whiz Kids*, 115.

45. Szalontai, *Close Shave*, 53.

46. Testa, *Sal Maglie*, 49.

47. Eladio Secades, "Un gran interrogación: El Habana," *Diario de la Marina*, October 20, 1946, 18.

48. Interview with Felo Ramírez, March 1994.

49. Márquez-Sterling, "Babe Ruth's Impact on Latin American Baseball and Latin American Ballplayers," 214.

50. Roberts and Rogers, *Whiz Kids*, 115.

51. Ibid.

52. Hemingway, *The Old Man and the Sea*, 21–22.

53. González Echevarría, *The Pride of Havana*, 293.

54. Figueredo, *Cuban Baseball: A Statistical History*, 263.

Chapter 2. Boxing Ernest Hemingway

1. Tygiel, *Baseball's Great Experiment*, 51–52.

2. Pietrusza, Silverman, and Gershman, *Baseball*, 939.

3. Harold Parrott, "When MacPhail Battled Rickey over Negro," *Sporting News*, July 24, 1976, 19.

4. Marren, "Branch Rickey and the Mainstream Press," 57.

5. United Press International, "Branch Rickey, 83, Dies in Missouri," *New York Times*, December 10, 1965, 1.

6. John B. Holway, "A Vote for Chandler, an Ignored Pioneer," *New York Times*, March 1, 1981, 2S.

7. "A Worthy Offspring," *Sporting News*, May 4, 1933, 1.

8. Pietrusza, Silverman, and Gershman, *Baseball*, 1, 185.

9. Allen and Walker, *Dixie Walker of the Dodgers*, 17.

10. Figueredo, *Who's Who in Cuban Baseball*, 154.

11. Burgos, *Playing America's Game*, 186.

12. Brown, "Cuban Baseball."

13. Burgos, *Cuban Star*, 160.

14. Barber and Creamer, *Rhubarb in the Catbird Seat*, 268.

15. Ibid., 268–69, 270, 273.

16. Swaine, "Jackie Robinson," 7.

17. Ibid., 8.

18. Rampersad, *Jackie Robinson*, 104–6, 109.

19. Ibid., 109.

20. Interview with Don Newcombe, January 1997.

21. Tygiel, *Baseball's Great Experiment*, 65–66.

22. Allen and Walker, *Dixie Walker of the Dodgers*, 28.

23. Ibid., 10–11.

24. Ibid., 11.

25. Durocher, *Nice Guys Finish Last*, 203.

26. Marlett, "Leo Durocher," 23.

27. Ibid.

28. Tygiel, *Baseball's Great Experiment*, 107–8, 106, 108, 109.

29. Wendell Smith, "Brooklyn Dodgers to Evade Race Issue, Train in Cuba," *Pittsburgh Courier*, September 28, 1946, 25.

30. Figueredo, *Cuban Baseball: A Statistical History*, 25–26.

31. Ibid., 241.

32. Durocher, *Nice Guys Finish Last*, 193, 172–74.

33. Ibid., 175–76.

34. Ibid., 176–77.

35. Hemingway, *The Old Man and the Sea*, 21, 23.

36. Fuentes, *Hemingway in Cuba*, 66.

37. Golenbock, *Bums*, 31–33.

38. Ibid., 33–34.

39. Ibid., 34.

40. Wolinsky, "Hugh Casey," 118.

41. Associated Press, "Brooks Leave for Havana Today; Leo Says Team Is Best in 9 Years," *Havana Post*, February 18, 1947, 6.

42. Marlett, "Leo Durocher," 25.

43. Durocher, *Nice Guys Finish Last*, 144.

44. Barber, *1947, When All Hell Broke Loose*, 97.

45. Wendell Smith, letter to Jackie Robinson, February 4, 1947, Wendell Smith Papers, National Baseball Hall of Fame Library collection.

46. Ibid.

47. Allen and Walker, *Dixie Walker of the Dodgers*, 147.

Chapter 3. Opening Day, Havana

1. J. G. Taylor Spink, "Game Booming in Cuba despite U.S. Slaps," *Sporting News*, January 22, 1947, 1, 6.
2. MLB.com, "Albert Benjamin 'Happy' Chandler."
3. Ray J. Gillespie, "O.B. Getting Dose of Own Medicine—Pasquel," *Sporting News*, February 28, 1946, 2.
4. McKenna, "Joe Cambria."
5. See note 3.
6. Theodore A. Ediger, "O.B. like Slave Market, Mexican Paper Charges," *Sporting News*, March 7, 1946, 2.
7. John Drebinger, "Gardella Reveals Jump from Giants," *New York Times*, February 19, 1946, 39.
8. "Mexicans' '$500,000 Offer' Ridiculed by Ted Williams," *Sporting News*, March 14, 1946, 2.
9. Shirley Povich, "Chandler Warns Mexican Jumpers to Return," *Sporting News*, March 14, 1946, 2.
10. John Drebinger, "Three Giants Jump to Mexican League," *New York Times*, April 1, 1946, 30.
11. Szalontai, *Close Shave*, 59.
12. Ibid., 60.
13. Dan Daniel, "Time to Rejoin O.B. Short, Chandler Warns Mexican Jumpers," *Sporting News*, April 11, 1946, 2.
14. Associated Press, "Players Who Jumped Contracts Ruled Automatically Suspended," *New York Times*, April 17, 1946, 41.
15. See note 13.
16. "Rizzuto Offer Disclosed," *New York Times*, June 9, 1946, 73.
17. Frederick G. Lieb, "Mexican Jumps Will Arouse Cards—Breadon," *Sporting News*, June 5, 1946, 5.
18. Alphonso Flores, "Pasquels to Toss Bigger, Better Bait at Musial," *Sporting News*, June 19, 1946, 2.
19. McKelvey, *Mexican Raiders in the Major Leagues*, 70–71.
20. MLB.com. "2012–2016 Basic Agreement."
21. "Army Draft Hits Nats' Four Latins," *Washington Post*, July 16, 1944, M6.
22. "Gil Torres Leaves for Cuba Seeking New U.S. Passport," *Washington Post*, July 17, 1944, 10.
23. "Pasquel Denies Gil Torres Is Signed by Mexican League," *Washington Post*, March 24, 1946, M6.
24. Shirley Povich, "Gil Torres, Guerra Report, Ending Mexican Rumors," *Washington Post*, March 29, 1946, 10.
25. Shirley Povich, "Torres, Guerra Protect O.B. Status by Joining New Circuit in Cuba," *Sporting News*, October 30, 1946, 12.
26. Chuck and Kaplan, *Walkoffs, Last Licks, and Final Outs*, 67.

27. Edgar G. Brands, "Gonzalez in Middle of O.B.-Cuban Controversy," *Sporting News*, October 23, 1946, 11.
28. René Cañizares, "Gates of New Million-Dollar Stadium in Havana Opened before 31,000," *Sporting News*, November 6, 1946, 14.
29. J. G. Taylor Spink, "Game Booming in Cuba despite U.S. Slaps," *Sporting News*, January 22, 1947, 1–6.
30. Isaac Rives, "Cuban League Outstrips New Circuit at Gate," *Sporting News*, November 6, 1946, 14.
31. "Alex Carrasquel y Agapito Mayor, los pitchers que actuarán esta tarde," *Diario de la Marina*, October 26, 1946, 18.
32. González Echevarría, *The Pride of Havana*, 86.
33. Torres, *La leyenda del béisbol cubano*, 16–17.
34. Ibid., 16.
35. Manzano, "Estadios."
36. Menéndez et al., *Libro azul*, 7.
37. González Echevarría, *The Pride of Havana*, 286.
38. Menéndez et al., *Libro azul*, 8.
39. González Echevarría, *The Pride of Havana*, 292.
40. Lasorda and Fisher, *The Artful Dodger*, 77.
41. González Echevarría, *The Pride of Havana*, 64–65.
42. René Cañizares, "Gates of New Million-Dollar Stadium in Havana Opened before 31,000," *Sporting News*, November 6, 1946, 14.
43. Figueredo, *Cuban Baseball: A Statistical History*, 223.
44. "Alex Carrasquel y Agapito Mayor, los pitchers que actuarán esta tarde," *Diario de la Marina*, October 26, 1946, 18.
45. Eladio Secades, "Play ball!! . . . Almendares y Cienfuegos," *Diario de la Marina*, October 26, 1946, 18.
46. René Molina, "Mas de 31,000 personas asistieron ayer a la inauguración del Stadium Habana," *Diario de la Marina*, October 28, 1946, 18.
47. Torres, *La leyenda del béisbol cubano*, 136.
48. Ibid.
49. Eladio Secades, "Así son los almendaristas," *Diario de la Marina*, October 26, 1946, 18.

Chapter 4. The American Series

1. Roscoe McGowen, "46 Players Reach Cuba for Training," *New York Times*, March 20, 1947, 34.
2. González Echevarría, "The '47 Dodgers in Havana."
3. Interview with Felo Ramírez, January 1997.
4. González Echevarría, *The Pride of Havana*, 45.
5. Interview with Felo Ramírez, January 1997.
6. Alexander, *John McGraw*, 17–18, 11–12.
7. Ibid., 13–17.

8. Ibid., 17–18.

9. Pérez, "Between Baseball and Bullfighting," 493.

10. Alexander, *John McGraw*, 18–19.

11. Monfort Soberats, "Recordando a José de la Caridad Méndez."

12. Ibid., 82.

13. Nieto Fernández, *José Méndez, el Diamante Negro*, 15.

14. Holway, *Blackball Stars*, 52–54.

15. Alexander, *Ty Cobb*, 98.

16. Ibid., 54–55.

17. Torres, *La leyenda del béisbol cubano*, 45.

18. Ashwill, "Ty Cobb in Cuba, 1910."

19. Figueredo, *Cuban Baseball: A Statistical History*, 90.

20. Burgos, *Playing America's Game*, 90.

21. Ibid., 95.

22. Alexander, *John McGraw*, 158.

23. Ibid., 159.

24. Holway, *Blackball Stars*, 55.

25. "Méndez Yet Great," *Sporting News*, January 25, 1912, 8.

26. Alexander, *John McGraw*, 160.

27. Ibid.

28. "Méndez Yet Great," *Sporting News*, January 25, 1912, 8.

29. Holway, *Blackball Stars*, 56.

30. Bjarkman, *Baseball with a Latin Beat*, 172.

31. McGraw, *The Real McGraw*, 239–40.

32. Holway, *Blackball Stars*, 36.

33. Figueredo, *Who's Who in Cuban Baseball*, 354–55.

34. Ribowsky, *Don't Look Back*, 61.

35. Ibid., 61.

36. Tye, *Satchel*, 133.

37. González Echevarría, *The Pride of Havana*, 185, 409.

38. Holway, *Blackball Stars*, 126.

39. Figueredo, *Who's Who in Cuban Baseball*, 82.

40. Ruiz, *The Bambino Visits Cuba*, 9.

41. Ibid., 9.

42. Holway, *Blackball Stars*, 128.

43. Ruiz, *The Bambino Visits Cuba*, 9.

44. González Echevarría, *The Pride of Havana*, 159.

45. Ibid., 160.

46. Holway, *Blackball Stars*, 125.

47. Ruiz, *The Bambino Visits Cuba*, 17.

48. González Echevarría, *The Pride of Havana*, 161.

49. Holway, *Blackball Stars*, 129.

50. Montville, *The Big Bam*, 225.

51. Marasco, "Our Giants in Havana."

52. Ibid.

Chapter 5. Living Legends

1. Wilson, *Early Latino Ballplayers*, 110.
2. Eladio Secades, "Un gran interrogación: El Habana," *Diario de la Marina*, October 20, 1946, 18.
3. Figueredo, *Who's Who in Cuban Baseball*, 45.
4. González Echevarría, *The Pride of Havana*, 145.
5. Wilson, *Early Latino Ballplayers*, 90.
6. Holway, *Blackball Stars*, 236.
7. Wilson, *Early Latino Ballplayers*, 41.
8. Ibid., 24.
9. Toot, *Armando Marsans*, 8.
10. Wilson, *Early Latino Ballplayers*, 26.
11. Ibid., 26.
12. Burgos, *Playing America's Game*, 92.
13. Ibid., 95.
14. Hemingway, *The Old Man and the Sea*, 23.
15. González Echevarría, *The Pride of Havana*, 143.
16. Wilson, *Early Latino Ballplayers*, 106.
17. González Echevarría, *The Pride of Havana*, 143.
18. Santana Alonso, *El Inmortal del béisbol*, 6–7.
19. Holway, *Blackball Stars*, 237.
20. Wilson, *Early Latino Ballplayers*, 29.
21. Burgos, *Playing America's Game*, 97.
22. Wilson, *Early Latino Ballplayers*, 30.
23. Burgos, *Playing America's Game*, 97–98.
24. Wilson, *Early Latino Ballplayers*, 70.
25. "Errors and Long Hits Beat Boston," *New York Times*, May 21, 1914, 12.
26. Wilson, *Early Latino Ballplayers*, 74.
27. González Echevarría, *The Pride of Havana*, 174.
28. John Kieran, "Mr. Terry Tells a Tale," *New York Times*, October 12, 1933, 36.
29. Arthur Daley, "The Cuban Curver," *New York Times*, July 14, 1957, 146.
30. González Echevarría, *The Pride of Havana*, 144.
31. Figueredo, *Who's Who in Cuban Baseball*, 46.
32. Wilson, *Early Latino Ballplayers*, 108.
33. Ibid., 111.
34. González Echevarría, *The Pride of Havana*, 44.
35. Wilson, *Early Latino Ballplayers*, 111.
36. Ibid., 36.
37. Ibid.
38. Holway, *Blackball Stars*, 244.

39. Burgos, *Cuban Star*, 50, 51.

40. Riley, *Encyclopedia of the Negro Baseball Leagues*, 233.

41. Figueredo, *Cuban Baseball: A Statistical History*, 212.

Chapter 6. Separate and Unequal

1. Wendell Smith, "The Sports Beat," *Pittsburgh Courier*, March 1, 1947, 16.

2. Ibid.

3. Ibid.

4. Hotel Nacional de Cuba, "Cuba's Hotel Nacional—A Historical Profile."

5. Ibid.

6. Ibid.

7. English, *Havana Nocturne*, 32.

8. Ibid., 36.

9. Ibid., 37.

10. Ibid., 33.

11. Ibid., 40–41.

12. Ibid., 5.

13. Ibid., 42.

14. Ibid., 42.

15. Eladio Secades, "No hay razón para alarmarse," *Diario de la Marina*, February 22, 1947, 18.

16. Sam Lacy, "Looking 'Em Over," *Baltimore Afro-American*, March 8, 1947, 12.

17. Wendell Smith, "The Training Camp Rhumba," *Pittsburgh Courier*, March 8, 1947, 17.

18. Dan Daniel, "Pasquel Goes After Whole Flock of Dodgers—and Draws the Bird," *Sporting News*, March 5, 1947, 17.

19. Roscoe McGowen, "Pasquel in Talks with 40 Dodgers," *New York Times*, February 26, 1947, 29.

20. Ibid.

21. Michael Gaven, "Lanier Has No Regrets for Jumping, Yet Yearns for Old Big League Days," *Sporting News*, March 19, 1947, 16.

22. Ibid.

23. "Lanier Fights Cut in Mexican Salary," *New York Times*, February 16, 1947, S5.

24. Lester Bromberg, "Lanier, Lacking Major League Stuff, Staggering Through Cuban Circuit," *Sporting News*, March 5, 1947, 18.

25. Dan Daniel, "Pasquel Goes After Whole Flock of Dodgers—and Draws the Bird," *Sporting News*, March 5, 1947, 17.

26. Roscoe McGowen, "Walker Devises First-Base Screen," *New York Times*, February 23, 1947, S1.

27. Roscoe McGowen, "Rickey on Trail of New Cuban Star," *New York Times*, February 25, 1947, 35.

28. Ibid.

29. Sam Lacy, "Activities of Stars under Cuban Sun," *Baltimore Afro-American*, March 8, 1947, 25.

30. Sam Lacy, "Baseball Is Cubans' Religion; Stars Live off Fat of Land, but Work Hard," *Baltimore Afro-American*, March 8, 1947, 13.

31. Ibid.

32. Ibid.

33. Sam Lacy, "Looking 'Em Over," *Baltimore Afro-American*, March 8, 1947, 12.

34. Tygiel, *Baseball's Great Experiment*, 165.

35. Rampersad, *Jackie Robinson*, 142.

36. Herbert Goren, "Dodgers Split on Robinson," *Sporting News*, March 12, 1947, 17.

37. Tygiel, *Baseball's Great Experiment*, 165.

38. Campanella, *It's Good to Be Alive*, 95.

39. Ibid.

40. Interview with Don Newcombe, January 1997.

41. Ibid.

42. Ibid.

43. Dan Daniel, "Pasquel Goes After Whole Flock of Dodgers—and Draws the Bird," *Sporting News*, March 5, 1947, 17.

44. Ibid.

45. Ibid.

46. Ibid.

47. "Rickey Snubbed by Pasquel—Jorge Tells Mexican Press," *Sporting News*, March 19, 1947, 2.

48. Kevin Merida, "Going to Bat for Robinson," *Washington Post*, June 11, 1997, D8.

49. Andrew Schall, "Wendell Smith: The Pittsburgh Journalist Who Made Jackie Robinson Mainstream," *Pittsburgh Post-Gazette*, June 5, 2011, B7.

50. Interview with Sam Lacy, January 1997.

51. Interview with Don Newcombe, January 1997.

52. "Air of Lavishness Pervades Game," *Sporting News*, March 19, 1947, 12.

53. Dan Daniel, "Plutocratic Life with the Opulent Dodgers," *Sporting News*, March 12, 1947, 14.

Chapter 7. Tale of Two Leagues

1. Figueredo, *Who's Who in Cuban Baseball*, 23.

2. Pietrusza, Silverman, and Gershman, *Baseball*, 639.

3. Frederick G. Lieb, "Mexican Jumps Will Arouse Cards—Breadon," *Sporting News*, June 5, 1946, 5.

4. Alfonso Flores, "Babe's Batting Demonstration Stirs Fight by Mexican Pilots," *Sporting News*, June 12, 1946, 2.

5. Riley, *Encyclopedia of the Negro Baseball Leagues*, 303.

6. O'Neil, *I Was Right on Time*, 11.

7. Riley, *Encyclopedia of the Negro Baseball Leagues*, 304.

8. Ibid., 304.

9. Figueredo, *Cuban Baseball: A Statistical History*, 224.

10. Figueredo, *Who's Who in Cuban Baseball*, 227.

11. Figueredo, *Cuban Baseball: A Statistical History*, 251.

12. González Echevarría, *The Pride of Havana*, 267.

13. Ibid., 258.

14. Ibid., 204.

15. Burgos, *Cuban Star*, 169.

16. González Echevarría, *The Pride of Havana*, 261.

17. Figueredo, *Who's Who in Cuban Baseball*, 228.

18. Ibid., 154.

19. Bjarkman, *A History of Cuban Baseball*, 71.

20. González Echevarría, *The Pride of Havana*, 237.

21. Riley, *Encyclopedia of the Negro Baseball Leagues*, 588.

22. Figueredo, *Who's Who in Cuban Baseball*, 66.

23. McKelvey, *Mexican Raiders in the Major Leagues*, 137.

24. Ibid., 141.

25. Dan Hall, "Pasquels to Land More Major Stars, Lanier Predicts," *Sporting News*, November 13, 1946, 20.

26. René Cañizares, "O.B.-Approved Cuban Loop Raps Major Run-Out," *Sporting News*, December 18, 1946, 2.

27. Ibid.

28. René Cañizares, "Perfect Game Spoiled by Hernández," *Sporting News*, December 25, 1946, 18.

29. "Cuban Pro Loop Bars Jumpers to Rivals—but Leaves Loophole," *Sporting News*, November 13, 1946, 22.

30. René Cañizares, "Cubans Shun Night Spots to Jam Winter Loop Tilts," *Sporting News*, December 4, 1946, 26.

31. Ibid.

32. René Cañizares, "Rival Cuban Leagues War over Raids on Players," *Sporting News*, November 27, 1946, 18.

33. See note 30.

34. Dan Daniel, "Don Dan Daniel Reports on Beisbol in Habana," *Sporting News*, March 5, 1947, 7.

35. René Cañizares, "Cubans Shun Night Spots to Jam Winter Loop Tilts," *Sporting News*, December 4, 1946, 26.

36. See note 26.

37. "Cuban Sports Leader Raps Happy, O.B. for 'Monopoly,'" *Sporting News*, December 25, 1946, 18.

38. Sid C. Keener, "Chandler Puts González on Bench for Five Years," *Sporting News*, December 11, 1946, 9.

39. Ibid.

40. "Cuban Pro Loop Bars Jumpers to Rivals—but Leaves Loophole," *Sporting News*, November 13, 1946, 22.

41. "Directiva del Club Habana," in Liga de Base-Ball Profesional Cubana, *Campeonato de 1950–51: Programa oficial*, 27.

42. "Mike Gonzalez Becomes Sole Owner at Havana," Sporting News, December 19, 1946, 2.

43. Wilson, *Early Latino Ballplayers*, 81–82.
44. René Cañizares, "Perfect Game Spoiled by Hernandez," *Sporting News*, December 25, 1946, 18.
45. Interview with Buck O'Neil, March 1999.
46. René Cañizares, "Cuban Series Canceled after First Contest," *Sporting News*, January 15, 1947, 16.
47. René Cañizares, "O.B.-Approved Cuban Loop Raps Major Run-Out," *Sporting News*, December 18, 1946, 2.
48. René Cañizares, "Cuban Winter League Rival Ends Season," *Sporting News*, January 8, 1946, 17.

Chapter 8. Hermit in Havana

1. Interview with Andrés Fleitas, January 1997.
2. Sam Lacy, "Playing with Colored Stars O.K.—Lanier," *Baltimore Afro-American*, March 8, 1947, 25.
3. Ibid.
4. Dan Daniel, "Happy, Laraine Lead Lippy to Sawdust Trail," *Sporting News*, March 12, 1947, 8.
5. Ibid., 1, 8.
6. Roscoe McGowen, "Dodgers Conquer Braves at Havana," *New York Times*, March 1, 1947, 18.
7. Ibid.
8. Roscoe McGowen, "Braves Triumph over Dodgers, 5–2," *New York Times*, March 2, 1947, 111.
9. "Catholics Quit Dodgers Knothole Club in Protest over the Conduct of Durocher," *New York Times*, March 1, 1947.
10. Jack Lang, "CYO Raps Lip, Quits Knothole Club," *Sporting News*, March 12, 1947, 8.
11. John Drebinger, "Yanks Bow in Exhibition at Caracas, 4–3; 2 Rivals Jailed When They Refused to Pitch," *New York Times*, March 2, 1947, 111.
12. John Drebinger, "Dodgers on Hand for Caracas Set," *New York Times*, March 4, 1947, 33.
13. John Drebinger, "Yankees Beat Dodgers under Lights at Caracas," *New York Times*, March 5, 1947, 33.
14. John Drebinger, "Brooklyn Victor under Lights, 8–7," *New York Times*, March 6, 1947, 32.
15. John Drebinger, "9,000 See Bombers Beat Brooklyn, 4–0," *New York Times*, March 7, 1947, 29.
16. Sam Lacy, "Dodgers Sign Mexican Second Baseman for Reported $5,000," *Baltimore Afro-American*, March 15, 1947, 12.
17. Burgos, *Cuban Star*, 95–96.
18. Ibid., 162.
19. Riley, *Encyclopedia of the Negro Baseball Leagues*, 554.

20. Sam Lacy, "Minoso Rejects Royals' Offer," *Baltimore Afro-American*, March 7, 1947, 12.

21. Roscoe McGowen, "Wensloff to Hurl for Harris Squad," *New York Times*, March 8, 1947, 18.

22. Barber, *1947, When All Hell Broke Loose*, 106–7.

23. Ibid., 107–8.

24. Wendell Smith, "A Pair of Kings . . . of 'Sock,'" *Pittsburgh Courier*, March 22, 1947, 14.

25. Sam Lacy, "Cubans Sour on Jackie; Unimpressive in Workouts," *Baltimore Afro-American*, March 15, 1947, 12.

26. See note 24.

27. Wendell Smith, "The Training Camp Rhumba," *Pittsburgh Courier*, March 8, 1947, 17.

28. Wendell Smith, "Knockdowns Thrill Cubans," *Pittsburgh Courier*, March 15, 1947, 16.

29. Ibid.

30. Wendell Smith, "Robinson May Need a Minor Operation," *Pittsburgh Courier*, March 15, 1947, 16.

31. Ibid.

32. Sam Lacy, "On-the-Scene: Dope on Jackie's Chances with the Dodgers," *Baltimore Afro-American*, March 15, 1947, 2.

33. Dan Daniel, "Lip vs. Larry Veracity Feud Grows Hotter," *Sporting News*, December 4, 1946, 15.

34. "MacPhail Added Blowhard Voice to My Critics—Lippy," *Sporting News*, March 19, 1947, 5.

35. Herbert Goren, "A Limit to New Leaf: Leo Shuns Gayety for Books, but He's the Same Lippy on Field," *Sporting News*, April 2, 1947, 8.

Chapter 9. New Year's Resurrection

1. René Molina, "Despidió el año el Habana con la acostumbrada paliza a los Azules," *Diario de la Marina*, January 1, 1947, 16.

2. Cuco Conde, "Iniciaron el año los Rojos con un triunfo sobre el Marianao, 6 Por 2," *Diario de la Marina*, January 2, 1947, 14.

3. Torres, *La leyenda del béisbol cubano*, 143.

4. Martínez Peraza, *Por amor a la pelota*, 34.

5. Casas, Alfonso, and Pestana, *Viva y en juego*, 57–63.

6. Figueredo, *Who's Who in Cuban Baseball*, 149.

7. Treto Cisneros, *The Mexican League*, 139.

8. Interview with Max Lanier, April 1994.

9. Riley, *Encyclopedia of the Negro Baseball Leagues*, 780.

10. Gerry Fraley, "Recalling Forgotten Man of '47," *St. Louis Post-Dispatch*, February 2, 2007, D1.

11. Riley, *Encyclopedia of the Negro Baseball Leagues*, 780.

12. Ibid.

13. See note 10.
14. Riley, *Encyclopedia of the Negro Baseball Leagues*, 780.
15. Frank (Buck) O'Neill, "Torres May Decide to Follow González on O.B. Blacklist Due to U.S.-Cuban Row," *Sporting News*, January 8, 1947, 17.
16. González Echevarría, *The Pride of Havana*, 34.
17. Figueredo, *Who's Who in Cuban Baseball*, 192.
18. Figueredo, *Cuban Baseball: A Statistical History*, 203–5.
19. Ibid., 218–19.
20. René Molina, "Lázaro Salazar supero a Jim Roy en un emotivo duelo que duro 10 actos," *Diario de la Marina*, January 8, 1947, 14.
21. Interview with Buck O'Neil, March 1999.
22. Riley, *Encyclopedia of the Negro Baseball Leagues*, 589.
23. Ibid.
24. Interview with Buck O'Neil, March 1999.
25. Interview with Max Lanier, April 1994.
26. González Echevarría, *The Pride of Havana*, 282.
27. Rucker and Bjarkman, *Smoke*, 15.
28. Figueredo, *Cuban Baseball: A Statistical History*, 256.
29. René Molina, "Dando batazos de todos metrajes y colores los Azules vencieron anoche al Cienfuegos 11 por 1," *Diario de la Marina*, November 23, 1947, 18.
30. René Molina, "Adolfo Luque y Mike González le dieron al juego un matiz emotivo," *Diario de la Marina*, January 21, 1947, 16.
31. Ibid.
32. Ibid.
33. Ribowsky, *The Power and the Darkness*, 292–93.
34. Riley, *Encyclopedia of the Negro Baseball Leagues*, 313.
35. Figueredo, *Cuban Baseball: A Statistical History*, 218.
36. Ibid., 219.
37. Ibid.
38. Ibid., 218.
39. Ibid., 223.
40. Interview with Agapito Mayor, January 1997.
41. Martínez Peraza, *Por amor a la pelota*, 29–30.
42. Bjarkman, *Diamonds around the Globe*, 469.
43. Interview with Gloria Mayor, April 2008.

Chapter 10. Panama and the Petition

1. John Drebinger, "MacPhail Aims Blast at Dodgers for 'Running Out' of Third Game," *New York Times*, March 11, 1947, 33.
2. Dan Daniel, "Larry-Lip War Heads for Showdown," *Sporting News*, March 19, 1947, 5.
3. "Chandler Tells Yanks Boss 'Think It Over' before Filing Written Charges against Rickey, Durocher and Parrott," *New York Times*, March 14, 1947, 29.
4. Ibid.

5. "Leo Surprised, but Will Talk," *Havana Post*, March 14, 1947, 6.
6. Associated Press, "Yanks Prexy Asks Chandler to Probe Rickey's Remarks," *Havana Post*, March 16, 1947, 10.
7. Sam Lacy, "On-the-Scene: Dope on Jackie's Chances with the Dodgers," *Baltimore Afro-American*, March 15, 1947, 2.
8. Tygiel, *Baseball's Great Experiment*, 168.
9. Ibid., 167.
10. Herbert Goren, "Dodgers Split on Robinson," *Sporting News*, March 12, 1947, 17.
11. Interview with Sam Lacy, January 1997.
12. Harold C. Burr, "Robinson Will Get Crack at First Base—and Chance with Bums If Impressive," *Sporting News*, March 19, 1947, 10.
13. Ibid.
14. Wendell Smith, "Royals, Brooklyn Basking in Sun," *Pittsburgh Courier*, November 29, 1947, 14.
15. Ibid.
16. Wendell Smith, "Robinson, 'Camp' Hot in Tropic Game." *Pittsburgh Courier*, March 22, 1947, 15.
17. Interview with Sam Lacy, January 1997.
18. Wendell Smith, "Robinson, 'Camp' Hot in Tropic Game," *Pittsburgh Courier*, March 22, 1947, 15.
19. Harold C. Burr, "Dodgers Players to Have Voice on Jackie's Climb," *Sporting News*, January 22, 1947, 16.
20. See note 10.
21. Interview with Buzzie Bavasi, January 1997.
22. Allen, *Jackie Robinson: A Life Remembered*, 96.
23. Interview with Bobby Bragan, January 1997.
24. Tygiel, *Baseball's Great Experiment*, 168.
25. Ibid., 205.
26. Bill Roeder, "Durocher Dashes to Sweetie as Robinson Goes into Action," *Sporting News*, March 26, 1947, 13.
27. Ibid.
28. Harold C. Burr, "Jackie's All Jake at First with Dodgers Coach Pitler," *Sporting News*, March 26, 1947, 13.
29. Cleto Hernández, "Hotel in Panama Jimcrows Jackie Robinson," *New York Amsterdam News*, March 29, 1947, 13.
30. Ibid.
31. "Robinson Segregated in Panama?" *Pittsburgh Courier*, March 29, 1947, 4.
32. Mann, *The Jackie Robinson Story*, 168.
33. Interview with Bobby Bragan, January 1997.
34. Roscoe McGowen, "Dodgers Play Tie with Royals, 1–1," *New York Times*, March 18, 1947, 37.
35. Associated Press, "Deadline Set for Robinson," *Havana Post*, March 19, 1947, 6.
36. Gayle Talbot, "Happy Chandler Denies Sports Writer's Story," *Havana Post*, March 19, 1947, 6.

37. Ibid.

38. John B. Old, "Miss Day to 'Show Cause' March 4," *Sporting News*, February 26, 1947, 10.

39. Ibid.

40. Ibid.

41. "Leo Keeps Lip Zippered While in California," *Sporting News*, March 26, 1947, 13.

42. Wendell Smith, "Robinson Sensational in Training Camp Games," *Pittsburgh Courier*, March 29, 1947, 15.

43. Ibid.

44. Interview with Bobby Bragan, January 1997.

45. Kahn, *The Era*, 35.

46. Allen and Walker, *Dixie Walker of the Dodgers*, 2.

47. Weiss and Wright, "Top 100 Teams: 92. 1947 Havana Cubans."

48. Ibid.

49. McKenna, "Joe Cambria."

50. Ibid.

51. Weiss and Wright, "Top 100 Teams: 92. 1947 Havana Cubans."

Chapter 11. Whoever Defeats Almendares Dies

1. Eladio Secades, "No estaba allí Max Lanier," *Diario de la Marina*, February 2, 1947, 18.

2. "Unidentified Major Star Cuba-Bound, Says Lanier," *Sporting News*, December 11, 1946, 22.

3. "Lanier Row Denied," *Sporting News*, February 12, 1947, 22.

4. González Echevarría, *The Pride of Havana*, 36.

5. See note 1.

6. René Molina, "Con sólo dos días de descanso, el zurdo Mayor le ganó al Cienfuegos," *Diario de la Marina*, February 6, 1947, 18.

7. Ibid.

8. McKelvey, *Mexican Raiders in the Major Leagues*, 147.

9. Ibid.

10. René Molina, "Desplegando un juego brillante en todos los órdenes ganó el Habana," *Diario de la Marina*, February 7, 1947, 14.

11. René Cañizares, "Press Balked, Cuban Player Strike Failure," *Sporting News*, January 12, 1947, 22.

12. René Cañizares, "O.B.-Approved Cuban League Loses $81,147," *Sporting News*, February, 19, 1947, 20.

13. René Molina, "Anotando dos veces en el séptimo, ganaron las estrellas americanas," *Diario de la Marina*, February 11, 1947, 18.

14. Ibid.

15. René Molina, "Agapito Mayor blanqueó al Habana, permitiéndole sólo tres sencillos," *Diario de la Marina*, February 13, 1947, 16.

16. Eladio Secades, "Injusto . . . y peligroso," *Diario de la Marina*, February 15, 1947, 7.

17. Eladio Secades, "El Habana no batea," *Diario de la Marina*, February 14, 1947, 16.
18. René Molina, "Mientras Lanier dejaba en 4 hits a los Rojos, McDuffie era bombardeado," *Diario de la Marina*, February 16, 1947, 7.
19. Interview with Max Lanier, January 1997.
20. Interview with Agapito Mayor, January 1997.
21. Eladio Secades, "Habana y Almendares," *Diario de la Marina*, February 23, 1947, 18.
22. Interview with Andrés Fleitas, January 1997.
23. Lester Bromberg, "Lanier, Lacking Major League Stuff, Staggering through Cuban Circuit," *Sporting News*, March 5, 1947, 18.
24. Ibid.
25. Interview with Max Lanier, January 1997.
26. Pérez, *On Becoming Cuban*, 75.
27. Elizondo, "History of the Cuban Liberation Wars."
28. González Echevarría, *The Pride of Havana*, 38.
29. Interview with Gloria Mayor, April 2008.
30. Interview with Agapito Mayor, January 1997.
31. Interview with Felo Ramírez, January 1997.
32. René Molina, "Escalo el Almendares el primer lugar del campeonato al vencer a los Leones," *Diario de la Marina*, February, 25, 1947, 16.
33. Interview with Max Lanier, January 1997.
34. Interview with Andrés Fleitas, January 1997.
35. See note 32.
36. Interview with Agapito Mayor, January 1997.
37. See note 32.
38. Ibid.
39. Ibid.
40. "Hoy: Habana vs. Almendares en el juego decisivo," *Diario de la Marina*, February 25, 1947, 16.
41. Ibid.
42. Interview with Andrés Fleitas, January 1997.
43. Interview with Felo Ramírez, January 1997.
44. Interview with Max Lanier, April 1994.
45. Ibid.
46. González Echevarría, *The Pride of Havana*, 145.
47. Lasorda and Fisher, *The Artful Dodger*, 75.
48. René Molina, "Venciendo por tercera vez consecutiva a la Habana, los 'Alacranes' ganaron el campeonato nacional," *Diario de la Marina*, February 26, 1947, 16.
49. Interview with Gloria Mayor, April 2008.
50. See note 48.
51. Interview with Andrés Fleitas, January 1997.
52. See note 48.
53. Interview with Andrés Fleitas, January 1997.
54. Interview with Leonardo Agüero, March 1999.

55. Interview with Andrés Fleitas, January 1997.

56. Interview with Max Lanier, March 1999.

57. Interview with Max Lanier, January 1997.

58. Interview with Max Lanier, April 1994.

59. Eladio Secades, "Un Verdadero Campeón!" *Diario de la Marina*, February 26, 1947, 16.

60. Interview with Agapito Mayor, January 1997.

61. Interview with Gloria Mayor, April 2008.

62. Interview with Andrés Fleitas, January 1997.

63. Interview with Buck O'Neil, March 1999.

64. Interview with Andrés Fleitas, January 1997.

65. Interview with Leonardo Agüero, March 1999.

66. See note 48.

67. Interview with Andrés Fleitas, January 1997.

Chapter 12. Opening Day, Brooklyn

1. Allen and Walker, *Dixie Walker of the Dodgers*, 3.

2. Ibid.

3. Interview with Don Newcombe, January 1997.

4. Interview with Buzzie Bavasi, January 1997.

5. Golenbock, *Bums*, 138.

6. "Lanier Fights Cut in Mexican Salary," *New York Times*, February 16, 1947, S5.

7. Ibid.

8. José Gómez, "Team Desertions Shake Wobbly Mexican League," *Sporting News*, March 19, 1947, 2.

9. Dan Daniel, "Pasquel Goes After Whole Flock of Dodgers—and Draws the Bird," *Sporting News*, March 5, 1947, 17.

10. See note 8.

11. Ibid.

12. Reginald Wood, "19 Outlawed Ex-Major Leaguers Not Returning to Mexican Loop," *Havana Post*, March 21, 1947, 6.

13. Interview with Max Lanier, January 1997.

14. See note 12.

15. Roscoe McGowen, "Dodgers Set Back All-Stars by 5–2," *New York Times*, March 23, 1947, 1–2.

16. Tom Meany, "Outside the Gas Chamber," *Sporting News*, April 2, 1947, 2.

17. Ibid.

18. Durocher, *Nice Guys Finish Last*, 253.

19. Ibid., 255.

20. Ibid., 256.

21. Dan Daniel, "Writing Ban for Lip Seen as Outcome of Hearing," *Sporting News*, April 2, 1947, 2.

22. Dan Daniel, "Rickey Skips Outside Ropes; Larry and Lippy Left in Ring," *Sporting News*, April 9, 1947, 6.

23. Ibid.

24. Joe Reichler, "Chandler Reserves Decision on Rickey, Yankees Prexy Case," *Havana Post*, March 25, 1947, 6.

25. Interview with Sam Lacy, January 1997.

26. Interview with Mike Sandlock, August 2011.

27. Roscoe McGowen, "Dodgers Defeat Montreal, 5 to 2," *New York Times*, March 29, 1947, 11.

28. Gayle Talbot, "Chandler, MacPhail, Rickey Meet Today," *Havana Post*, March 28, 1947, 6.

29. Gayle Talbot, "Rickey, MacPhail Rift Seems Over," *Havana Post*, March 29, 1947, 6.

30. Ibid.

31. Durocher, *Nice Guys Finish Last*, 259.

32. See note 29.

33. See note 22.

34. Ibid.

35. See note 21.

36. "U.S. Stars Missing as Mexican Loop Lifts Lid," *Sporting News*, April 2, 1947, 11.

37. Ibid.

38. Associated Press, "Cuban Hurler Wins Opener As Season Starts in Mexico," *Havana Post*, March 28, 1947.

39. See note 36.

40. Reginald Wood, "19 Outlawed Ex-Major Leaguers Not Returning to Mexican Loop," *Havana Post*, March 21, 1947, 6.

41. Roscoe McGowen, "Dodgers Shut Out Montreal, 7–0, As Kirby Higbe Hurls 5-hitter," *New York Times*, March 30, 1947, 1–3.

42. Wendell Smith, "Jackie Robinson Will Play First Base for Brooklyn Dodgers," *Pittsburgh Courier*, March 29, 1947, 1.

43. Falkner, *Great Time Coming*, 156.

44. Roscoe McGowen, "Brooks Are Halted by Gerheauser, 6–5," *New York Times*, March 31, 1947, 17.

45. Roscoe McGowen, "Dodgers to Drop 10 Men by Sunday," *New York Times*, April 1, 1947, 35.

46. Ibid.

47. Roscoe McGowen, "Only 3 Dodgers Certain Starters," *New York Times*, April 2, 1947, 35.

48. "Rickey Puts Down Anti-Robinson Move," *Baltimore Afro-American*, April 5, 1947, 13.

49. Roscoe McGowen, "Dodgers Trounce Montreal, 12 to 2," *New York Times*, April 3, 1947, 33.

50. Ibid.

51. Interview with Don Newcombe, January 1997.

52. Durocher, *Nice Guys Finish Last*, 257.

53. Ibid.

54. Louis Effrat, "Dodgers Purchase Robinson, First Negro in Modern Major League Baseball," *New York Times*, April 11, 1947, 20.

55. Arthur Daley, "Play Ball!" *New York Times*, April 15, 1947, 31.

56. Richard Sandomir, "In Print, Cheerleading and Indifference," *New York Times*, April 13, 1997, S9.

57. Sam Lacy, "Dodgers Sign Up Jack," *Baltimore Afro-American*, April 12, 1947, 1.

58. Sam Lacy, "'It's Wonderful,' Says Jackie's Better Half," *Baltimore Afro-American*, April 12, 1947, 23.

59. "No Locker for Robinson," *Sporting News*, April 23, 1947, 4.

60. Harold C. Burr, "Dixie Walker Draws Boos at Jackie's Flatbush Bow," *Sporting News*, April 16, 1947, 18.

61. "'Misquoted,' Says Dixie," *Baltimore Afro-American*, April 15, 1947, 12.

62. "J. Robinson, Ballplayer," *New York Times*, April 12, 1947, 16.

63. "The Press on Jackie," *Baltimore Afro-American*, April 15, 1947, 12.

64. Mike Klingaman, "Robinson Was Covered in Mainstream Papers Mostly by Invisible Ink," April 15, 1997.

65. See note 63.

66. Sam Lacy, "Looking 'Em Over," *Baltimore Afro-American*, April 19, 1947, 12.

67. Sam Lacy, "Greeted with Cheers As He Opens Season," *Baltimore Afro-American*, April 19, 1947, 25.

68. Rampersad, *Jackie Robinson*, 169.

69. Eig, *Opening Day*, 50.

70. See note 67.

71. Eig, *Opening Day*, 55.

72. Ibid., 59.

73. See note 55.

74. Arthur Daley, "Opening Day at Ebbets Field," *New York Times*, April 16, 1947, 32.

75. Robinson, *I Never Had It Made*, 59.

76. Ibid., 61.

77. Stanley Woodward, "General Strike Conceived," *Sporting News*, April 21, 1947, 4.

78. Ibid.

79. "Says Cards' Strike Plan against Negro Dropped," *New York Times*, March 9, 1947, 27.

80. "Robinson Reveals Written Threats," *New York Times*, March 10, 1947, 16.

81. Durocher, *Nice Guys Finish Last*, 205.

82. Burgos, *Cuban Star*, 179.

Chapter 13. A House United

1. Roscoe McGowen, "Gonzales May Sell Cuban Team and Become Coach with Dodgers," *New York Times*, February 28, 1947, 18.

2. Ibid.

3. Dan Daniel, "Don Dan Daniel Reports on Beisbol in Habana," *Sporting News*, March 5, 1947, 7.

4. Dan Daniel, "Cuban League Makes Peace with U.S. Ball," *Sporting News*, April 30, 1947, 1.

5. "Majors Friendly to Cuban League," *New York Times*, May 13, 1947, 32.

6. "Cuban League Wins Recognition in U.S," *New York Times*, July 12, 1947, 8.

7. J. G. Taylor Spink, "Cuban Pact to Spur Game in Latin-America," *Sporting News*, July 16, 1947, 1.

8. George M. Trautman, "The Cuban Winter League" letter, July 22, 1947, National Baseball Hall of Fame Library collection.

9. J. G. Taylor Spink, "Cuban Pact to Spur Game in Latin-America," *Sporting News*, July 16, 1947, 2.

10. "Lanier Seeks Offers from Semi-Pro Clubs; Through Dickering with Mexican Circuit," *New York Times*, April 20, 1947, S3.

11. "Job Wanted: Max Lanier," *Sporting News*, April 30, 1947, 34.

12. "Feller Tour Lists Five Games in Cuba," *New York Times*, August 12, 1947, 28.

13. "Chandler Ruling on Cuban Tours Seen Hinging on Clubs' Approval," *New York Times*, August 13, 1947, 30.

14. J. G. Taylor Spink, "All Big Leaguers Barred from Cuban Loop," *Sporting News*, August 20, 1947, 1.

15. Ibid.

16. "Ruling Puzzles Feller," *New York Times*, August 16, 1947, 8.

17. "Pension Fund Gift Planned by Feller," *New York Times*, August 17, 1947, 99.

18. René Cañizares, "Players to Share Profits in New Cuban League," *Sporting News*, June 18, 1947, 1.

19. René Cañizares, "O.B. Approved Cuban Loop Holds Edge As Outlaws Open Season," *Sporting News*, October 29, 1947, 13.

20. René Cañizares, "Players Battle May Force Cuban Loop into Courts," *Sporting News*, November 5, 1947, 19.

21. Figueredo, *Béisbol cubano*, 272.

22. Ibid., 270.

23. René Cañizares, "Cuban Outlaw Loop Opens Before 36,000; Rival Draws Only 3,000 on Same Night," *Sporting News*, November 12, 1947, 21.

24. "Sanguily Charges O.B. with Failure to Give Cuban Loop Qualified Talent," *Sporting News*, November 5, 1947, 19.

25. "Sanguily Denies Giving Interview Rapping O.B," *Sporting News*, November 12, 1947, 21.

26. Pedro Galiana, "Cuban Horizon Broadened by Easing of O.B. Rules," *Sporting News*, December 24, 1947, 20.

27. González Echevarría, *The Pride of Havana*, 53.

28. Pedro Galiana, "Cuban Outlaw Loop to Stick, Say Directors," *Sporting News*, December 31, 1947, 22.

29. Pedro Galiana, "Cuban O.B. Loop Outdraws Rival Two to One at Gate," *Sporting News*, January 14, 1948, 19.

30. Pedro Galiana, "Calvert Changes Cuban Uniform to Rejoin O.B.," *Sporting News*, January 21, 1948, 20.

31. "Mexicans Await Chandler's Aide," *New York Times*, January 21, 1948, 32.
32. "All Differences with U.S. Baseball Leagues Ended, Says Mexican Loop Head," *New York Times*, January 23, 1948, 29.
33. "Awaits Mulbry Report," *New York Times*, January, 23, 1948, 29.
34. "Lanier, Other Exiled U.S. Stars Elated by Chandler's Attitude," *New York Times*, January 23, 1948, 29.
35. "Here with President's Son, Says He'll Sign Players in U.S.—Calls Himself League Boss, So Commissioner Aguilar Resigns," *New York Times*, January 27, 1948, 32.
36. "Feud Within Mexican League," *New York Times*, January 28, 1948, 29.
37. Pedro Galiana, "Mexican Jumpers Balk over Pasquel Pay Cuts," *New York Times*, February 25, 1948, 21.
38. Pedro Galiana, "New Stadium Bars Outlaw Cuban League," *Sporting News*, March 10, 1948, 24.
39. Ibid.
40. Figueredo, *Béisbol cubano*, 270.
41. René Cañizares, "Cuban Outlaw League Defies Legal Threats," *Sporting News*, December 17, 1947, 20.
42. Figueredo, *Béisbol cubano*, 271.
43. Pedro Galiana, "Court Victory Gained by O.B., Loop in Cuba," *Sporting News*, March 31, 1948, 24.
44. Pedro Galiana, "Clubs from Four Countries to Play Caribbean Series," *Sporting News*, September 1, 1948, 37.
45. "De La Cruz Plans 3-Nation Series," *Sporting News*, June 9, 1948, 1.
46. Pedro Galiana, "Meeting Called on Latin Series," *Sporting News*, August 18, 1948, 32.
47. Ibid.
48. "Gonzalez Visits Cardinals; Seeks Reinstatement to O.B.," *Sporting News*, June 28, 1948, 16.
49. "No Change in Gonzalez' Status in Organized Baseball," *Sporting News*, August 1, 1948, 2.
50. Alfonso Flores, "Player Raids 'Only the Beginning,' Says Pasquel," *Sporting News*, April 4, 1946, 4.
51. Jorge Alarcón, "Mexican Loop Ends Its Race 5 Weeks Early," *Sporting News*, September 29, 1948, 30.
52. Ray Gillespie, "Pasquels Give Up Control of Mexican League," *Sporting News*, November 3, 1948, 14.
53. Pedro Galiana, "Chandler Ban on Cuban Players Rapped by Havana Sports Paper," *Sporting News*, March 2, 1949, 26.
54. Pedro Galiana, "'50 Caribbean Series to Puerto Rico; Bigger Split Arranged for Players," *Sporting News*, March 9, 1949, 28.
55. Edgar G. Brands, "Lanier and Martin Now Pitching in U.S. Court," *Sporting News*, March 16, 1949, 2.
56. "Complete Text of Judge Conger Decision," *Sporting News*, April 13, 1949, 8.

57. "Gardella Plea to Enjoin Baseball Is Denied in Federal Court Here," *New York Times*, April 20, 1949, 36.

58. "Gardella, Lanier and Martin Lose Appeal for Quick Reinstatement," *New York Times*, June 3, 1949, 32.

59. "Ban on Major Leaguers Who Jumped to Mexico Lifted by Chandler," *New York Times*, June 6, 1949, 24.

60. "Cuba Cheers Ruling," *Sporting News*, June 15, 1949, 12.

61. Pedro Galiana, "Cuban Natives Spice Up Games after Chandler O.K. to Play in Winter League," *Sporting News*, November 2, 1949, 16.

Bibliography

Interviews

Agüero, Leonardo. Telephone interview by author, March 1999. Tape recording.

Bavasi, Buzzie. Telephone interview by author, January 1997. Tape recording.

Bragan, Bobby. Telephone interview by author, January 1997. Tape recording.

Fleitas, Andrés. Telephone interviews by author, January 1997 and March 1999. Tape recordings.

Lacy, Sam. Telephone interview by author, January 1997. Tape recording.

Lanier, Max. Telephone interviews by author, April 1994, January 1997, and March 1999. Tape recordings.

Mayor, Agapito. Telephone interviews by author, January 1997 and March 1999. Tape recordings.

Mayor, Gloria. Interview by author, Tampa, Florida, April 16, 2008. Tape recording.

Miñoso, Orestes. Telephone interview by author, June 2000. Tape recording.

Newcombe, Don. Telephone interview by author, January 1997. Tape recording.

O'Neil, Buck. Telephone interview by author, March 1999. Tape recording.

Ramírez, Felo. Interview by author, Viera, Florida, March 1994. Tape recording.

———. Telephone interview by author, January 1997. Tape recording.

Sandlock, Mike. Telephone interview by author, August 2011. Tape recording.

Tiant, Luis, Jr. Telephone interview by author, November 2001. Tape recording.

Books and Articles

Alexander, Charles C. *John McGraw*. New York: Viking, 1988.

———. *Ty Cobb*. New York: Oxford University Press, 1985.

Allen, Maury. *Jackie Robinson: A Life Remembered*. New York: Franklin Watts, 1987.

Allen, Maury, and Susan Walker. *Dixie Walker of the Dodgers: The People's Choice*. Tuscaloosa: University of Alabama Press, 2010.

Ashwill, Gary. "Ty Cobb in Cuba, 1910." Agate Type. agatetype.typepad.com/agate_type/2008/08/ty-cobb-in-cuba.html.

Barber, Red. *1947, When All Hell Broke Loose in Baseball*. Garden City, N.Y.: Doubleday, 1982.

Barber, Red, and Robert Creamer. *Rhubarb in the Catbird Seat*. Garden City, N.Y.: Doubleday, 1968.

Bjarkman, Peter C. *Baseball with a Latin Beat: A History of the Latin American Game*. Jefferson, N.C.: McFarland, 1994.

———. *Diamonds around the Globe: The Encyclopedia of International Baseball*. Westport, Conn.: Greenwood, 2005.

———. *A History of Cuban Baseball, 1864–2006*. Jefferson, N.C.: McFarland, 2007.

Brown, Bruce. "Cuban Baseball." *Atlantic Monthly* 253, no. 6 (1984): 109–14.

Burgos, Adrian, Jr. *Cuban Star: How One Negro-League Owner Changed the Face of Baseball*. New York: Hill & Wang, 2011.

———. *Playing America's Game: Baseball, Latinos, and the Color Line*. Berkeley: University of California Press, 2007.

Campanella, Roy. *It's Good to Be Alive*. Boston: Little, Brown, 1959.

Casas, Edel, Jorge Alfonso, and Alberto Pestana. *Viva y en juego*. Havana: Editorial Científico-Técnica, 1986.

Chuck, Bill, and Jim Kaplan. *Walkoffs, Last Licks, and Final Outs: Baseball's Grand (and Not-So-Grand) Finales*. Skokie, Ill.: ACTA Sports, 2008.

Craft, David. *The Negro Leagues: 40 Years of Black Professional Baseball in Words and Pictures*. New York: Crescent, 1993.

Díez Muro, Raúl. *Historia del base ball profesional de Cuba*. Havana, 1949.

Durocher, Leo. *Nice Guys Finish Last*. With Edward Linn. New York: Simon & Schuster, 1975.

Eig, Jonathan. *Opening Day: The Story of Jackie Robinson's First Season*. New York: Simon & Schuster, 2007.

Elizondo, Ed. "History of the Cuban Liberation Wars." CubaGenWeb. cubagenweb.org/mil/war-hist.htm.

English, T. J. *Havana Nocturne: How The Mob Owned Cuba—and Then Lost It to the Revolution*. New York: William Morrow, 2008.

Falkner, David. *Great Time Coming: The Life of Jackie Robinson, from Baseball to Birmingham*. New York: Simon & Schuster, 1995.

Figueredo, Jorge S. *Béisbol cubano: A un paso de las grandes ligas, 1878–1961*. Jefferson, N.C.: McFarland, 2005.

———. *Cuban Baseball: A Statistical History, 1878–1961*. Jefferson, N.C.: McFarland, 2003.

———. *Who's Who in Cuban Baseball, 1878–1961*. Jefferson, N.C.: McFarland, 2003.

Fuentes, Norberto. *Hemingway in Cuba*. Translated by Consuelo E. Corwin. Secaucus, N.J.: Lyle Stuart, 1984.

Golenbock, Peter. *Bums: An Oral History of the Brooklyn Dodgers*. 1984. Mineola, N.Y.: Dover, 2010.

González Echevarría, Roberto. "The '47 Dodgers in Havana: Baseball at a Crossroads." In *1996 Spring Training Baseball Yearbook*, 20–25. Chapel Hill, N.C.: Vanguard Sports Publications, 1996.

———. *The Pride of Havana: A History of Cuban Baseball*. New York: Oxford University Press, 1999.

Hemingway, Ernest. *The Old Man and the Sea*. New York: Scribner, 1952.

Holway, John B. *Blackball Stars: Negro League Pioneers*. 1988. New York: Carroll & Graf, 1992.

Hotel Nacional de Cuba. "Cuba's Hotel Nacional—A Historical Profile." hotelnacio naldecuba.com/en/history.asp.

Kahn, Roger. *The Boys of Summer*. New York: Harper & Row, 1972.

———. *The Era: 1947–1957, when the Yankees, the Giants, and the Dodgers Ruled the World*. New York: Ticknor & Fields, 1993.

Keane, Robert N., ed. *Baseball and the "Sultan of Swat": Babe Ruth at 100*. New York: AMS, 2008.

Lasorda, Tommy, and David Fisher. *The Artful Dodger*. New York: Arbor House, 1985.

Liga de Base-Ball Profesional Cubana. *Campeonato de 1950–51: Programa oficial*. 1950.

Mann, Arthur. *The Jackie Robinson Story*. New York: Grosset & Dunlap, 1956.

Manzano, Rogério. "Estadios." Desde Mi Palco de Fanático. desdemipalcodefanatico. wordpress.com/estadios.

Marasco, David. "Our Giants in Havana." The Diamond Angle. web.archive.org/web/20131016145510/http://www.thediamondangle.com/archive/feb04/havana.html.

Marlett, Jeffrey. "Leo Durocher." In Spatz, *The Team That Forever Changed Baseball and America*, 22–27.

Márquez-Sterling, Manuel. "Babe Ruth's Impact on Latin American Baseball and Latin American Ballplayers: Cuba—A Case Study." In Keane, *Baseball and the "Sultan of Swat,"* 211–17.

Marren, Joe. "Branch Rickey and the Mainstream Press." In Spatz, *The Team That Forever Changed Baseball and America*, 57–61.

Martínez Peraza, Marino. *Por amor a la pelota: Historia del béisbol amateur cubano*. Miami: Ediciones Universal, 2009.

McGraw, Mrs. John J. [Blanche S.]. *The Real McGraw*. New York: David McKay, 1953.

McKelvey, G. Richard. *Mexican Raiders in the Major Leagues: The Pasquel Brothers vs. Organized Baseball, 1946*. Jefferson, N.C.: McFarland, 2006.

McKenna, Brian. "Joe Cambria." Society for American Baseball Research. sabr.org/bioproj/person/4e7d25a0.

Menéndez, José M., et al. *Libro azul: Resumen general campeonato base-ball profesional 1946–47*. Havana: Arrow Press, 1947.

Miñoso, Minnie. *Just Call Me Minnie: My Six Decades in Baseball*. With Herb Fagen. Champaign, Ill.: Sagamore, 1994.

MLB.com. "Albert Benjamin 'Happy' Chandler." mlb.mlb.com/mlb/history/mlb_history_people.jsp?story=com_bio_2.

———. "2012–2016 Basic Agreement." mlb.mlb.com./pa/pdf/cba_english.pdf.

Monfort Soberats, Charles. "Recordando a José de la Caridad Méndez." *Carteles* 37, no. 3 (1956): 82–87.

Montville, Leigh. *The Big Bam: The Life and Times of Babe Ruth*. New York: Doubleday, 2006.

Nieto Fernández, Severo. *José Méndez, el Diamante Negro*. Havana: Editorial Científico-Técnica, 2004.

Nowlin, Bill, and Kit Krieger. "La Tropical Park, Then and Now." *National Pastime* 25 (2005): 3–8.

Oleksak, Michael M., and Mary Adams Oleksak. *Béisbol: Latin Americans and the Grand Old Game*. Grand Rapids, Mich.: Masters Press, 1991.

O'Neil, Buck. *I Was Right on Time: My Journey from the Negro Leagues to the Majors*. With Steve Wulf and David Conrads. New York: Simon & Schuster, 1997.

Pérez, Louis A., Jr. "Between Baseball and Bullfighting: The Quest for Nationality in Cuba, 1868–1898." *Journal of American History* 81, no. 2 (September 1994): 493–517.

———. *On Becoming Cuban: Identity, Nationality, and Culture*. Chapel Hill: University of North Carolina Press, 1999.

Pietrusza, David, Matthew Silverman, and Michael Gershman, eds. *Baseball: The Biographical Encyclopedia*. Kingston, N.Y.: Total/Sports Illustrated, 2000.

Rampersad, Arnold. *Jackie Robinson: A Biography*. New York: Knopf, 1997.

Ribowsky, Mark. *Don't Look Back: Satchel Paige in the Shadows of Baseball*. New York: Simon & Schuster, 1994.

———. *The Power and the Darkness: The Life of Josh Gibson in the Shadows of the Game*. New York: Simon & Schuster, 1996.

Riley, James A. *The Biographical Encyclopedia of the Negro Baseball Leagues*. New York: Carroll & Graf, 1994.

Roberts, Robin, and C. Paul Rogers III. *The Whiz Kids and the 1950 Pennant*. Philadelphia: Temple University Press, 1996.

Robinson, Jackie. *I Never Had It Made: The Autobiography of Jackie Robinson*. As told to Alfred Duckett. New York: Putnam, 1972.

Rogosin, Donn. *Invisible Men: Life in Baseball's Negro Leagues*. New York: Atheneum, 1983.

Rucker, Mark, and Peter C. Bjarkman. *Smoke: The Romance and Lore of Cuban Baseball*. Kingston, N.Y.: Total/Sports Illustrated, 1999.

Ruiz, Yuyo. *The Bambino Visits Cuba, 1920*. San Juan, Puerto Rico: Yuyo Ruiz, n.d.

Santana Alonso, Alfredo L. *El Inmortal del béisbol: Martín Dihigo*. Havana: Editorial Científico-Técnica, 2007.

Spatz, Jeffrey, ed. *The Team That Forever Changed Baseball and America: The 1947 Brooklyn Dodgers*. Lincoln: University of Nebraska Press, 2012.

Swaine, Rick. "Jackie Robinson." In Spatz, *The Team That Forever Changed Baseball and America*, 6–14.

Szalontai, James D. *Close Shave: The Life and Times of Baseball's Sal Maglie*. Jefferson, N.C.: McFarland, 2002.

Testa, Judith. *Sal Maglie: Baseball's Demon Barber*. DeKalb: Northern Illinois University Press, 2007.

Toot, Peter T. *Armando Marsans: A Cuban Pioneer in the Major Leagues*. Jefferson, N.C.: McFarland, 2004.

Torres, Ángel. *La historia del béisbol cubano, 1878–1976*. Los Angeles: Ángel Torres, 1976.

———. *La leyenda del béisbol cubano, 1878–1997*. Los Angeles: Ángel Torres, 1997.

Treto Cisneros, Pedro. *The Mexican League: Comprehensive Player Statistics, 1937–2001 = La Liga Mexicana: Estadísticas comprensivas de los jugadores, 1937–2001*. Jefferson, N.C.: McFarland, 2002.

Tye, Larry. *Satchel: The Life and Times of an American Legend*. New York: Random House, 2009.

Tygiel, Jules. *Baseball's Great Experiment: Jackie Robinson and His Legacy*. New York: Oxford University Press, 1997.

Virtue, John. *South of the Color Barrier: How Jorge Pasquel and the Mexican League Pushed Baseball Toward Racial Integration*. Jefferson, N.C.: McFarland, 2008.

Weiss, Bill, and Marshall Wright. "Top 100 Teams: 92. 1947 Havana Cubans." MiLB.com: The Official Site of Minor League Baseball. www.milb.com/milb/history/top100.jsp.

Williams, Stephen. *Cuba: The Land, The History, The People, the Culture*. Philadelphia: Running Press, 1994.

Wilson, Nick C. *Early Latino Ballplayers in the United States: Major, Minor and Negro Leagues, 1901–1949*. Jefferson, N.C.: McFarland, 2005.

Wolinsky, Russell. "Hugh Casey." In Spatz, *The Team That Forever Changed Baseball and America*, 113–18.

Index

Fleitas, Andrés, 94*i*, 136–37, 148–53, 157–60, 182, 185–87, 189, 191–95, 197–201, 223–24, 228, 230, 246–47

Florida International League, 40, 143, 145, 176, 233, 235, 244

Formental, Pedro, 148, 160, 185, 192–93

Fortuna (Unión Atlética), 70, 163–64

Foster, Andrew "Rube," 64–65

Franklin, Murray, 224, 240, 262*t*

Fránquiz, Julio, 51

French, Larry, 7, 32

Frisch, Frankie, 28, 46, 69, 85

Furillo, Carl, 170, 174

Gaines, Jonas, 253*t*

Galan, Augie, 32, 205

Galiana, Pedro, 50, 234, 236–37

García, Eloy, 128, 231

García, Manuel "Cocaína," 119–21, 126, 132–33, 153–54, 157, 159, 163, 181, 183–84, 188, 190, 195, 197, 200, 229, 236, 253–54*t*, 255–58*t*

García, Pablo, 193

García, Silvio, 23–24, 45, 55, 88, 90*i*, 121–23, 126, 134, 141, 152, 227, 234

Gardella, Danny, 12, 39–40, 42–43, 104*i*, 185, 205, 209, 231, 235, 237, 240–41, 262*t*

Gehrig, Lou, 5

General Electric (Panama team), 165, 168–69, 174, 202, 259*t*, 261*t*

Gibson, Homer, 75, 159, 251*t*

Gibson, Josh, 12, 120, 132, 154, 161–63

Gionfriddo, Al, 239

Gladu, Roland, 43, 52, 204, 224, 235, 240, 262*t*

Gómez, Preston, 44, 74

Gómez, Rubén, 84

Gómez, Vernon "Lefty," 227

González, Catayo, 229, 257*t*

González, Gervasio "Strike," 60, 63, 68

González, Miguel Ángel, 14, 42, 89*i*, 133, 154, 183, 224, 227–28, 236; Adolfo Luque and, 31, 55, 74, 76, 78–79, 121, 131, 160–61, 185, 238, 241; Brooklyn Dodgers and, 221–22; final series against Almendares and, 190, 192–94,

195, 197; protest against Héctor Rodríguez, 186–88; Martín Dihigo and, 80, 163; St. Louis Cardinals and, 6, 30, 45–46, 72–73, 84–85, 130

González Moré, Luis "El Conde," 51, 161

Goren, Herbert, 113, 142, 147, 167, 169, 206–7, 209

Gran Stadium Cerveza Tropical, 7. *See also* La Tropical

Gray Monks (Monjes Grises)(Cuban League), 11, 76, 86, 127, 132, 154, 162, 179, 181, 183, 185, 188

Greenberg, Hank, 12, 40

Griffith, Clark, 39, 116, 177

Guerra, Fermín, 44–45, 47, 99*i*, 121–22, 152, 177–78, 225, 227, 239

Guilló, Nemesio, 1, 48

Habana (Cuban League), 7, 10–12, 23, 29, 47, 48–49, 58–60, 62, 64, 66–71, 81, 87, 92*i*, 95*i*, 104*i*, 106, 112, 118–19, 126–27, 132–34, 148–64, 179–89, 209, 219, 221–24, 234, 239, 241, 246, 251–55*t*, 262*t*; Dick Sisler and, 6, 13–17, 42; Eternal Rivals with Almendares, 8, 17, 48, 55, 65, 76, 125, 243; final series against Almendares, 190–95, 197–200; Miguel Ángel González and, 6, 42, 45–46, 72–73, 78–80, 84, 89*i*, 130–32, 121–24, 227–28, 236. *See also* Lions

Hausmann, George, 40–41, 43, 112, 184–85, 189, 193, 197–89, 205, 209, 224, 233, 237, 240, 262*t*

Havana Cubans (Florida International League), 40, 143, 145, 167, 176–78, 233–35, 244, 259*t*, 261*t*

Havana Military Academy, 111–12, 143

Havana Reds (Liga Nacional), 45, 47, 121, 124–25, 128, 134, 177

Hayworth, Myron "Red," 153, 159 181, 224, 262*t*

Head, Ed, 170

Hemingway, Ernest, 18, 31–34, 78

Herman, Billy, 32–33, 107

Hermanski, Gene, 207, 215

Hernández, Alberto "Sagüita," 126, 133, 152, 194, 227